Punishment Without Crime

SVETLANA GRINBERG

ARKADY GRINBERG

ScarletSails Press

TO THE DESCENDANTS:

Elena
Olga
Yasha
Sasha
Mia

Punishment Without Crime

Families are like little nations. They mold themselves from people and circumstances. Their joy and sorrow alternate with a curious and fascinating constancy, sometimes caused by family members, sometimes by chance that picks them as unexpected participants, often dispensing hardship for no apparent reason but for belonging to a particular lot. And, like nations, families are a mixed breed.

PUNISHMENT WITHOUT CRIME

Book I. Czarist Russia

"Wretched and abundant,
Oppressed and powerful,
Weak and mighty,
Mother Russia!"

Nikolai Nekrasov

Part One

1

A boy appeared on a street of Olshana, where tailor Abram's house faced the synagogue. He probably cut across vegetable gardens as he came from the woods, which surrounded the place like guards. The street was not very long, and the boy walked toward its crowded part. The long shadows made by the setting sun started to crawl, hugging the small houses facing the street, hugging the trees and bushes. This time of day, the street was full of playing kids. The boy walked slowly and deliberately until he stopped in front of a house where a little girl sat on a bench by the door, consumed with eating a pancake. A sudden pull on it startled her. She looked up and saw her pancake disappearing into a boy's mouth so quickly she could not believe it was possible. Tears were just about to roll from her eyes when the boy, finished with the pancake, started to make funny faces and jump around her like a street clown. The girl's lips moved in a second from crying to giggling. The boy was funny, and she could not stop laughing. She liked her new friend and wanted to show him her toys. Two rag dolls appeared—one male, one female—and the boy was invited to play with them.

The kids were having a good time when a voice from the house yelled out, "Lyuba, time to eat." The little girl, Lyuba, yelled back, "Coming," but continued to play with the boy.

Soon a middle-aged woman appeared from the house with a stern look on her face. "Lyuba, how many times should I tell you we are waiting for you? Come right now!" The woman noticed the boy standing next to Lyuba. She had never seen him before in the village. "Whose child are you, boy? Go home."

The boy did not move and did not answer the question. His head dropped down. To her surprise, he was sobbing. She also noticed that his clothes were torn and dirty and that he looked thin. Compassion for this child rose inside her.

"Would you like to eat with us? What is your name?"

"My name is Senya," the boy said. He walked toward the door; he could not wait to eat.

Inside the house, Senya discovered a room similar to what he had seen before: a large table in the middle with several people sitting around it. His gaze spanned all corners of the room in search of an icon—he had to make the sign of the cross upon entering a house—but no icon was present. Surprised but hungry he found an empty spot on a long bench by the table and was just about to grab some food when the woman's authoritarian voice pronounced, "Senya, what are you doing? First wash your hands!"

Surprises never stop in this house, Senya thought as he saw an older girl approaching him with a jug full of water and a bowl. As he washed his hands in water poured from the jug, the water in the bowl became almost black. The girl had a towel draped over her arm. Senya wiped his hands dry very quickly, for the sight and smell of the food on the table made him incredibly hungry. He could not wait to start eating, but since nobody else did, he had no choice but to wait. In addition to the woman and Lyuba, he saw a man, two girls, and a boy, all of different ages. The children's looks questioned who he was, but the man actually put it in words.

"Sarah, who is this boy?"

"I don't know. Let him eat; we'll talk later."

Senya consumed the food he received with such speed that everyone else around the table stopped eating for a while and watched him. They had never seen anybody eating that fast before, and they were puzzled about how so much food could go through a child's little mouth at such speed.

After the meal, Sarah called Senya into another room that served as a bedroom. Again, he looked into every corner of the room and found no icon. He heard a voice:

6

"Senya, tell me about yourself. Who are your parents? Where are they?",

Senya was quiet, for he was afraid to say something inappropriate and be thrown out of this house. He liked the family, he liked the food, and he wanted to stay with them.

"I don't have any parents."

Sarah decided not to badger him, but to bathe him and wash his clothes. She asked her son Fima to heat some water and told Senya to undress. He was so thin one could easily count his ribs, and deep bloody scratches covered his back. To prevent a potential infection, Sarah took out some of the herbs she always kept in the house to treat various illnesses, boiled them, and added them to the bathwater to sanitize Senya's skin. After Senya had bathed, Sarah rubbed some aloe juice into his wounds to speed up their healing. Finished with the boy, she turned her attention to his clothes. They were not only dirty, but were also damaged and worn to the degree that repairing them would not be practical. She threw his tatters away and produced some of Fima's clothes to replace them.

Sarah also discovered a cross on a chain around Senya's neck. The boy was a Christian. Her initial thought was that he wandered off somehow and his relatives must be searching for him. She now knew what to do next: she had to take Senya to the local priest, who could help to find his family. But she could not do it tonight, for the Jews were prohibited from being in the Ukrainian part of town in the evening. She kept the boy overnight.

The next morning, she took Senya to see the priest. The road from Sarah's house to the church on the Ukrainian side of Olshana was not long, and she held the boy by the hand without asking any more questions.

Where is she taking me? Senya asked himself as they walked in silence. Why cannot I stay with them? Concerns about his future made his head tight with apprehension, and he walked with a heavy heart.

The local priest knew Sarah well, as did many people on both sides of the town. Her reputation was of a wise woman, and she had a nickname: One Thousand Tips. People came to her for advice on medical and other matters. She greeted the priest.

"Senya is clearly a Christian. If you cannot find his family, it would only be appropriate to place him with a Christian family. He is a good boy, and I would not mind keeping him, but it would not be fair to him."

"I will take care of the boy for a few days and look for his family," the priest said.

Sarah went home feeling sad about the boy's situation. She liked this quiet, good-looking boy, and she knew that he'd impressed Lyuba. Nevertheless, she told herself, taking Senya to the priest was the right thing to do.

In the meantime, the priest questioned Senya about his family, and Senya told him of his mother's death and how he had fled the neighbor, who was not kind to him, to look for a better place. He described his wandering from village to village, from market to market, stealing some food, and how the local boys had sometimes beaten him. It was summertime, so he could sleep in the woods, where he stayed away from thugs and found plentiful berries that quenched his hunger. He no longer knew how long ago he had left his native village, only that it was after the winter, and he did not know if he had any relatives.

Since looking for the boy's parents was not an option, the priest tried to think of someone who could take Senya into their family. This was not easy. The second part of the nineteenth century was unkind to peasants in the Russian Empire. Most peasants had big families of their own and adding another mouth to feed was not simple. The priest knew his flock and searched his mind for a possible fit. For the time being, though, Senya stayed with the priest's family.

2

Lyuba was sad when she learned about Senya's fate. She was only five, but Senya had been good to her, and he was funny. Lyuba was fretful and constantly nagged her mother about Senya. Sarah did not know what to do with her little daughter. She tried to explain that Senya had a family somewhere looking for him and that it would be unkind to keep him away from them. This is what she told the little girl, while to herself she justified her actions by thinking that it was tough to be a Jew in Russia and there was no reason for a Christian child to suffer needlessly when there was plenty of suffering even without being Jewish. Sarah was convinced she had done the right thing, but Lyuba wanted Senya back. How surprised both of them were when Senya showed up at their house one morning.

"Senya, what are you doing here?" Sarah asked.

"I want to live with you, Aunt."

"But what about the priest? Did he find your family?"

"I don't have any family." He started to cry.

As Sarah hugged him and gave him a kiss on the forehead, she noticed bruises on his face and hands. "What happened, Senya?" she asked, and Senya told her how he did not like it at the priest's house because the older boys picked on him and called him a bastard.

"Please, please, Aunt, let me stay with you. I will be good!"

Sarah liked the boy and really wanted to keep him. The only problem was that Senya was not a Jew. She was not sure how to raise him or how the Ukrainians would look at this situation. She thought they could afford to feed another mouth, as her husband Yankel was a good shoemaker and earned enough money for the family's care.

"Senya, I know you are a good boy. Why don't you play with Lyuba, and I will be back soon."

Sarah went to talk to her husband, whose little shop was at the end of their backyard. Yankel listened carefully to his wife and said, "Sarah, I think under the circumstances God would want us to keep the boy. It will be a mitzvah, I am sure. Don't worry about what people would say. I will teach him the skills of a shoemaker, and we will manage somehow. Let's do it!"

Now, Sarah's family was not big by the standards of that time. Yankel Kagan and she had been married for almost twenty years, but they had only four children—three daughters and a son. All the children had Russian names: son Fima and daughters Vera, Nadezhda (Nadya), and Lyubov (Lyuba), names that mean Faith, Hope, and Love. Lyuba was the youngest, Vera the oldest. Sarah gave her children Russian names because she felt it would make their lives a little easier in the land where Jews were second-class citizens. She wanted them to feel a part of the country that had become their homeland.

Both Lyuba and Senya rejoiced at the news. They grabbed each other's hands and threw themselves into a dance. They laughed and moved in a circle. This was the beginning of a real friendship.

Sarah had to address many issues that dropped on her head like a bunch of stones. Senya needed clothes and a place to sleep, she needed to let the rabbi and the neighbors know, she needed to tell the priest. Then Senya needed to start his education.

Sarah had a lot to do.

3

A new life surrounded Senya in the Kagan household. First, the shoemaker's shop, where in time Senya would learn his profession, required hustling. Yankel was a good shoemaker and might even be the best in the area. His shop smelled of leather and polish and was usually crowded. Then there was the language that people in the house spoke most of the time. Senya did not understand it and did not know what to make of it, as he spoke the mixture of Russian and Ukrainian that peasants in Central Ukraine used. Lyuba could not satisfy his curiosity about the language because she was too little, but Fima explained that they were Jews and had their own language, Yiddish. This was Senya's first glimpse into the Jewish culture.

The Kagans were a typical Jewish family, where the man had an occupation that put food on the table. Yankel spent most of his waking hours working in the shop. On Shabbat, he went to the synagogue to pray and study. He was not an extremely religious Jew, but he maintained the traditions passed down to him through generations of his ancestors. The traditions were to serve God, support the family, educate the children, and help the poor and the weak.

While a man was the nominal head of a family, his wife—his Jewish wife—was usually the real decision maker. The wife reared the children, took care of the house, cooked, controlled social events, and generally directed the life of the family. The traditional saying is that a man is the head of the family, but his wife is the neck: the neck turns and the head follows. Sarah was just such a wife, and she took care of her family with all her heart and all her energy. She brought in some additional cash, which she earned by cooking for other people. She was such a good cook that her services were always in demand.

The male children in a family began studying the basics early in their lives. They had to in order to read the Torah. The boys also helped at home, especially as they grew older. The girls usually studied with their mothers. After a few days of getting familiar with the family and its rules, Senya followed Fima into the local *yeshiva* and began his formal studies.

Schooling was not easy for Senya in the beginning, as he had to learn enough Yiddish to understand what was going on. Then he had to learn the Hebrew alphabet. He also studied Russian in school.

At home, both Fima and Senya learned the shoemaker's trade. They loved to work in the shop with Yankel. He was a kind, witty man and they enjoyed his company. He taught his boys every detail of the business: how to nail a sole, how to take a measure of a foot, how to prepare a polish, how to talk to a customer, how... There was no end to what they had to learn to become shoemakers, but they were taught by one of the best, and so their skills developed rapidly.

Yankel had another skill that gave him and his family joy: he had played the violin since he was a child and loved music. When Jews came together for a celebration of any sort, music and dancing always kept their spirits high, helping them forget the troubles they experienced in their daily lives. Yankel played the violin at home when he had time, and sometimes he joined a band, which consisted of local fellows playing violins, drums, clarinet, and accordion... whoever was available.

11

When Jewish youth gathered on a nice summer night for a dance and comradeship, even a single musician playing a violin or an accordion was greatly appreciated. But the band... ah, the band! This was heaven, when the drum gave a strong beat and an accordion and a clarinet poured a melody, each in its own color, echoing and then diverging from one another, and the violin went higher and higher as if reaching heaven. Who could stand still and not dance when a band was playing?

Yankel's boys were proud and wanted to be just like him. It became one of his life passions to teach all his children to play the violin, and he also wanted to buy each of them their own instrument so they could all play together. Vera and Nadya, as the oldest siblings, already had their violins. Fima was next in line and expected to have one soon. Meanwhile, all the children learned to play the violins the family already owned.

Most of the family togetherness took place in winter, when the days were short and most of the outside work was on hold. Now Yankel could spend some time teaching the kids to play. They also had long conversations about many interesting subjects, including Jewish history and traditions. Senya seemed to absorb what he heard through his pores.

One story made a long-lasting impression on Senya because it reminded him of his very first day with the Kagan family, when he was forced to wash his hands before eating. He had been surprised by the attention given to what he thought was an unimportant ritual. He had grown used to it by now, but this story related hand washing to issues of life and death.

As usual, Yankel's story was inspired by an innocent remark. When Vera noted, in reference to some encounter, that not everyone was as principled about washing their hands as the people around her, Yankel looked at her and asked, "Do you remember when we talked about the Spanish Inquisition and how many of our people lost their lives?"

Vera's look betrayed her lack of confidence in the subject.

Yankel found a convenient spot on a bench, leaned slightly forward, as he usually did while telling a story, raised both hands, and began:

"When the Jews were dispersed from Palestine by the Romans about two thousand years ago, they left their homeland in all directions. Some went south toward the deserts and eventually reached the Sea of Arabia. Some went north toward Persia, the Caucasus Mountains, and the Caspian Sea. Many went west to Egypt and beyond, all the way to Spain. The Jews prospered in Spain. They contributed much to Spanish commerce, and their life was good. When the rule in Spain passed from Muslim Moors to Christian Kings in the Middle Ages, the Jews stayed."

Here Yankel became more emotional, and his arms, which he always used to enhance a story, moved expressively.

"Things were going well for the Spanish Jews until the Inquisition, which was created to fight heresies within Christianity. But it quickly affected non-Christians. Jews became the subjects of constant attacks and persecutions. Life got tougher, and remaining in the country without converting to Christianity was risky for the Jews. Many of them went north to France and Germany, and then some traveled east toward Poland and Russia, which is probably how our ancestors ended up here in Russia. Some Jews did not want to leave Spain. They converted, but at heart many of them felt they were still Jews and still followed their familiar traditions. The Church leaders found out about this and decided to search for and persecute those converts who just pretended to become Christians for survival. Because such people preserved their Jewish traditions, one of the easiest ways to uncover the pretenders was to see if they always washed their hands before eating. If they did so, they were Jews masquerading as Christians, and they were burned at the stake. You see how deep this tradition is with our people?"

Yankel's stories were fascinating. Full of history and emotion, they kept listeners in awe of the past and of the man who knew so much. As he spoke, vivid pictures of days long gone appeared in his children's minds. Traditions were rooted in real events, and the history of humankind came out in its full magnificence.

Another story that left a strong impression on Senya was told one evening, when the family gathered by the furnace to keep warm. Yankel told them about the last Shabbat service in the synagogue and mentioned that he was a Cohen. Senya did not know what a Cohen was and asked Yankel to explain. He assumed the word had something to do with the Bible, and while he had already read some parts of the Old Testament and was familiar with the main characters in the religious drama that took place thousands of years ago, his knowledge was spotty. He did not know much about the way the stories in the Bible were translated into the reality of life. Now he was about to hear about one such example.

"When Moses took the Jews out of Egypt," Yankel began, "he did it under the command of God. While traveling to the Promised Land, God talked to Moses many times and offered the Ten Commandments, visions of future happiness, and specific rules of behavior and worship. God told Moses to make Aaron, his brother, a priest, which would be the highest position among the Israelites because he would serve God directly at the altar. The sons of Aaron were also made priests, and from that time on all Aaron's male descendants were priests, or *cohanim* in Hebrew."

Yankel stopped, looked around, and reached for the old Hebrew Bible lying on the table.

"Here, I will read you something from the Bible." His fingers quickly went through the pages to find the right passage. "This is from Numbers. *And Lord spoke further to Aaron: Of all the holy things of the sons of Israel I have given them to you and to your sons as a portion, as an allowance to time indefinite.*"

Yankel put the Bible back and looked at his children. "You see? It happened more than three thousand years ago, and we still remember that some Jews have a special place before God and therefore special obligations. Many descendants of Aaron have the name Cohen, but as our people scattered all over the world, some of them adapted their names to local languages. Sometimes, the names were changed completely and are not even close to Cohen, but people know who they are, as this fact is passed by families from generation to generation."

Yankel stopped again to allow the story to make an impact on his children. Then he continued:

"Do you know our neighbors, the Levitskys? Their name is also significant as a part of our history. When God told Moses to make Aaron and his family priests, he also directed Moses to make the tribe of Levy into assistants of the priests who would help the priests with various activities around the altar. This was the second group of Jews, called Levites, selected by God. Everybody else was referred to as Israel."

4

Every fall after the harvest, a fair took place in Elizavetgrad that attracted peasants and artisans from the entire region. The vendors offered produce, tools, clothes, and toys—anything people needed for their lives. Yankel usually went there with his sons to sell shoes and some of the leftover fruits and vegetables from their garden. He also bought presents for his entire family. This time, he promised if he made enough money, to buy Senya a violin.

Yankel and his boys enjoyed the ride to town and did not mind leaving early in the morning to find a good spot in the market. They packed a bag of apples, a bag of pears, two boxes of vegetables, a few pairs of shoes, and started toward the town in their old wagon drawn by a black horse while the rest of the family was still sleeping.

The road to Elizavetgrad snaked through several small, unassuming villages. Yankel had driven through such villages many times and always thought of the mostly poor and uneducated peasants still living in illiteracy and drunkenness. They loved their Czar-father and survived with the hope that he would somehow make their lives easier… just as soon as he found out how his officials oppressed common folk. The Russian peasants waited and hoped, year after year, with few results, but such was their character that Czar and Church were above everything else in life.

The market was already swarming with people soon after sunrise. The day promised to be fair, and the townsfolk had a good opportunity to spend time at the fair, not only buying things, but also enjoying street performers and sweets, which were sold everywhere. A fair like this one usually attracted clowns, jugglers, and other entertainers. And no fair in Russia would be without its bears. Bear-guides took their animals from fair to fair to entertain visitors, and entertain they did. These were brown bears, some adults, big and ferocious, and some cubs, cute and cuddly. They performed many tricks. Fima and Senya were much impressed with the bears, especially their dancing, and wanted to make time to see them. But first they had to sell and earn money.

On a nice day, selling was easier, as people enjoyed the surroundings and were in a mood to spend more money. Fruits and vegetables were sold quickly, and so Yankel let the boys walk around the fair while he still had shoes to sell. The brothers wandered through the market looking for clowns and bears and watching them with amazement. By the time they came back, Yankel sold all his merchandise.

Now it was time to buy presents for everybody. First, Yankel had to buy his sons some new clothes, as they grew out of the old ones fast. Then he had to find some fine fabric to make dresses for the girls. Sewing at home was cheaper than buying ready-made clothes, and Sarah could sew well. Next, he wanted to buy something lovely for his wife. He found the ideal gift at the stall of a jewelry vendor: a string of the red coral beads that were popular in Ukraine. They were dark red, the color of rubies. And finally—Senya dared not ask, but anxiously waited for this moment—Yankel said that it was time to find a new violin. That would be a violin for Senya! The boy could not believe his luck. Soon he would own a real violin!

Yankel was looking for the fellow who sold violins. He had already bought three violins from him and counted on a good price from this vendor. He found him near the edge of the market and was glad to see several violins still sitting on a shelf. When Yankel selected the winner violin, he and the merchant haggled over the price for a little while, then finally shook hands. And Senya became the owner of an instrument whose music could make people dance and cry. There was no end to his happiness.

The road home seemed longer than usual to Senya. He could not wait to show his new violin to his little sister, Lyuba. As soon as the wagon stopped in front of the house, he jumped down. Screaming "Lyuba, see what I got!" he burst into the house. Lyuba was already running toward him. Senya showed the violin to her. "This is our violin!"

Later that night, the family played some of their favorite melodies. Now they had five violins, which meant that whoever was not playing a violin would beat on the table and on pots as drummers to achieve the effect of an orchestra. This was a happy family.

5

What does it take for a poor Jew to be joyful? A little music, a lot of friends, but a lot of music is even better.

At sixteen, Fima finally was old enough to play in a band. After his first try-out with more experienced musicians, he was accepted as a good fiddler, and every time the band needed a violinist Fima was ready. He played well and audiences—especially the girls—liked a handsome young man. Fima enjoyed the music and the attention he received. He also discovered Rivka, whom he already knew well, but had not noticed when she became a beautiful young woman. While Fima played, Rivka watched him, even if she was dancing with someone, and Fima always tried to keep her in the corner of his eyes, too. After the dance was over, Rivka waited for Fima, and he walked her home very slowly to savor more time together. They were definitely growing fond of each other.

In the meantime, Vera and Nadya were close to marrying the boys they were in love with. Their parents expected such an event and were happy with the choices the daughters made, but they were also sad that two daughters were leaving the nest together. But the timing was right. Vera was almost twenty, Nadya—eighteen. Sarah cried and laughed when she thought of the upcoming weddings and the future of her daughters. Such is the emotional makeup of Jews, developed through generations of persecution. They always look for something funny in a hard situation and are always ready to cry when they are happy.

Both Vera and Nadya were married in September on the same day. The entire village came to the wedding to wish the newlyweds Mozel Tov. Eating, drinking, singing, and dancing went on until the early morning hours. The Kagan family members reached their homes tired and happy.

After the wedding, when Vera and Nadya packed their belongings and moved in with their husbands, Sarah cried and Yankel told everyone with a forced smile on his face that he now had a bigger house and could finally have enough space for his books, although everyone knew that Lyuba would now get her own room.

The girls knew that their departure was hard for the parents and tried to soften the blow by visiting them often. They would come in the evening or on a weekend and describe their new lives, bringing some food they had cooked and cheering their parents. This worked for almost a year until one spring evening when Vera and Nadya came with their husbands with the usual offerings of food, but without the usual excitement in their eyes. Sarah noticed something different and in her typical direct fashion asked, "What is going on, Vera? Did someone die?"

"No, Mother, nobody died. Why do you need to think of the extreme?"

"But you look like somebody died! What is the matter?" Sarah kept questioning while Yankel was quietly and nervously observing the scene.

"We need to talk," Nadya said. "Let's sit down."

"Okay, let's talk," Sarah said and sat down.

18

"Mom, Pop," Vera started, "we've decided to move to Elizavetgrad. It is difficult for us to earn enough money here to live normally. We keep hearing it is easier to find good-paying jobs in the city, and we want to move there."

"Are you crazy?" Sarah shouted. "You want to move to the city where the pogroms started? Don't you know what happened there just a few years ago? The city is full of anti-Semites who look for any opportunity to attack Jews."

"Mom, you are overreacting. The time is different now, and the Jews who live there are not complaining of any major disturbances. We do need to provide for ourselves, you know." Nadya spoke with the conviction of a person who has already made up her mind.

Clearly, the decision to move had been made and there was no way to convince the girls and their husbands to change it. Sarah had to give in. As soon as she recognized this, the conversation shifted to the discussion of the details.

The departure was planned to take place in two weeks. When the time arrived, Sarah prepared a big dinner for her family and the in-laws. Everybody came to wish the youngsters good luck in their new place. The next day was Sunday, when part of the family, part of Sarah's and Yankel's hearts, moved into something new. As usual, it was easier for those who left than for those who stayed. All the girls were crying. Fima and Senya wanted to cry, too, but they had to maintain their manly expressions and refused to cry. Yankel told his usual jokes while swallowing tears, and Sarah, strangely, was calm. She had made her peace with this decision and now just wanted her children to be happy. After a lot of kissing and hugging, after a lot of tears, after a lot of good wishes, the two young families started on their road to a new life.

6

As the older girls moved away, Sarah's attention turned to the next in line, Fima. She knew he spent a lot of time with Rivka. Sarah liked the girl, but Rivka's family was Orthodox, very religious, unlike Sarah's.

This meant that everything would have to be done according to the strictly traditional rules. Well, thought Sarah, we'll see when the time comes. It is too early to worry about anything now.

What Sarah did not notice was that Senya and Lyuba, who always liked being together, looked at each other a little differently now. Senya was around fifteen, judging by his stature, and Lyuba was thirteen—too young for anything serious, but not too young to discover new and wonderful emotions. With time, Sarah more sensed than noticed that the air around them was changing, but as for finding life companions for her children, she was more attentive to Fima's life.

"What a nice young man!"

This is what people usually said about Fima. He was handsome, good-natured, had a good profession—a good shoemaker is not easy to find—and also played the violin well. And how well-mannered he was! Everybody liked him. People did not even notice the slight limp that he had had since his early childhood when he had broken his leg and it had not healed properly. In fact, this limp was a benefit: he could not be recruited into military service because of it. Any young woman would be glad to be his wife, but he liked Rivka. In the last couple of years, Rivka and Fima had become so close that the all-knowing and all-noticing women of Olshana already called them a soon-to-be couple.

How surprised Sarah was one evening to find Fima in a bad mood. This did not happen often.

"Lyovushka, what is it with you? Are you ill?"

"No, Mother. I just think that I will never be married to Rivka."

"Why is that? Did you two break up?"

"No, but her parents keep reminding her that she cannot get married until Runa does, and you know how ugly Runa is! She will never find a husband, and Rivka will never marry because of her. This is terrible!"

"Are you sure you are not overreacting?"

"You know Runa is older than Rivka. Her strict parents do not want to break the tradition of not marrying younger daughters off until the older ones are married."

20

"Fima, don't fret. I promise you, this is a simple matter. I will fix it, trust me."

Fima hugged his mother and said, "My wise mommy, you probably already have a plan."

But Sarah was not exactly sure what to do. It is one thing to convince a stubborn man to change his mind; it is a different matter to convince a religious person to forgo a long-standing tradition. How to resolve this problem? She decided to sleep on it.

By the next morning, she knew what to do and how to talk to Rivka's mother Hannah, who would have to be convinced first. She prepared her famous meat cakes and went to Hannah's house.

Hannah greeted Sarah with a wide smile. "Hello, Sarah! It's nice to see you!"

"Hello, Hannah! We did not talk in a long time. I made some cakes. Can we talk?"

"Of course. Come in, sit down. Let me make some tea. How are you? Your family? How are your girls in the city?" Hannah was genuinely glad to see Sarah.

"I am fine, except, you know, with age it is more difficult to work in the garden. The children help me, but I know they have other things in mind. They are growing fast. Vera and Nadya write often and say they are happy in Elizavetgrad. They miss us, and I hate to think about the time when they will start having children and I am not around to help. But what can you do? Children have their own lives, and we cannot stand in their way if we wish them happiness."

"Yes, you are right, Sarah. But you also have to protect them." Hannah bustled around, preparing tea, putting glasses and silverware out, making the dinner table look inviting for a guest.

"Right you are, Hannah. This is why I came to talk. You know Fima and Rivka are in love. We need to think about their wedding because this will make our children happy."

"Sarah, you know we cannot do anything about Rivka's wedding until Runa is married!"

"Why not?"

21

"What do you want us to do? Break with tradition? Why doesn't Fima marry Runa? We would be in-laws just the same!"

"What are you talking about? Marry Runa! He loves Rivka! What is this—a bazaar to negotiate our children's happiness?"

"Come on, Sarah! You know I was joking. Help me find a good husband for Runa and we will have two weddings at the same time. But we cannot break with our tradition. Runa marries first. Rivka second."

"Tradition, tradition! Do you want to let down your daughter? Besides, traditions change. As we say, new times, new songs! You have to change with the times, Hannah. Otherwise, it's like you are stuck in a spider web. I don't think you want all your younger daughters to be old maids if Runa never finds someone to marry. Do you think the boys who like them today will wait forever? Do you want to risk never seeing any of your daughters married and never having any grandchildren?"

Sarah's hard-hitting questions startled Hannah and her confidence began to tremble. She was not sure how to react to Sarah's arguments anymore. Like all mothers, she wanted to see her children happy, but it was difficult for her to contemplate an act against tradition.

Sarah sensed Hannah's state of mind and kept pushing. "Hannah, you know my Fima is a bachelor any girl would like to have for a husband. He likes your daughter. Let's strike a deal now so he would not need to look for another bride."

Thoughts flew through Hannah's head. Emotionally, she already agreed with Sarah; she was just looking for an intellectual justification for the change she was about to accept.

"Sarah," she finally said, "I think you are right. But what about my husband? He will not agree to this."

"Yes, he will. If you get to him the way you know how, he will." Sarah winked an eye and made a face that Hannah understood well. "I am sure of it. Let's talk about the wedding."

Both women laughed now, and with that, in anticipation of the joyous event, started to discuss preparations for the wedding. They decided on a date before Rosh Hashanah, hugged each other as close relatives, shed a few happy tears, and parted. As expected, Hannah convinced her husband that this marriage was good and appropriate, and preparations for the wedding soon began in earnest.

A few days before the wedding, Yankel asked Fima to sit down with him for a talk. He wanted to share some of his life experiences with his son and talked about many things, including the respect and support the wife deserves. He ended with something that had been passed through generations in their family: "If you want to be the King in the family, treat your wife like the Queen."

"Father, I have always observed this at home. I cannot behave any other way."

<h2 style="text-align:center">7</h2>

Olshana was changing. And not only Olshana, but many other small towns where Jews traditionally lived were affected as more and more people left. Some went to America, and others, especially younger Jews, to bigger cities in Russia, closer to educational and economic opportunities. For those small entrepreneurs who stayed, it was more difficult to survive financially with fewer customers. Two of Sarah's children had already followed the trend of moving away. After his wedding, Fima also decided to leave, as Yankel's business was slowing down and did not generate enough orders to support two families. Sarah did not even put up a fight this time; she knew her son had made the right decision and that he would live close to his sisters, who were already established in Elizavetgrad. Again, tears and cries, hugs and kisses, wishes of good luck in a new place... and finally Fima and Rivka's little wagon departed. Sarah and her remaining children, Lyuba and Senya, watched until the wagon completely disappeared from view. Yankel could not bear to watch and went to his shop as soon as the young couple started to drive away. He wanted to drown himself in work and have no time left to think about this separation with his beloved son.

Elizavetgrad was a city of decent size, and Fima was pleased with his business achievements in a short time. He found space for his shoemaker's shop and soon had enough customers to keep him working almost full time. It was only a matter of time before Fima invited Senya to join him in the city and help with the growing business. At first, Senya was not willing to leave Lyuba, but with time, as Fima's descriptions of life in the city excited his interest, moving to the city and joining his brother became more and more attractive. He could still visit Olshana, and when Lyuba became old enough, they could marry. He decided to move. When Senya told his family about it, nobody liked the idea, even though everyone understood that this was going to happen. He just needed his official papers. All Russian citizens were required to have a document like a passport for traveling and moving to new places, but while a peasant stayed local, the passport was kept in a police station. Now Senya needed it so he could legally move to Elizavetgrad.

Being sixteen or so (he did not know his birthday), Senya had lived in Olshana for nine years, but he had rarely seen the local authorities, as the Jewish part of the town did not require a lot of attention from the police. But now he had to meet the local officialdom. He decided to do it on his own, without any help from Sarah or Yankel. He stated to Sarah, who wanted to accompany him, that he was a grown man and could handle such a simple task by himself.

One afternoon he put on his best shirt and went to the place where all official business was conducted. He found the office in the center of town, opened the door, and walked in. In a small town like Olshana, the officials were not bothered much. When Senya walked in, the clerk sitting at the desk behind a railing looked up with an expression typical for a bureaucrat in any corrupt society: *Who is here to interrupt the slumber of an important man?* It was also typical for such a man to be affected by the presence of a strong and confident person. Senya was tall and handsome, and his confident demeanor resembled that of a nobleman.

"Good afternoon," Senya said.

24

By now the clerk had enough time to examine the visitor and decide that, noble demeanor or not, nobles do not dress like this man and so he must be a peasant, which meant he could give the young man little courtesy.

"What do you want?"

"I need my papers."

"You need papers! You can just barge in and I will drop everything important I do and give them to you? Oh, these people, when will they learn?" The clerk went on loudly complaining about the interruption in his routine, but finally he asked, "What is your name?"

"Senya."

"Senya who?"

This was the first time in Senya's life that his first name was not sufficient. He was startled, but composed himself quickly and responded, "Senya Kagan."

"What? Kagan? Are you a Jew?"

"I have lived with the Kagans since I was a little boy."

"Wait a minute—what is that cross doing on your neck if you are a Jew?"

"I was born Christian, but I live with the Kagans. What difference does it make?" Senya's natural confidence boosted his defenses. His voice started to sound stronger.

"If you are not a Kagan, I need to know your real name. How can I give a document without your real name? Don't you see, peasant?"

Senya understood. He sensed that a change in his life was approaching. He dropped his head. "I forgot my real name."

"Well, then, we will call you Nepomnyashchy. Let me just write it down, Senya Nepomnyashchy from Olshana." The clerk spent some time writing. Then he looked up at Senya again. "How old are you, Senya Nepomnyashchy?"

"I am sixteen," Senya answered after a brief hesitation.

"What? Do you think I am stupid? I have a son who is sixteen. He looks a lot less mature than you do. You must be at least eighteen. Maybe more."

"I am sixteen!"

"Sure you are. Let me see. I don't think we've had enough military recruits. I am going to sign you up to defend the Motherland, Nepomnyashchy. We will let you know when to be ready. Good-bye."

The conversation was over.

Senya was confused and upset. Something had just happened here, and he did not know how to react. Back home, he described the incident to Sarah and Yankel.

The prospect of Senya becoming a soldier at his age was frightening to Sarah. She had heard from people before about the hardships that conscripts suffer, and Senya was not mature enough, she thought, for life without the guidance of his parents and far away from everything he knew.

About three weeks after his attempt to receive his formal papers, Senya and a few other Olshana boys were picked up by a military representative. Now he was called by his new name—Nepomnyashchy. His new friends made fun of this name as it meant someone who does not remember. Senya did not want to go through the explanation of how he got this name, and it did not matter, anyway. From now on, it was his name. He had arrived in Olshana as a little boy without a family name, and he departed as a confident, strong young man.

Leaving the people he loved to face the unknown was difficult for him. Saying good-bye to Lyuba was the hardest part of all, even though she tried to be brave and optimistic. In addition to the food Sarah prepared for Senya to take with him on the long road, Lyuba packed a violin to help him in difficult moments and to lift his spirits. She also said quietly, when just a few moments were left to them, "I had a dream, and I think it was a prophetic one. You will be back in a couple of years, and we will be happy for many years until we die together. Remember this and be strong."

8

Senya's military service took him to middle Russia. He wrote home as often as time allowed and in his letters he described his new life and friends and how much he missed the family. He never complained about anything and always finished with *I hope to see you soon.* How soon he could see his family was not clear. A private in the Russian Czarist Army could serve up to twenty-five years. That is a long time. He would come back a middle-aged man. Would Lyuba wait for him that long? Could he even ask her to wait?

Fate intervened and cleared the situation faster than any hired lawyer could. It was a gray and gloomy day when Sarah answered a knock on the door with her usual, "It's open, come in." The door did not open. Another knock demanded her attention. Surprised by somebody's strange behavior, Sarah ran to the door and opened it. On the doorstep stood a tall, handsome man smiling from ear to ear. He was in a soldier's uniform. It was Senya! Sarah did not recognize him immediately, as he looked much older now, but his big blue eyes spoke clearly who he was.

"Yankel, Lyuba," Sarah yelled, "come! Look who is here!"

Yankel and Lyuba came running from wherever they heard Sarah's voice. Realizing the reason for the yelling, their facial expressions quickly changed from alarm to pleasure. Everyone was hugging and kissing Senya, but he could not take his eyes off Lyuba, who had grown into a beautiful woman. He wanted to kiss her not as a sister but a lover.

They spent the evening sharing stories of their lives since Senya's departure. Senya explained the reason for coming home after spending only two years in the army: the injury he had sustained during training exercises, which caused some loss of mobility in the leg. Then he revealed details about his life as a soldier. Face to face, he could tell his family the truth about the bad food they had to eat and the humiliations the soldiers suffered from the officers. He also told them about how some officers drank too much, hit the soldiers right in their faces, and laughed because those soldiers had no power to defend themselves. Life in the army was hard for enlisted men, especially for Jews, who not only suffered the same or worse treatment from the officers as their fellow soldiers, but were also attacked by their fellows. Jewish conscripts often found a way to protect themselves from other soldiers by offering writing and reading services. Jews could read while most other conscripts could not as they were largely peasants with no education.

When the elders finally decided to go to bed, Senya and Lyuba had some time to themselves. Lyuba was elated to see her friend and future husband, as she imagined him in her dreams.

"My dear Lyuba, how is your life? Tell me more about yourself."

"It was difficult for me during this time. My siblings are all away. I see them only on holidays. And you I could not see at all. I had imagined how you spent your days, how you wrote your letters. It's been difficult for me without you, Senya."

He smiled at her. "Every single day I was thinking about seeing you again. When we had to run a lot or do some hard work, thinking of you always gave me strength. I thought that all of life's difficulties would disappear if I could only come back and be with you. Lyuba, let's get married! Would you be my wife?" Senya stepped closer and hugged Lyuba with all his youthful strength.

"Yes, I will gladly be your wife!"

Tears appeared in Lyuba's eyes. Senya hugged her again and kissed her lips for the first time.

The next day, Sarah and Yankel learned about Lyuba and Senya's decision to marry. They were already expecting it. The young couple would stay with them, and Sarah would hear little kids running around again. She missed having little kids in her house. All her grandchildren lived in Elizavetgrad, and she did not see them often. But Lyuba's children would be here, right here, where Sarah could be with them all the time. And Yankel, whose health was declining, liked the idea of slowly transferring his business to Senya. Everybody was filled with joy and looking forward to the wedding, which they set for the end of August.

Life became busy in the Kagan household. Plans for the wedding and the preparation of the house for a young family occupied everybody. Now Senya became not just a vendor in the biggest market in the city, but also a buyer. One day not long before the wedding, when Yankel, Senya, and Lyuba were all at the market, Sarah, who was working outside her house, noticed an unknown, strangely dressed woman rapidly approaching. She was surprised when the woman stopped and asked, "Are you Sarah?"

"Yes."

Sarah was studying the woman. She was quite tall and very beautiful. There was something familiar in her face, especially her eyes. Sarah just could not pin it down, but she had a feeling she had seen these eyes before. The eyes, these large, blue eyes—they were so familiar!

"My name is Elena," the woman said. "I am looking for my lost brother, and people tell me I need to talk to you. My brother's name is Senya."

Sarah almost dropped to the ground. Intuitively she knew this was Senya's sister, but wanted proof.

"Why don't we go inside and sit down," Sarah said.

Inside, she offered Elena a seat by the table. Both women were nervous, Sarah preparing treats for the guest, Elena looking around the house. When the tea and sweets were ready, Sarah poured a glass for Elena and sat down with her. Elena could not wait any longer and continued the conversation she had started outside.

"I am looking for my brother, Senya. He disappeared when he was about seven. I was living in America at that time. I have been trying to find him with no success until someone who had seen your son said he looks just like our father, except for the blue eyes that are like our mother's."

"Well," said Sarah, "this kind of resemblance is not enough to say that my Senya is your brother."

"My brother has a birthmark right behind his left ear," Elena said.

Now Sarah realized that this was indeed the sister. She gasped for air and said, "I think you've found your brother."

Part Two

1

Elena's eyes filled with tears as she struggled to maintain her composure. Sarah waited a few moments in silence for her guest to calm down and then told her Senya's story, starting with his appearance on her doorstep and continuing through his life with her family. She explained how she had taken Senya to the priest in an attempt to find his family, and how he came back, how he grew up and served in the army. Elena was listening, crying and smiling.

"Senya is away in town," Sarah said, "together with my husband and daughter. They are buying things for the wedding and should be back soon."

"The wedding?" Elena asked.

"In a few days, Senya marries my youngest daughter."

Their conversation halted when the loud voices of the returning family members penetrated the tense spirit inside the house. As soon as Yankel, Senya, and Lyuba walked in, their lively conversation abruptly stopped when they saw a beautiful, young, and, judging by her dress, rich woman sitting at the table with Sarah. All three were baffled. Their silent faces said, *What is this stranger doing in our poor house?*

The woman stood up, and something turned in Senya's soul, something whispered in the back of his mind that this woman was here because of him. As he kept looking at her, a vague vision of another woman, who resembled this one, patting him on the head emerged from the deep recesses of his memory. She looked more closely at Senya and began crying. Then she stepped close and hugged him tightly. When she looked behind his ear and saw the birthmark, she cried harder.

"I was searching for you so long, my dear brother," she said when she could control her speech. "I found you, found you!" And she kept hugging and kissing Senya as the rest of the family silently watched.

"You are my sister?" Senya asked when his shock diminished.

"Yes, yes. I am Elena, your older sister." After her initial euphoria subsided, she added, "You look like an exact copy of our father, Count Voronov, only your eyes are like our mother's."

2

"You are the son of a count and a serf."

These were Elena's first words when she and Senya were alone. So much craved Elena to be with her lost brother and share the past that she had accepted Sarah's invitation to stay with them as long as she wanted. Sarah prepared one room for the guest, while Elena sent the coach back to the Elizavetgrad hotel to bring her belongings to Olshana. After the rest of the family had settled for the night in their rooms, Elena spoke those opening words.

"You are the son of a count and a serf. Our father, Count Voronov, owned an estate not too far from here that included the village of Sotkino. The Voronovs were a noble family, but the Count left no legitimate heirs because you and I are his illegitimate children."

Senya interrupted, "So, who are we? Tell me about our parents. I don't remember much, except when I look at you, something familiar stirs in my memory."

"People say I look a lot like our mother. That is why I look familiar to you. I will tell you what I know and what I remember about them." Elena shifted in her seat and composed herself for a long story.

Senya was fidgeting in anticipation of learning about his roots. He touched his sister's hand.

"Our father was a hero of Sevastopol. You may know about the Crimean War that Russia lost. Father was an officer. He was injured but made it back home to Sotkino. Mother mentioned to me once that he took the loss to heart and remembered his friends who had been

32

killed for as long as he lived. Soon after he returned home, his father died of a sickness that could not be cured. Father was the last member of his family as his mother had died in childbirth. He was alone now except for a close friend, Baron Kivirov, whose estate was close to Sotkino. That is where he met our mother, who was Kivirov's serf.

"When I asked our mother how she met our father, she smiled and described to me how she and the other girls were serving Kivirov and his friends, who were playing cards, eating, and drinking. They did not pay much attention to the girls, but she noticed more than the men knew. She noticed that Count Voronov's face was often sad and that he was drinking a lot. And then she noticed that he could not take his eyes off her."

"If you resemble our mother, she was quite beautiful," Senya said.

"Thank you, Brother. I think she was beautiful, but also different from the other serfs. When I was a child in Sotkino, I spent time in the kitchen and heard the women there talking about her. To them, she did not look like a serf, but like a free woman. I asked them why they thought so, and they told me that when she came to Sotkino with our father, she looked so confident, so proud, that they thought he had brought a wife home....I asked our mother later about this, and she laughed and said that she was scared of the new situation but hid her feelings by pretending to look pleased."

"Why was she scared? It's not like she was going to prison or another country."

"Well, a new situation can be scary. She was very young. And *scared* might have been just a part of it. She had had it quite good with the Kivirovs, taking care of their little daughters. They loved her. She did not want to lose that. And another thing: Kivirov's wife, Sophia, was a well-educated woman from Moscow who loved the arts. She wrote plays and staged them at their estate. Our mother acted in those plays. I guess Sophia liked her as an actress because, Mother told me, she played rich women. Imagine—a serf girl dressed in beautiful, expensive clothes, playing princesses, queens, and other nobles. She loved it!"

"I see," Senya responded. "Our father also saw her playing those roles?"

"Of course he did. He visited his friend often, and a couple of times our mother heard him asking the Baron to sell her to him. But the Baron refused because his wife and children liked her. And then—when she was telling me this part of the story, her face became sad—one day she was directed to pack her things and go with the Count. The housekeeper told her that the Count had won her in a card game. Like a dog or a horse. She was upset for years when she remembered how it had happened.

"But her life in Sotkino was good. The Count assigned her easy duties and spent a lot of time teaching her to read, write, and count. He made her into an educated woman. She told me how they walked together and he told her about his friends who had died during the war with such strong feelings that she could sense his humanity. She fell in love with him then, and... and that is where I came in."

Elena looked down as if trying to hide something. Senya felt that his sister was overwhelmed with emotions. He waited. After a few minutes, Elena lifted her head, smiled, and continued.

"Since I was a little girl, I have remembered our small cottage covered in ivy. There was a green meadow nearby where I liked to run and pick flowers. The Count gave our mother that cottage after I was born. Can you imagine? A serf living in a cottage, doing almost nothing for the estate, and even having the old nanny help with her baby! I learned later that this was unprecedented. But the Count wanted it that way because, I think, he loved her." Elena paused. "He loved her, but he also went to St. Petersburg to look for a wife. You know, our mother could not be good enough for a count. That was expected, but she was quite upset. Although he took good care of us, he needed a legitimate heir to continue the family line."

"If he looked for a wife who was not my mother, where did I come from?" Senya asked.

Elena laughed. "Wait. I will get to you in time. Our father went to the capital where his closest relative, Aunt Leeza, lived and began looking for a wife. Our mother told me he stayed in St. Petersburg with his aunt for almost a year. Then one day she heard from people on the estate that he was coming home with a new wife. She saw the new wife from a distance when they arrived. A young, beautiful woman. With a kind face, she told me. Her name was... her name was... Olga. Our mother soon learned she was rich and brought much money to improve the estate's business. I was little when she came to Sotkino, but I remember her standing by our cottage and talking to our mother. She started to come more and more often, and after a while spent every day with me, either in our cottage or in the mansion. She had taught me all kinds of stuff. I could speak French when I was a teenager, and play the piano, too. And of course, she taught me to speak proper Russian and history and about the arts. You see, she could not have her own children. No one knew why, but she could not. So she spent time with me. I owe her so much gratitude because her involvement in my upbringing is what made me into who I am now. And I was also in awe of her knowledge."

"From what you're telling me, you and our mother did not live like serfs. It's amazing! I've never heard such a story."

"You're right. We were lucky that way. We were lucky...." Elena touched her forehead and her expression changed as if she were trying to weigh how lucky her childhood had been. She resumed her story.

"Our father visited us often. He loved me. Later I came to understand that he was falling in love with our mother again. Even though I was still a child, I could see the difference in how Father looked at Olga, with respect and admiration, and at our mother with excitement. When she became pregnant, Olga learned about it and left. And then you were born!"

Elena stopped talking so Senya could absorb the story. She was happy to tell it to her brother, and he was ecstatic to hear it.

"Go on," Senya nudged his sister.

"Olga left the Count. We stayed in the cottage. Our parents loved each other, but they were still a noble and a peasant, as by this time the new law had abolished serfdom. It would have been good, but eventually years of sadness and drinking to cover it affected Father's health. I was old enough to remember his complaints about pain, then he had difficulties walking, then...."

Elena's eyes became moist. The retelling of a painful part of the story was not easy for her.

"Then we moved from the cottage to the mansion so our mother could deal with our father's pain at any time of day or night. The doctors came and went, not helping much.

She paused again, then smiled and continued: "Father liked seeing you around. You were little, but you looked more and more like him as you grew. Everybody said so. I can see it now in my mind, how you would run into his bedroom shouting something silly and it would bring a smile to his face. And then one night he died. Everyone cried because he was not a bad master, kind to many people, but also because nobody knew what would happen next, who would manage the estate."

"Didn't he have a wife?"

"He did, but she was far away. Olga was also a city woman and knew nothing about agriculture or running an estate. She could marry someone who would mistreat the peasants. Who knew? People were apprehensive, even though when Olga stayed in Sotkino, they liked her. Anyway, she did come to the estate and sold it. We were blessed, however, as Father had signed all the proper papers before his death and our mother actually owned the cottage and a little land around it. That was how we survived after his death. We grew vegetables and fruits on our piece of land, but had no dairy or meat or grains of our own. The estate had provided those things when the Count was alive, but after his death—no more."

"So how did we manage?"

"We did what other farmers were doing: we sold what we had in abundance and bought what we needed. We started selling our fruits and vegetables in Elizavetgrad at the same market you just came home from. The Count had also given our mother a horse and a small wagon well before his death, and we used it to take produce to the market.

And you helped, too! You helped me pick mushrooms in the forest and flowers in our yard. Do you remember?"

Senya was visibly struggling to envision the past, his face showing the working of the mind.

"No, I cannot recall that. But how did you get to America?"

"From the marketplace!"

"What?"

"I always rode to the market early in the morning to sell what we had at the time from the garden and the forest. One day, a young fellow stopped by and asked about the price of the flowers. I did not think he needed the flowers. He wasn't even looking at them. He was looking at me all the time with an expression I understood very well. I sold him some flowers but did not engage in the conversation. He came back again and again. We finally started talking, and he told me that he lived in America and came home to Elizavetgrad every time he saved enough money for the trip. Nikolai—that was his name—told me a lot about America. How people are free to do what they want, how many opportunities exist there for those who want to work. He was an engineer and made enough money to live on and even save some. I was fascinated by his descriptions, and when he asked me to go to America with him, I seriously thought about it. Every question I had, he answered.

"How can I buy a ticket?

"You can work on a ship.

"Where would I live?

"You can stay with me for a while.

"I do not speak English!

"You know French and can learn English fast.

"And so on. When I told my mother about it, she encouraged me to go, and I decided to take my chance. The thought was I would get there, start making money, and send some home to help Mother and you. Then I would eventually pay for your trip to America, too. So, I went.

"Everything happened as Nikolai had predicted. I got a job on a ship washing dishes. In New York, I quickly found a position in a women's clothing store. My education helped me with English and my looks attracted attention from people involved in modeling clothes. I became a model and soon was making more and more money, sending some to you. Do you remember any letters from me?"

"No. I guess I was too little."

"Well, I wrote a lot of letters. But our mother replied less and less often, though she did write to me for a while. And then the letters stopped coming. I was so worried! I didn't know what to do besides continuing to write to her. Eventually, I decided to travel to Sotkino. When I got there, I found strangers living in our old cottage. They knew nothing about your fate. Talking to the villagers, I learned about our mother's death and your disappearance. Then I asked a local priest to look for you and promised to pay him well for his efforts. I left him my address in New York and went back to America.

"In time, I married a wealthy businessman and had two sons, all the while still waiting for news about you. I kept writing to the priest in Sotkino, but his responses were not promising. You had disappeared without a trace. Until, finally, I received a letter from him relating a story he had heard from his wife about an old peasant-woman who saw a young man in the market who looked just like the last Count Voronov. The woman had even approached the youngster to see him better. She was shocked by the resemblance. Shocked, because this boy was clearly part of a Jewish family. She asked him where he was from, made the sign of the cross, and left. After I read this, I decided to take this chance and go to Russia again to check it out. I talked to the priest and his wife, and they directed me to the old woman who had seen you. Slowly, step by step, I learned about the market and the profession of the young man. I came to Olshana and finally—thank God!—I found you, my dear brother."

3

It was almost dawn when Senya stumbled to bed after hearing his sister's long story. The story was extraordinary. Tired as he was, sleep did not come. Senya was rerunning the most fascinating parts of his family's history in his mind. A son of a count and serf! He was not the first child of such a union in Russia, but still, he had never thought of himself as having any noble blood. And now he was about to marry a Jewish girl. What would his noble father think of his son producing Jewish children? I'd like to see his reaction, Senya thought with a smile.

But he also felt a certain pride, strange as it was. He was a descendant of an influential count in a huge empire. He could have presented himself to other nobles as Semyon Voronov, and they would have shaken his hand, offered him a drink, talked to him as an equal. Senya's imagination took him on a wide ride as he fantasized about participating in the kinds of activities the nobles do.

Elena had said the Voronov family had deep roots in Russian society. His ancestors were close to the Russian Czars, they commanded troops in wars, received gratitude and riches from the sovereign, built estates. They were part of the Russian elite!

Senya was contemplating: How would I perform in the circumstances my ancestors faced? Would I have been a hero of Sevastopol, like my father? We lost that war, but brave Russian soldiers and officers did their duty.

Then his attention turned to the other ancestors: the serfs. He knew about serfdom, even though Czar Alexander II had abolished it in 1861. People remembered, and some peasants still could not get away from their environment because they had no means to start a new life. Elena had told him that she'd seen their mother's parents a few times while she lived in Sotkino. They were poor. The land they had to feed themselves was not as good as the Baron's because it was full of rocks and required much effort to harvest anything they planted. And they had to spend time working the Baron's fields before they could even attend to their own. Living had been harsh, and there was no escape.

If I were a serf, Senya thought, either working the fields or doing something else, I might not stand for it. I might end up doing something that would get me punished.

Reconciling the histories of both his parents became difficult for the weary young man. He fell asleep thinking how strange his fate was and how he would live with the three pillars of his personality: a Russian noble, a serf, and a Jew.

Part Three

1

The wedding was approaching fast. Everything seemed to be ready, but Sarah was nervous anyway—she wanted her daughter's, her baby's, marriage to be perfect. When the wedding day arrived, the couple was blessed with beautiful weather. All guests arrived promptly, and after the marriage ceremony and celebratory dinner, the fun began. The band played, the guests danced, and the just-married young couple danced more than anyone else. They loved this day, they loved each other, and they loved life.

Elena observed the celebration with a mixture of happiness and sadness. She was happy for her brother who was marrying someone he loved, but, although this was not mentioned to anyone, she would rather see her brother marrying a Christian and following Christian traditions. With the current situation, she was not sure whether he considered himself Jewish or Christian. He was wearing the cross she had left him, and she was content with that, but he had just gone through a Jewish marriage ceremony full of religious significance for a different people. She understood that the Jews gave him shelter, education, and, most importantly, love. Nevertheless, he was her only brother, and she wanted to talk to him about joining her in America, maybe even on the same ship she was to depart on from Odessa soon.

The celebration with its dancing and singing went on all night. It was only when the last guests finally left that Elena caught Senya alone and said, "I am going back home soon. I would be overjoyed if you moved to America with your wife. America is a country of opportunities and I could help you there. You are young and talented; you could be rich, happy, and living close to me."

"I cannot leave my parents here," Senya replied and Elena winced at the word *parents* but said nothing. "They raised me and I am what I am because of them."

"They can join you later," insisted Elena.

"I don't think Lyuba would want to leave them behind either. Besides, they may not want to go at all."

"Look, Senya. I am the only sister you have and it would be better for us to be close to each other. When I left Sotkino, I promised our mother to help move both of you to America. Unfortunately, life has not completely cooperated with our plans, but we found each other, so let's stay together."

"My dear sister. I know how painful it is for you to understand, but I do have a brother and two more sisters—you saw them, aren't they great? I wish you were close too, but I cannot leave all of them, especially my parents. You can come visit us, and maybe someday we will travel to America, but I cannot do it anytime soon."

Elena began to comprehend the attachment her brother had to the entire Kagan family, not just Lyuba. She grasped the impossibility of what she wanted her brother to do and was upset about it. However, life is a good teacher and Elena had her lessons too, such as learning to live with frustrations and unfulfilled expectations. She loved her brother and wanted to keep their upcoming separation tension-free.

"I understand, my dear. I just don't want to lose you again. Let's write often and stay in touch. I want you to promise that if you need money, you will let me know. I can help. I also want to leave some money for your young family now, as a gift." Elena gave Senya a wallet, which was filled with something, presumably money.

"Thank you, sister. I promise to write and keep in touch." He did not want to argue about the gift after already rejecting Elena's offer to move to America.

"Senya, where is Lyuba?"

"She is probably in the house helping her mother. I will call her."

When Lyuba appeared, happy and tired, Elena hugged and kissed her saying, "Lyuba, my dear, take care of my little brother. He is the only brother I have. Let me know if I can help with anything. Come visit us soon and please accept this from me."

She took off a gold necklace with a pearl pendant and put it on Lyuba's neck. The sisters-in-law hugged and, to avoid crying together, went to help the others clean up. Senya also joined them. It was one of the happiest days in his life and he did not want it to end.

After the wedding, Elena left, the Kagan siblings with their families went home to Elizavetgrad, and the young couple found itself in the old, familiar house under new, unfamiliar circumstances. Now everyone looked at them differently, as a single unit, not as before when they were Lyuba and Senya. Now they were the Nepomnyashchys—the name of the new family.

The young couple settled into a family routine quickly. Their living arrangements changed somewhat, but they remained in the same house and were surrounded by the same people. Lyuba continued helping her mother with daily work at home and in the yard, while Senya became a full-time shoemaker working with Yankel. By now, Senya's skills in fixing and making new shoes were considerable. Yankel was sure that his business would stay alive with such a good craftsman taking care of it. If only people stopped leaving Olshana, Senya would provide a good living for Lyuba and their children.

Children. Little feet shuffling, tiny voices making funny sounds, and their contagious laughs that remind one of the beauty and meaning of life—how much both Yankel and Sarah waited for all this commotion to start again in their house. But when the first anniversary of Lyuba's wedding came along, there was still no sign of grandchildren. Sarah and Yankel talked about this among themselves, but never mentioned it to Lyuba or Senya. God willing, there would be many kids, but at his age Yankel was wondering how much longer he would be around, especially since his health kept deteriorating. He had trouble with his feet for quite a while, but recently they were swelling more and it was hard for him to walk. He also developed breathing difficulties. Yankel stayed in bed a lot and was spending less time in the shop, leaving it to Senya's care.

Almost two years after the wedding, Lyuba finally broke good news to her parents—she was pregnant. The elder Kagans were ecstatic. At last their dreams were coming true. Sarah could not wait to see a little one and become a grandmother in her own home. With the announcement of the family growing soon, Senya wanted to earn more money and began spending more time in the shop making shoes and then going to the market to sell them. He turned out to be a good salesman; his good looks and pleasant demeanor attracted women who liked talking to him and ended up buying his products. Sometimes when he went to the Elizavetgrad market he saw his brother Fima, who came to the market just to chat with Senya and share family news. Everyone was excited about the youngest in the family becoming a mother, and the city relatives wanted to know all the details.

Lyuba was six months pregnant when, on a Sunday morning, Senya was preparing to go to Elizavetgrad. He wanted to sell the new shoes he just made and buy some things Lyuba had asked for. He packed his wagon early in the morning, kissed his wife good-bye, and left in a very good mood. Things were going great: they would be parents soon, he was looking forward to seeing Fima, and the weather was pleasant. The ride was expected to be joyful and the selling swift.

It was late morning. Lyuba and Sarah were cleaning the house when they heard noise outside. There was loud shouting; somebody was yelling "Oh my God! What are you doing?" Then came the sound of broken glass, a burst of wild laughter, and all of a sudden their door opened and a big man appeared inside the house. He was obviously drunk and behaved like someone who decided he was the ruler of this world and could do anything he wanted.

"Ah, Jewish bitches," were his first words. "You think you can insult and offend us Ukrainian peasants. You like eating our bread and meat, and you think your greed can swallow everything. We will teach you who is the boss here!"

The man looked around the house, came to the table full of dishes, and turned it over. The sound of broken dishes rang out like a church bell. Lyuba shouted, "Get out of here, you are drunk! Or I will call the police."

The man looked at her and laughed. "The police? I am the police! Do you think someone will help you?" Then he looked at her again and something different from rage reflected in his eyes.

"Come here, you little slut. Let me taste how sweet a Jewess is. I've heard you are very tasty." With these words, he approached Lyuba and tried to rip her clothes off. Everything was happening fast and Sarah, shocked by the intrusion, had not said a word yet, but when she saw the drunkard attacking Lyuba, her fury was like that of a lioness defending her cubs. She jumped on the man and started hitting him with a pan she was still holding in her hands. The man was caught by surprise, but not for more than a moment. Then he pushed Sarah away from him and hit her so hard with his fist that she fell down like a cut tree and hit her head on the overturned table. She fell and stayed motionless. Lyuba wanted to run toward her mother, but the man intercepted her, brought her down, and jumped on top of her. He pinned her arms with one of his and with another began tearing her clothes off. Lyuba struggled, but there was no use; the man was too big and strong for her. She started crying and shouting, "Get off me, get off me, son of a bitch!" but her struggle made him only more determined to achieve his goal.

Suddenly, Lyuba felt his grip on her arms weaken and she was able to move. The man did not react at all and Lyuba pushed him away with disgust. She looked up and saw her father standing above her with a shovel in his hands. Lyuba stood up, wanting to see her mother, who was still not moving, but Yankel, in a strange quiet voice, said, "Time is short, it is a pogrom and that means other thugs are going to be here any minute. You must protect yourself; we will take care of ourselves."

Yankel took her to the backyard, opened the entrance to the ground cellar where they kept food to avoid spoilage, let her in, and closed the lid in such a way as to prevent it being noticed. Then he went back to the house to check on his wife.

Senya's day was good. Shoes were selling well; he saw Fima and they discussed family affairs for a while. He was in a great mood. It was about midday when he noticed that shoppers were looking strangely at Jewish vendors and whispering something to each other. He asked a woman who just bought a pair of shoes about it, and she nervously replied, "There is word on the street that today Jews are to be beaten."

Senya understood immediately. He packed his belongings quickly and ran the horse almost to the brink of expiration by the time they entered Olshana. Upon reaching their street, he understood what had happened there. People he had known for a long time were running around their houses trying to collect whatever possessions were still intact. Some were sitting next to motionless bodies, crying and trying to revive them. Broken glass was everywhere. Senya approached his house with a heavy heart, expecting the worst. He stopped the wagon at the entrance, ran inside, and saw destruction. Everything was ruined, broken into pieces, and some items were gone. It was as quiet as a cemetery. No voices were heard, no whispers, no sound—just silence. And then he noticed two bodies lying in a pool of blood: Sarah and Yankel. In shock, Senya burst out sobbing. His body slowly dropped to the floor, hands covering his face, refusing to believe the gruesome scene. All he could do was repeat the same question that Jews had been asking for many years, "Why, why did this happen? What were they guilty of to be punished so?"

After a few moments, as though awakened from a bad dream, he shook his head and cried out, "Lyuba, Lyuba, where are you?" But there was no response. Senya ran to the backyard and looked around—nothing. Then he remembered about the cellar. When he opened the lid to the cellar, he saw Lyuba. She was crying and her skirt and hands were bloody.

"Senya, we lost our child."

2

Burying people you love is like cutting out a piece of your body and putting it in the ground. The violent and unexpected manner of death only adds to the grief of those still alive. This was not the first pogrom in Russia, but it was the first in Olshana, where many people died and many were injured. Nobody even talked about the broken and stolen stuff. Who cares about that when you are burying your loved ones and seeing their faces for the last time? Never again will they laugh, never again will they complain about a hard life, never again can someone humiliate them. They are saints now. The living are the ones left to struggle. They bury the dead, their souls torn asunder by guilt. Why was I not here to help? Why did I have to go somewhere?

The Kagans and many neighbors finished their solemn duty within three days of the pogrom. The authorities came, looked around, and left. Nobody was arrested, nobody was punished. People talked about moving to America. Everyone had a story to tell about this great country, which accepted immigrants and provided opportunities. Everyone knew someone who made it over there across the ocean in the new world. Lyuba's sisters and their husbands made a quick decision: it was time to leave Russia and find a place where pogroms do not happen. They were confident in their decision and attempted to convince both Senya's and Fima's families to move together. But the brothers were not sure. Fima's business was becoming quite profitable and he did not want to lose it. Senya and Lyuba meanwhile decided to move closer to their brother in Elizavetgrad.

Vera's and Nadya's families collected their belongings and left for America into a new life, while their brothers stayed behind, working together and living near each other. Nobody could know when the family would be together again, and the separation was hard.

With time, love heals wounds and makes people whole again. Lyuba's disposition improved, slowly but irrefutably. She was beginning to smile at her husband again and laugh at Fima's jokes. She noticed children again and enjoyed watching them play, and the desire to have her own baby came back. Maybe this time God would be kind to her and she would have a baby. Lyuba's prayers were answered when she noticed the pregnancy signs again.

A healthy baby came right on schedule. The girl was named Zhenya. She looked just like Senya, except for her big brown eyes that resembled her mother's. And two years later a son, Yasha, enlarged the family again. Yasha was a carbon copy of Lyuba. Luckily for him, a cousin was born at about the same time. Boris, Fima's second child, would be Yasha's companion. The boys grew up side by side. They were crawling, walking, and saying their first words as though competing with each other. And by the time Yasha and Boris were two, Lyuba had another baby. It was a girl again, named Anna. If Sarah could only see her! Anna took after her grandmother so much that sometimes Lyuba cried looking at her and remembering her mother.

Zhenya and Yasha were quiet and obedient children. But not Anna. There was nothing she would do when asked; that would be obeying and Anna's will could not accommodate it. She was the one who decided what to do! If her mother asked her to sweep the floor, she would refuse and run away with an expression of insult on her face. But a few minutes later she would come back and offer to sweep the floor as if nobody mentioned that before. And she would do a great job too, but it had to be done on her terms. Everyone in the family liked Anna, the youngest one. She was sweet, cute, and her strong character in combination with her theatrical behavior only added to her adoration.

At five years of age, the children began studying Yiddish and Russian. At the same time, following the family musical tradition, the violin was still the instrument that the children learned to play. That is, all except Anna, who again wanted to be different and asked for a guitar. As the children were growing up, a new family band was taking shape. Between Lyuba's and Fima's families there were four adults and five kids, all of whom were musical and all, except Rivka, played an instrument. Now, as before, some hands were holding violins—with one little pair of hands clutching a guitar—while others were beating on tables and pots as drums, all making music and participating in the shared happiness.

But joy was not always present in their lives. They were used to the feeling of being second-rate citizens; they were used to hard work; they were used to the social limitations of Russian Jews. They could not get used to the pogroms though, which were occurring more frequently. This was not just the fear of physical harm to one's family, but mental anguish over their total humiliation and helplessness in the face of evil. When rumors of new pogroms in the Elizavetgrad area started again, the emigration discussion renewed.

"Time to leave, time to find a better place for our families," Fima offered when they gathered to plan their future. "I see no hope here. Let's move."

"Where do you propose to go?" asked Lyuba.

"America, of course! Our sisters write that they all work and make enough money to live on. We can do the same. And we would not need to worry about upcoming pogroms anymore."

A brief silence and then Senya spoke, "Probably the right decision. But where is the money for all of us to leave together?"

"We can borrow whatever is missing," proposed Rivka.

"Borrow from whom? I bet you whoever has the means to leave is contemplating it as we do. No one would lend us money," replied Senya.

"I am afraid he is right," Fima agreed. "We need to find a solution."

"Right. If we pool our resources, maybe one family can move. And when we make enough, the other will follow," proposed Senya. "I think you guys should go first. Establish yourself in America and we will join you later."

Rivka said, "Senya, didn't your sister offer to help if you needed money?"

"She did," said Senya, "but I do not see it as an option now."

"Why not?" jumped in Fima.

"This idea does not feel right. We met only once, and she has a rich husband, but how would he react if she sends us a lot of money, which who knows when we can repay? Just not right. Besides, how long would it take for all this to work? Aren't you eager to leave soon?"

"Well then. We are back to the plan to move separately," concluded Fima.

The decision was made.

It was hard for them to part. There is always attraction in something new, and there is hope—plain, nourishing hope for people who made a difficult decision to start a new life and are looking forward to the future. But those who stay now face the same unchanging environment minus the loved ones who are not present to share and help. In Lyuba and Senya's case, the situation was even grimmer since all their close relatives were now far away and they felt completely alone in the hostile world.

Before the departure, after the hugs and kisses and tears, Fima turned to Senya and said, "Senya, you will come to America when we settle there, promise?"

Senya wiped the tears from his eyes and replied with a typical Russian answer: "Time will tell."

3

The first days after the parting were total hell for Senya and Lyuba. The difficult everyday routine became harder to cope with when the safety net of the extended family disappeared. And then the letter from Fima arrived. It was such a joy to open this letter and read the words put on paper by the people they loved. Senya read it aloud.

> Hello my dearest Senya, Lyuba, and the children!
> I want to tell you we are okay. The trip was long, but our sisters met us when we arrived in New York and it was great to hug them. They rented a tiny apartment for us and also supplied some basics: furniture, household items, and, of

*course, food. In two weeks I found a job in a shoemaker
shop. This was a Jewish shop and I could communicate with
the owner in Yiddish. Then Rivka found a job as a
seamstress in a factory. She works hard, but together we
make enough money for rent, food, and even to buy some
new clothes. The children started school and Boris also
delivers newspapers in the morning to help a little.*

*We love it here. Our new life is not easy, but there is no
threat of pogroms and the children are safe! I hope with time
to save enough money to open my own shop, and then you
can join us and we will live as one big family again.*

We all miss you and cannot wait to kiss you.

Your brother and uncle, Fima.

Senya finished reading the letter to the entire family, who were
hungrily listening to every word. It was a good letter but everyone was
sad they were far away. Senya also thought that the decision to stay was
the right one. He did not want Lyuba to work hard. If that was what
she would be doing in America, he did not want to go there. Here, in
a familiar place with a familiar language and customs, he would provide
and protect.

Soon after Fima's, another letter from America arrived—from Elena.
She had learned about Fima's move and wanted to add her voice to the
chorus that was asking Senya to move his family to America. She also
sent money and wanted Senya to use it to buy tickets and whatever they
needed for the trip. But Senya had already decided: instead of moving
to America, they would move to a better part of town. In bigger cities,
Jews usually lived on the outskirts. Senya did not look like a Jew at all.
If anything, he resembled Russian aristocracy and he always carried
himself with the confidence inherited from his parents. He wanted to
use his favorable appearance to impress the rich and powerful in the
city. They were lucky to find an affordable place not far from the city
center, where the aristocracy lived, and the family moved. They
expected to earn more money with richer customers.

51

The first steps in business are usually difficult. Although Senya retained some of his former customers, his income was hardly enough to sustain the family and the shop. To speed up the acquisition of new customers, Senya decided to go door to door in the wealthiest neighborhoods and show his shoemaking capabilities. He recognized that news travels fast in the relatively small circle of the rich and powerful. The aim was to impress his first customers with the hope that they would tell the others of his great skills. Soon his efforts were rewarded—he did impress a couple of significant citizens of Elizavetgrad with his talent. He made good shoes fast, and the clients, in addition to their satisfaction with the product, were also pleased to be served by a good-looking young man who never missed promised delivery dates.

A year later, Senya's business grew a great deal and he had to hire two helpers to take care of all the orders. Senya was happy that he could provide enough for the family and Lyuba did not have to work. That was his goal: to protect Lyuba from as much of life's troubles as possible. She was his Queen and he treated her as royalty. In Senya's household, there was always love and affection accented by ever-present flowers, which Senya supplied as a sign of admiration for his wife.

4

Fima and all the sisters regularly sent letters. And the message was always the same, "Come join us!" Senya and Lyuba felt their relatives' love even across the ocean. But they lived in Elizavetgrad, building their own business, raising children, growing as a family toward a future that all of them wanted to be better than the present. What was important was that the children grew up in an atmosphere of love, affection, respect, and hunger for knowledge.

Zhenya and Yasha demonstrated more discipline and striving for knowledge than Anna. Zhenya's dream was to become a doctor, even at a time when the most a woman with medical aspirations could achieve in Russia was to be a nurse. The human body fascinated her and she wanted to learn all about it: how it grows, what makes it sick, how to prevent disease, how to make people live longer.

Yasha loved books. He read everything he could find, above all history and philosophy. The issues affecting not the human body but the development of the human race were of most interest to him. His immediate dream was a library—a big library containing books on all subjects written by great writers, historians, philosophers, and scientists. At times, Yasha thought he could spend all his waking hours reading. Even the smell of books, the sharp smell of glue and ink, sometimes mixed with a distinct leather aroma, lifted his spirit, reminding him of the treasures hidden between the books' covers that he could partake of as soon as he had free time.

Anna manifested more of a street-smart attitude to life than her siblings. She had a strong, stubborn character that did not like discipline and repetition. Her grades in school were fine, as she was quick and sharp, but she did not have her siblings' drive to learn. Playing a guitar, helping her father in the shop with selling and buying—this she liked and was good at. She had the instinct for the right business transactions and the ability to talk a customer into buying. But she could not handle taking directions from others.

In the case of the Nepomnyashchy children, their young years contained strong indications of their futures.

5

Yasha had a friend in school—Sergey. Their friendship started unexpectedly. Yasha was a small, quiet Jewish boy, constantly barraged by insults and threats of beatings by the street thugs, while Sergey was one of those street guys who would not be called a thug, but could defend himself—he was big, strong, and grew up in the streets, as his single mother worked long hours. Sergey noticed Yasha in school and took a liking to the smaller boy, who was smart but defenseless against physical attacks. Once, when Yasha's trip home was about to be interrupted by the thugs' attempt to ridicule and beat him, Sergey stood in front of Yasha and said, "You want to start with me?" The guys did not want to mess with Sergey and left the boys alone. Since that day, they became an indivisible pair and spent most of their time together. After school, they usually went to Yasha's home. Lyuba fed the boys and then they studied or played. Watching Yasha, Sergey developed a great interest in books. Sergey's mother was quite upbeat about this arrangement. She was satisfied that her only son spent time not on the street with thugs, but with a nice and well-mannered boy.

One day, Sergey did not show up for school and Yasha ran to his house to find out why. Sergey was home alone, sitting in the corner of the room as if in a trance.

"What is the matter, Sergey?"

"Last night my mother got sick. I took her to the hospital. She could hardly walk. She died soon after."

Yasha took his friend home. Lyuba looked at the boys and understood something terrible had happened.

"His mother died," said Yasha quietly.

Lyuba hugged Sergey, who could not hold it any longer and started sobbing aloud. Lyuba's eyes filled with tears. The feeling of losing a mother was familiar to her. She hugged Sergey even stronger without saying a word, just allowing him to express his grief the best he could.

From that day on, Sergey stayed with Yasha's family. Senya and Lyuba acquired another son. And when Sergey asked, "Uncle Senya, may I call you Daddy?" Senya replied, "I'd be delighted if you call me Father. Look, your hair is the same as mine, your eyes are the same color as mine—blue; you resemble me more than Yasha. No doubt you are my son!"

Sergey was happy. He'd never known his father, who died when he was a baby, and the desire to have one was overwhelming for the boy. Now he had gained one. It was different with Lyuba; he had called her "Mama Lyuba" from day one to distinguish her from his real mother.

At age fourteen, the boys finished their secondary school education. It was time to decide what to do next. Yasha's love of books led him directly to a print shop. He became an apprentice and was pleased to be consumed by the book world. Sergey followed him and the friends continued to be together. Every two weeks they received their pay and took it home to Lyuba. They felt proud to contribute to the family's coffer, but did take a little out of their pay and spend it on flowers for the parents, candies for the sisters, and books for themselves.

Lyuba could not be happier with her sons. She took the money not because she needed it, but because she understood how important it was for the boys to feel they contributed a portion of what the family needed. She added Yasha's money to the family budget, and she collected Sergey's money separately, planning to present it all to him as a surprise when he eventually became independent.

While the boys were working hard in the print shop, Zhenya, following her dream of medicine, was admitted into the training school for medical nurses and was on the way to achieving her goal, although still a distant one. Anna was a different matter. She was not particularly interested in the sciences or words, but rather in the creative and social aspects of life. While still in school, the help she provided in Senya's shop suited her personality nicely. When school was over at fourteen, she naturally drifted more toward her father's business, who enjoyed the help of his youngest child. He saw that Yasha was not going to learn the craft of shoemaking and was fine with that. "New times, new songs," as the old saying went, was still true. Senya always knew that he was working hard for his kids to have better lives through education. Lots of changes were occurring in the world and in Russian society. New technologies, new ideas, old problems, ancient desires of freedom and life uninhibited by lack of money—everything was mixing into a huge ball of emotions that was more and more difficult to untangle.

Among the clients Senya acquired after moving into the center of the city was Countess Rudinsky. She was a heavyset, sickly woman who lived in one of the largest mansions on the best street of Elizavetgrad. Her personality was also heavy, full of arrogance, irritability, and dissatisfaction with everyone around her. She ordered many shoes for her swollen feet and paid promptly, but she was difficult to satisfy and so petty with all the details, that many a time Senya hoped that she would find another shoemaker to badger. No such luck. She liked Senya's work and kept buying more. Once, she ordered a pair of shoes for the anticipated ball and Anna was with Senya when he took her measurements. Something in Anna's demeanor and appearance impressed the Countess, and in her usual arrogant tone of voice, she inquired, "Who is this girl?"

"My daughter, Anna."

The Countess fixed her gaze on Anna for a few seconds and finally pronounced, "Well, she is a nice-looking girl!"

"Thank you!" Senya was shocked. The Countess never talked to him about anything that was not part of the transaction at hand.

"Anna, have you finished school?" continued the Countess in a tone of diminishing harshness.

"Yes, Countess."

"You read and write well, don't you?"

"Yes, I can read and write." Anna was still smiling, but the interrogation was upsetting her.

"Well, I need someone to read to me at night and write some notes and letters. My eyes are weak. I'd like you to do that, and I will pay you well."

"Thank you, Countess, I will ask my mother," replied Anna, although she already decided that she could not stand the arrogant woman and would not work for her. With her strong and independent nature, Anna's tendency would be to give a more daring answer, but her upbringing provided a calming leverage and reminded her of good manners she had learned at home.

When Anna shared the news with her mother, she said, "Anna, I think it's a good opportunity for you to make some money. It is not a difficult job and you can also learn something new."

"Oh yes, it is a difficult job," Anna replied. "You know that she is not a nice lady."

Then Senya put his hands on Anna's shoulders and, looking straight into her eyes, said, "Why don't you try, and if you don't like it, leave. You don't need her permission to leave, you are not a slave!"

Senya's eyes became moist as he was talking to Anna. All of a sudden, he remembered Elena's story of their life and how his mother had been bound to her master as a thing, not a human being. He hugged Anna, kissed her on the forehead, and then, in a trembling voice, continued, "I will not let anybody harm you, my little princess. And don't let them put you down either; they are not gods, just humans with better luck."

Anna was listening intensely and weighing her parents' words against what she knew about the Countess. It was common knowledge she had lost her husband. He had died, her daughter recently married and moved to her husband's remote estate somewhere close to the Caucasian Mountains, and her only son was in a military school in Kiev. She was alone, which was probably why she wanted the companionship of an intelligent and well-behaved girl. Although Anna did not want to work for the Countess, making more money was always welcome in the uncertain world of small business.

"Ok, I will do it. As long as she treats me well," concluded Anna.

Two days after the Countess made the offer, Anna, accompanied by her mother, was knocking on the front door of the Rudinsky mansion. A servant opened the door and inquired the reason for their visit. The Countess heard the conversation and shouted from the upper floor, "Who is that? I don't expect anybody at this time."

"It is Anna Nepomnyashchy," the servant answered. "She says you offered her a job."

"Oh, Anna." The Countess's heavy breathing as she was coming down the stairs was nearing. "Let her in. And explain that she should enter from the back door. She had probably never visited a home like this before. She wouldn't know."

Anna turned around to leave the place at once but Lyuba stopped her. "Wait, Anna, give yourself a chance. You can always leave later."

Anna stayed. After the initial shock of her first entrance into the mansion, Anna's relationship with the Countess actually turned out to be reasonable. The Countess was arrogant and intolerant of any mistakes her servants made. She cursed them, called them rural idiots, and asked rhetorical questions such as, "Why am I punished with such stupid servants?" But she did treat Anna with a certain respect, as she probably realized that otherwise Anna would not stay. Whatever the reason, the Countess and Anna got along fine.

Nevertheless, Anna always looked forward to her day off. The family showered her with love—she was still the youngest—and she preferred the simplicity of her parents' home to the luxury of the mansion, where she felt watched all the time. Coming back to work was usually a chore. One day, when she entered the mansion, she noticed something different about the place. There seemed to be more commotion than usual, and the servants looked a little more enthusiastic doing their tasks.

"What's going on?" Anna asked one of the servants.

"The young Count just arrived home for his summer vacation from the military school."

The future officer apparently was liked a lot more than his mother, and the servants took pleasure in doing something for their young master.

Later that day, the Countess introduced Anna to Victor. "Anna, this is Victor Andreevich."

There was unexpected dignity for Anna in that introduction. The Countess was proud of her son and so happy he was home that she introduced him even to a person below her rank in life. Her joyful mood affected everything she did. Victor was of average height, slim, with a great head of dark brown hair and piercing brown eyes. Anna liked him and because of that hid in her room at the first opportunity.

Victor noticed Anna as well. His initial reaction was to her natural beauty, but quickly he was also struck by her proud demeanor. Anna did not fit the characteristics of the typical servant Victor was accustomed to seeing. She carried herself as a confident young woman and had opinions about many things. The combination of Anna's appearance and behavior appealed to Victor. He hunted for a reason to see her, and, when a servant was dusting library books, he eagerly requested the servant to be replaced with Anna. She seldom performed duties such as this, only when an invasion of guests required additional help. This time, however, she was even glad to do it because she was as interested in meeting Victor again as he was in seeing her. There she was, pretending to carefully dust off the books, while actually enjoying her conversation with Victor, who kept asking questions about her family, her interests, and her accomplishments.

"My brother, Yasha, loves books so much, and his dream is to have a good library at home," Anna said.

"Why don't you bring him here sometime? I'd love to meet him."

"I will, if you wish. He'd be thrilled! And I play guitar," Anna responded.

Victor disappeared for a few minutes, leaving Anna wondering what happened. When he reappeared, a typical Russian seven-string guitar was in his hands, and he offered it to Anna. She took the guitar, played a few chords, and then went through a couple of her favorite melodies. The first *date* went smoothly, and they both parted with a warm feeling of desire to meet again.

Victor fulfilled his promise and invited Yasha for a visit. Both Yasha and Sergey showed up at the appointed time. A servant let them in and called for Victor and Anna, who came quickly to greet them. Anna introduced them as her brothers to Victor, who liked them both immediately, and introduced Victor to her brothers with the words, "And this is Victor Andreevich," which prompted the Count to reply, "Please, just call me Victor."

Notwithstanding the huge differences in social standing between the Count and the brothers, there seemed to be something that united them. Maybe it was their mutual desire for knowledge or the appreciation of the new times that were soon to come. Victor belonged to the type of young nobles who were thinking of changing their society into a more inclusive, more democratic one. He wanted to be fair and sensitive to other people's needs.

But before going to the library, an incident, painful to the brothers, occurred. It happened when the young people were conversing in the hallway. They heard a sharp voice: "Who are your guests, Victor?" It was the Countess.

"They are Anna's brothers. I invited them to see the library."

The Countess did not like such a development. It was one thing to have Anna as a servant; it was another for her son to become friendly with her family. Her nasty, disagreeable nature displayed itself again when she turned around to face Masha, the servant who had opened the door for Yasha and Sergey, and declared sternly, "Masha, how many times have I told you that the front door is for nobility? Next time, when someone like these boys comes for any reason, send them to the back door!"

Yasha was shocked, Victor was embarrassed, Anna was fuming, and Sergey felt completely denigrated. The Countess wanted to reinforce the social distance between her son and them. Victor recovered quickly and invited them to come to the library. The Countess left and the young people moved into the library, where they had an interesting discussion about many issues—that is, everyone except Sergey, who was greatly upset by the Countess's attack. He could not calm down and did not say much more than "yes" or "no" during the entire time they were together. And he associated Victor with his mother, imagining him to be no better than she was. He thought, "An apple does not fall too far from the apple tree." Since that day, Sergey was unable to forgive Victor and the Countess for the incident.

6

Victor liked coming home from school on vacation. The security and familiarity of the house where he spent his childhood created a feeling of belonging. Here he had learned to walk, played with his sister, found friends, developed interests—here were the roots of his life.

He was a member of the powerful ruling elite, and the umbilical cord tying him to this institution existed here, at home. But usually it took about a day or two for him to absorb the memories, and then he would spend the rest of his time with friends, who were also on holiday. The Countess did not see enough of her only son and used every opportunity to be with him. Strangely, during this visit Victor spent more time at home. The Countess was happy until she suspected the reason for the change and her apprehension grew.

The Countess was on the right track; she was not the reason for Victor spending more time at home, Anna was. Victor constantly conceived new tasks that only Anna, as he was presenting the situation, could accomplish well. He kept asking her to play the guitar, and the young people truly enjoyed each other's company. A few days before his departure to school, he found Anna in her room and said, "Anna, I am graduating soon and coming home. And I want you to know... This was the most pleasant vacation I remember because I met you."

Anna's cheeks reddened and she looked down.

"I would like to write to you. Could I send letters to your parents' house? I want to make sure you definitely receive them."

"Sure." Anna tried to stay cool as much as possible and not show her true emotions.

"Will you write to me?"

"Yes."

Victor left the mansion and it felt empty with him gone. Anna had kept her cool while Victor was talking to her, but since his departure she was looking forward to each Sunday to go home and read a letter from him. And the letters were steady in coming—every week there was one. Anna's response was just as efficient, and every Monday there was a letter ready, addressed to the military school in Kiev. It would be difficult for Anna's mother not to notice her new behavior associated with the letters, and one day Lyuba asked her daughter, "What is going on, Anna? Why so many letters from the Count?"

"Victor wanted to write to me and I want to write to him. I feel close to him and I think he really likes me."

"You know you belong to a completely different class of people and Victor would never marry you?" It was not really a question, but a statement of fact, the way Lyuba saw it.

"Why not?"

"This is as old as life itself. He can have fun with you, but will marry within his circle, don't you understand? Just remember the story of your grandmother, your father's mom."

"She was a serf!" asserted Anna.

"So what? For them you are as good as a serf. We love you very much and do not want you to suffer."

Lyuba was trying to alert Anna to stay away from a romance that in all likelihood would not last long and leave her disappointed. Anna wanted to believe her feelings and Victor's good intentions. She did not completely discount her mother's admonition, but she liked Victor and wanted to hope they could be together.

Waiting for Victor's homecoming was tougher as the date was approaching. The days were monotonous and boring. While at home on her days off, Anna spoke very little with her parents and siblings. Her emotional state was fragile and she wanted privacy, which her family respected.

Victor's return was just a few long days away. He was expected to arrive on Sunday, and the Countess invited her friends to join in a celebration in his honor. Since the occasion required extra help, the Countess asked Anna to stay in the mansion on Sunday. Anna was cheerful. She could not wait to see Victor again.

At last, Victor appeared in the front door, lively and smiling. The Countess was hugging him, but his eyes were shooting all over looking for someone else. That someone else was not in the welcoming party; it was not her place. When the opportunity arose after dinner for Victor to disappear, he went to the library and asked one of the servants to send Anna there. Anna walked into the library. Victor approached her. She stood quietly, as if removed from real life, and could not look straight at him. The desire to hug him and the understanding that it would not be right created a confusion within her that resulted in a state of immobility that was quite unnatural for Anna. Victor took Anna by the hand, walked her to the couch, and sat her down.

"Anna, I missed you. I could not wait to see you again. Have you missed me?"

Anna nodded and remained quiet.

Victor took out of his pocket a little box and placed it in Anna's hands.

"What is it?"

"Open it." Victor shook his hand encouraging her.

Anna opened the box and there appeared a pair of beautiful gold earrings with malachite. The earrings were magnificent and obviously expensive. She loved them! Even more than the earrings, she loved the fact that Victor spent a lot of money for the present because of her importance to him.

"Do you like them? Put them on."

Anna's hands trembled and she could not manage to insert the earrings into her ears.

"Let me help you," said Victor.

When the earrings took their proper place, Victor pulled Anna to his chest and kissed her, lips to lips. It was a long, sweet kiss.

Suddenly, an angry voice disturbed the quiet of the room.

"Victor, what are you doing? Have you lost your mind? How can you kiss a servant and a Jew?"

A thunderbolt could not have had more of an effect on Anna than this short exclamation. With a look of disdain, she turned to the Countess and said, "I am not your servant! I am nobody's servant!"

With that, she went to her room, collected her belongings, and left the mansion, promising herself never to return and speak to Victor again. Her mother was right after all; the distance between them was too great for anything good to come out of their relationship. This way was better. The Countess made everything simple.

The earrings stayed in the mansion.

7

When Anna told her sad story at home, everybody expressed their agreement with the way she acted in a difficult situation. They still remembered how the Countess disliked Yasha and Sergey fraternizing with her son, and her mean-spirited "Go through the back door," and her arrogant attitude to anybody below her on the social ladder. This family and many other people, whose lives intersected with the Countess, did not like her. Sooner or later it was bound to happen that Anna would have to leave her employ.

"My dear, you did right," Lyuba said. "It's better to end it sooner rather than later. He is not for you anyway."

Senya summed up the family's feelings and support. "We are not counts, but we will not let them harm us. Good going, daughter."

The next day, Lyuba opened the door upon hearing a knock and saw a well-dressed man, obviously a noble. The visitor introduced himself, "My name is Victor Rudinsky," omitting the word "count." He behaved modestly and Lyuba actually liked him.

"I would like to talk to Anna."

"She is busy."

"Then please tell her I am sorry for what happened, but I did not do anything to offend her, and I cannot be responsible for what my mother did," Victor said and left.

This was the first time Lyuba met Victor and he impressed her not as much with his looks as with his modesty and humility. She actually suggested that Anna talk to him if he came again, but Anna did not want to hear about it.

A few weeks later, Victor showed up again, this time in a military uniform.

"I came to see Yasha."

Surprised, Senya showed Victor in. It was Saturday evening; everyone was home, including a fellow who was trying to impress Anna with his wit. When Victor walked into the room, Senya immediately said, "Yasha, a young man is here to see you."

Yasha took Victor aside. "How are you?"

"I came to say good-bye."

"Where are you going?"

"I was called to join the army and leave tomorrow. The war is still going on. It is my time to share the burden." Victor hesitated a second. "I am worried about my mother. She is alone and may need help if something really bad happens. This is not the old Russia we grew up in; things are changing fast. All this talk about the revolution and then the war.... I'd like someone to take care of my mother in case she needs help."

"Don't worry, Victor. I promise to visit her and see if she needs anything."

They shook hands and the young Count Rudinsky, in a new military uniform of the Russian Czarist Army, left the small house, which had never completely accepted him. He was ready to contribute to the devastation that was the First World War.

Soon after Victor's departure, Yasha and Sergey were also drafted into the army. The country, invested in the continuing war, needed new canon meat. While Victor joined the officers' ranks, Yasha and Sergey were privates. Senya and Lyuba were beside themselves when the draft notices arrived, but there was nothing anybody could do about it—their turn came.

When the boys were ready to leave, Lyuba kissed them and said, "I had a dream. You boys will be all right, but you must stay together and help each other. You will be all right."

Senya added, "It will be as your mother says. Believe me, I know."

The boys left, and everything familiar was changing fast in Russia. Nobody could predict where it would end. They all remembered what Victor had said before leaving about the looming changes.

The year was 1917.

Victor did not know how right he was.

Book II. Soviet Russia

"Revolutionaries who take the law into their own hands are horrifying not because they are criminals, but because they are like machines that have got out of control, like runaway trains."

Boris Pasternak.
Doctor Zhivago

Part One

1

It was still dark when Yasha woke up. The wind was howling outside as if trying to scare off unwanted visitors, and the uncomfortable sleeping arrangements made resting difficult. It was dark. Dark inside the peasant cottage, dark outside, dark in Yasha's mind. Life had been surreal ever since he was drafted into the Russian Army. Many things had happened since that time—unexpected, exciting, strange new things. Yasha was trying to go back to sleep, but he could not, and the loud snoring of his fellow Red Army conscripts was not helping. Yasha moved a bit on the bench he occupied with another soldier and tried to see around, but it was pitch black—dark, a good sign that there was still plenty of time before dawn. What a pity he could not sleep. After spending a while in a military uniform Yasha got used to many uncomfortable situations—insufficient sleep, long marches with heavy loads, rotten food, terrible sanitary conditions, and other such pearls of soldiering in war times. But sleeping fully clothed in his uniform with a gun close by—this was still difficult. No relaxation, no rest, no change from day to night.

Yasha was lying with his eyes open and trying to remember his dream. He was in an unfamiliar but beautiful place. There were people around, moving slowly and seeming content with themselves. An air of peacefulness saturated the place. A young woman approached him and offered something she had in her hands. He could not remember what it was, just that it was something good. And her smiling face was very pleasant. She was waving to him to follow her, and he did. She picked a path somehow through all the strange formations that surrounded them and kept turning her head to see if Yasha was still following her. He was, very diligently, as if a magnet was pulling him toward this woman. And then, suddenly, she fell and disappeared in the bottomless pit. Yasha saw it when he came to where the woman had been standing just a moment ago; he looked down and saw nothing. The feeling of peacefulness vanished and grief took its place. It was disturbing and he woke up. Now he was lying in bed trying to understand the meaning of this dream. Did it have anything to do with his future? Or was it something happening to his family right now? Or what else could it have been?

From reflecting on the nightmare, Yasha's mind wandered into the memories of his life over the last several months. It all looked like a dream too. He remembered September 1917, when both he and Sergey were drafted into the Russian Army and were sent to basic training. They were nineteen at the time and did not want to go to the front, but obviously they were not the ones making decisions. Their basic training had taken place in Poltava—a city that was also in the southern part of Ukraine. This city had a special place in Russian history as it was there in 1709 that the first significant victory over the Swedes led by their famed King Charles XII made Peter the Great a hero. Poltava was a symbol of Russian military prowess and human strength.

All history aside, Yasha and Sergey did not want to fight in the war. It was one thing to defend the motherland from invading armies, but it was entirely different when the reason for the war and the killing was not clear at all. They wanted to do something to help people live better, not kill or be killed. Most soldiers felt that way. In their battalion there were a couple of young privates who talked often about the war, its cruelty, and the complete lack of reason for peasants and workers to participate in it. They were Bolsheviks and they talked to the soldiers they could trust, explaining that fighting for the Russian Czar was stupid and soldiers should use their weapons against the Czar and his regime instead of supporting him. Yasha and Sergey had heard of Bolsheviks before, but in the army they actually met them face to face and heard their story, which sounded right. The Bolsheviks were preaching liberty, peace, equality—all the traits of the society that Yasha and Sergey wanted also. They listened; they listened carefully and absorbed much of what the Bolsheviks were saying. However, training was a short program and the boys were ready to be shipped to the front and join hundreds of thousands of other men already in the trenches. Many of them would be dead by the time the young recruits were ready to take their place, only to die or be maimed quickly. But fate had a different design for Yasha's and Sergey's lives.

Early on October 26th, soldier Konev, one of the Bolsheviks agitating against the Czar, stood on a podium which the officers usually used for observing training and through a megaphone appealed to the soldiers to move closer to him and listen to what he had to say. The officers were nowhere to be seen and the crowd was growing. The situation was strange, as if all of a sudden the privates were dropped into the middle of a desert with no direction and no commanders. Private Konev seemed to be taking that command.

"Comrades!" Konev bellowed when a big group of soldiers had assembled. "Many of you know I am a Bolshevik and my party advocates peace and equality for all people. And you know well, this war is not our war. I am here to tell you that yesterday the heroic workers of Petrograd, with the help of soldiers and sailors, stormed the Winter Palace and threw out the government that kept the war going and the people suffering. From now on Russia is free! People will govern, instead of the Czar and his family. No Czar! No war! Bread, peace, and land!"

The crowd was stunned and stayed unusually quiet, until someone in its midst shouted, "Long live the Bolsheviks! Down with the Czar! No more war!"

As if the right button was pushed, the crowd became one and started repeating the slogans. Men cried and smiled, throwing their hats in the air to celebrate an event the significance of which they did not comprehend yet, but it felt like something good. The sense was that the war was over and they did not have to be afraid of dying in it.

Konev allowed the crowd's collective energy to show itself and continued, "From now on, you—the soldiers, peasants, and workers—are in charge of the country. You have the guns and should use them to help the Bolsheviks establish control over the towns and villages, to throw away all those counts and barons and other nobles who have drunk people's blood for too long. Now, it is our time, comrades! Let's join in the construction of a new communist society that treats everyone equally. Long live the Bolshevik Party! Long live Comrade Lenin!"

Yasha was surprised and pleased at the same time. He looked around for Sergey—somehow they had managed to lose each other in the commotion. Soldiers, mostly young recruits, were excited and energized by what they just heard. Yasha kept going through the crowd shouting, "Sergey! Sergey!"

He observed some former peasants now in uniform discussing the fastest way of getting to their villages. He heard some discussions about what to do with the guns, and then he saw Sergey standing next to Konev, listening to something he was saying to the group of soldiers. Yasha moved closer and listened too. Apparently, the political and military power in the capital now resided with the Bolsheviks and their leader, Vladimir Illich Lenin. This information was communicated via telegraph to all locations in Russia, and local Bolshevik organizations were taking charge. This is why the officers in this Poltava regiment had disappeared—they feared for their lives. Konev was urging the listeners to join them and help establish the local soviets for governance. Yasha could not wait to share his thoughts with Sergey.

"How do you like this?" Yasha asked when they were finally together.

"I think this is terrific! What do you think?"

"I am surprised that it happened so soon, but I am not surprised that it did happen. This is great! All our dreams can now be fulfilled. Can you imagine, no more nobles and we elect people who represent us and make sure things are fair for everyone? Fairness—we are all equal!"

"I agree! And we can participate in this life as equals, not some second-rate people."

"What do you think we should do now, Sergey?"

"I'd like to join the Bolsheviks as Konev said and help build a new country. He said we could sign up to become revolutionary guards. Let's do it!"

"Agreed!" Yasha replied, and they started elbowing their way closer to Konev and the other Bolsheviks, who were surrounded by soldiers asking questions.

All the memories Yasha was now recalling while lying on a bench in the middle of the night were very vivid. He remembered specific situations, words exchanged, feelings he had, because this period was utterly different and truly important in his life. The faces of people dear to him sometimes appeared in his mind while he was going through his memories as if watching a movie.

He and Sergey had signed up with Konev as revolutionary guards. They became a part of the military detachment that supported the Bolshevik representatives in setting up the rule of local soviets. Not everyone in the country liked the revolution, and many different parties and groups of former soldiers or bandits were vying for political and material benefits from the disarray caused by the revolution. Many people had guns: officers of the Czarist army, former police, military men, not all of whom were on the side of the Bolsheviks, and they were all shooting at each other. These were dangerous times; a bullet could come from anywhere and end this paradise on Earth for anyone in a second, especially when you were moving from town to town, village to village, and participating in setting up a new rule. Sergey and Yasha took part in quite a few exchanges of shots with different bands— usually they did not even know who—but so far fate was kind to them and neither was wounded. They kept together as Lyuba told them and watched each other's back while moving from place to place. When they came to a new town or village, their political leader would call a meeting and make a speech about the wonders of the new society they were building. Then they would set up a soviet, usually from the poorest citizens, to run the place. Animosities, bad memories, and old offenses were on people's minds, as the new governing bodies were taking full control of their lives with significant consequences for all involved. After the meeting and organizational activities, the detachment would usually disperse through the village looking for places to stay and eat.

Yasha's retrospection was interrupted by a rooster announcing a new day. Pre-dawn light came through the windows and slowly some details were materializing from the darkness: the sleeping faces of his comrades, their guns nearby, crude wooden furniture handmade by peasants, a huge oven painted white and therefore coming out of the darkness more visibly than other items. Yasha knew that soon these people would be up, preparing to move on. He learned the morning routine well, when soldiers begin collecting their things, discussing what the new day can bring.

Today could be a difficult day. They were supposed to enter a town rumored to maintain close ties with the Whites—vestiges of the former uniform Czarist army aided by those from the intelligentsia and bourgeoisie dead set against the revolution. Today a fight might be forthcoming, and this possibility always created additional tension among the revolutionary guards. Who knew who would survive?

2

When Lyuba and Senya learned of the revolution they were not sure what to make of it. And this was the second revolution in less than a year. This word—*revolution*—became known to the masses from 1905 and projected either hope or threat, depending on a person's standing in the society. After the February 1917 revolution things did not change much for the majority of the people. Yes, the Czar had abdicated and some new, strange political entities appeared, such as the soviets. But Russia was still in the war and most people did not feel much of a difference in their lives.

And after the second revolution in October there was no visible change for Lyuba and Senya on the streets, not immediately, anyway. But concern for their sons only increased. They received a letter from Yasha about the Poltava training base, but nothing more after the revolution. The change of government and its impact on their lives was difficult for them to grasp. And this time the change was profound—the Bolsheviks had made it known from day one that everything would be different from now on. The situation was uncertain, as was the fate of all those away from their homes. It was becoming more evident that the new state was being born in blood, deceit, and power struggles.

One gray day in December Anna decided to check on Victor's mother. She was wondering about Victor and wanted to find out if his mother had new information. Anna came to the mansion she knew well and knocked on the door. Nobody answered. Anna waited a little and knocked again. The air was chilly and she was shivering in her coat while waiting for someone to open the door, but nothing was happening. She knocked again and started screaming, "Masha, anybody! Please open the door!"

Finally, the sound of someone moving inside the house reached her ears and the door opened. Anna could not believe her eyes. It was the Countess herself, and she looked awful. The Countess was wearing a fur coat, wool shawl, and fur hat, under which strands of hair were sticking out. She looked terrifically unkempt, but the worst was in her eyes: despair and bewilderment. She was not her confident and arrogant self.

Recovering from the initial shock, Anna asked, "Countess, where is Masha?"

"Masha is gone. Everyone disappeared. I don't know where they are; I am all alone."

"What do you mean—disappeared?"

"They said they are leaving to build new Russia. Why new? What is wrong with old Russia? I do not understand.... I do not understand."

"Countess, why are you wearing a coat at home?"

"Oh, it's cold. Everyone is gone and I don't know how the heat works."

The Countess was completely lost without help. Anna, still remembering the insults, felt pity for this lonely woman. Besides, she was Victor's mother and she loved him. Anna made a decision. She asked the Countess to find a key, collected some of her clothes in a suitcase stored in the bedroom, locked the mansion, and took the Countess to her home.

Seeing Anna letting Countess Rudinsky inside their modest home was eerie for Senya and Lyuba. This was not the person they remembered; this was an old woman who could not understand where she was. Anna offered the Countess a chair to sit down in and made a sign to her parents to follow her into another room, where she explained the situation and said, "I think she should stay with us until Victor is back. She is going to die without somebody's help."

It is not easy to elevate oneself above the offenses of everyday life and give a supporting hand to another human being who would probably never do it for you. It takes a special spirit, and Anna's parents were proud of her for being such a person. Since the boys were away and their room was unused for anything else, the decision was made to let the Countess use that room and take care of her until Victor came back.

In fact, taking care of another person would not be easy for them. Senya's business was dormant: his rich clients had vanished and the lower classes did not have the means to buy shoes or the inclination to pay a professional to fix old ones. The family was eating through their savings, and they would not be able to use the Countess's money because the banks had been nationalized by the new government. The Countess had nothing and she did not even realize it. A difficult winter was approaching with many unanswered questions looming ahead.

3

Count Victor Rudinsky became an officer in the Russian Czarist army in 1917 and was shipped to fight in the Austrian territory. By the time he hit the trenches, the war was in a state of stagnation. Neither side was trying to advance much while both sides were shooting at each other with all kinds of materiel made to kill. And kill it did. Every day Victor observed injured and dead soldiers; every day he was not sure if he would see the sunset.

The war was difficult for all involved as it was not clear what it was about. Russian officers attempted to maintain discipline in the army, but it was becoming difficult. There were Bolshevik agitators among the troops constantly preaching to the enlisted men about the uselessness of this war and the need to go home and till land. When such agitators were discovered, they were usually arrested and sometimes shot for treason. But every once in a while, an officer especially diligent in searching out the disgruntled soldiers would be killed during a shooting exchange with the enemy, mysteriously having been shot in the back.

When the news of the October revolution reached the troops where Victor served, some soldiers disappeared, probably acting on the agitation of Bolsheviks to return home. But the majority of the troops were still loyal to the idea of the government as they knew it. While the armistice talks were going on, many officers left the troops and joined the groups of monarchists attempting to destroy the new system. These were the Whites. After the peace treaty with Germany was signed, many officers and a significant number of privates swelled the White ranks and made this monarchist movement a force the new Russian government had to deal with. The Civil War had started.

Count Rudinsky joined the Whites in March 1918, together with most of his regiment—officers and privates. The regiment was operating not far from its original positioning: in Western and then Central Ukraine. Together with others, the regiment was squeezing the Red Army. Since people needed to eat, visiting villages was imperative, and that is where unexpected fights with the Reds broke out many times. The country was becoming like a checkerboard with temporary red and white fields, depending on who was in town. Local loyalties also played a role, as a particular town or village could lean one way or another based on many circumstances.

When Victor's regiment entered Berki, it was met with bread and salt—the traditional Russian symbols of hospitality. That meant that the majority of the populace had pro-monarchist leanings and the soldiers would be in no danger of a sneak attack. Victor gave the command to his troops to disperse and, as soon as he dismounted his horse, was invited into a big house with the other officers. This was the house of a local leader, a peasant of means, who was overjoyed at seeing White officers at his table. Victor was shown to a clean room where he could stay overnight, and he allowed himself the pleasure of lying in a real bed for a few moments until the call for dinner.

At the table, besides a colonel, a captain, and two lieutenants, one being Victor, there were the host and two other men from the village who were part of the common leadership. Traditional Ukrainian dishes covered the entire table, and one would never guess that somewhere in this country people were starving.

After a short prayer the host poured vodka in glasses and offered a toast, "Long live the Czar-father!"

Everyone stood up, the officers saluted, and all drank. Then silence fell—it was not every day that the soldiers could eat well. In a few minutes, the conversation started. The host turned to the colonel and asked, "Your excellency, when do you think the Reds will disappear? We are tired of them!" And he laughed a little.

"If it were in my power, I'd get rid of them quickly," said the senior military man at the table. "You know, they don't really have officers who understand military business. I am surprised they lasted up to now, but I don't think it will be for long. We had just heard of General Denikin opening a new front, and additional ammunition supplies from other countries are expected any day. I think in a couple of months they should be finished."

"Good, good. I am glad to hear that, because we hear rumors that the Bolsheviks are killing everyone who is not with them and they make everything common—the land, the clothes, even the wives."

"These peasants know nothing about government, nothing about the discipline required to make money, nothing about any matters

78

important in a country. How could they hope to govern?" This was a question raised by another of the local men.

"And that is why they won't win!" replied the captain. "Let's drink to the hosts of this celebration."

Victor entered his room in a strange mood. He enjoyed the food and drinks and the quiet of the normal human residence. The setting reminded him of the gatherings in his mansion in Elizavetgrad, and the dancing and mingling that were usually part of such festivities. But back then he did not have anything else on his mind: no worries about staying alive, or about the wellbeing of his mother, or about the future of his country. The conversation about the Reds at the table disturbed him more than he would imagine. He wanted the Reds defeated, and yet he was not sure he wanted Russia to be a monarchy again. But was this revolution the answer? It did not seem that way either. He saw destruction everywhere. Nothing constructive was going on, just killings, killings. He was tired of these killings. First, at the front shooting at Germans, now here shooting at fellow Russians. This was terrible and there was no end in sight. He did not agree with the colonel that the Reds would be defeated soon.

4

Yasha's detachment of the Red Guards was about to leave the village when a rider on horseback appeared in the distance. He galloped toward the commander of the detachment. The commander, Comrade Trunov—a short, stout man in his thirties, wearing a black leather jacket and a similar cap—was a serious man who had been sent to lead this detachment, consisting of about a hundred soldiers. The rider got off his horse near Trunov and proceeded to meet the commander. In a few minutes, Trunov ordered the detachment to line up and said, "Comrades, I just received the confirmation that Berki is occupied by the Whites. They have been staying there since last Monday and seem comfortable. Our task is to destroy them and free Berki from the counterrevolutionaries. I want to see the platoon commanders. We will depart soon."

Trunov allowed the soldiers to disperse and sat down under the tree with the platoon commanders to develop a plan of action. They finished in twenty minutes, and the detachment was ready to march to Berki. Sergey, as one of the platoon commanders, gathered his troops, explained their role in the forthcoming fight, and with the words "Good luck!" indicated it was time to move. Berki was about seven miles away—a couple hours' march—but by the time the Reds took positions around the village and were set to attack the Whites, the spring sun was already high.

The plan was to surround the village and overwhelm the enemy by surprise. However, the Whites' sentries had discovered their presence and the surprise component was gone. Now it was a fight between troops that were almost equal in number, with the key difference being that the Whites were squeezed inside the village and could not maneuver easily, while the Reds had more room for movement. The shooting game began in the middle of a sunny, windy day, and quickly people on both sides were dying. Trunov's revolutionary guards tried to attack frontally, but the resistance was too fierce. The biggest problem was a machine gun that the Whites had situated on a small hill close to the center of Berki. It had a good view of the battlefield and its crew inhibited the attacks very professionally. Sergey's platoon was positioned right in front of the gun and he was looking for ways to destroy it. Yasha was close to Sergey and saw him intensely observing the enemy position and then all of a sudden shaking his head in disbelief.

"Yasha," Sergey shouted over the sound of gunfire, "take a look at that position where the machine gun is." And he offered his binoculars to his friend.

Yasha took the binoculars, looked in the indicated direction, and froze. He saw through the power of optics an officer in a military uniform, giving orders to soldiers manning the machine gun. He had known this officer in his former life. It was Victor, Count Victor

Rudinsky. Yasha had a strange feeling in his stomach. He could be killed by someone he had known as a nice guy in their former life! Or he could potentially kill this nice guy right now!

The fight continued for another couple of hours. Trunov tried to attack in different directions with no success. The Whites also tried to beat the enemy in a frontal attack, but the defenses were equally strong on both sides and, after being sprayed by a shower of bullets, their attack subsided. With the sun setting and darkness filling Berki, Trunov ordered his troops to move out. He wanted to save his troops until reinforcements arrived, and they marched away to find a place in the woods to eat and rest.

Sergey and Yasha were riding next to each other without uttering a word. Both were thinking about Victor. Sergey broke the silence first. "Do you remember, Yasha, what Victor had said about equality? About the abolishment of the titles that the nobility loves so much? But that was just talk and now he is fighting to preserve this old Russia. He is a hypocrite!"

"You cannot be sure of his reasons. Besides, there are a lot of problems with our side too. That's why many people are afraid the Bolsheviks may be worse than the Czar."

"You know better, Yasha, than to compare what we are building with the old Russia. In the new society, we will be working for our benefit, not those who exploited us before. And the difficulties we experience—they are temporary difficulties. You'll see how much better the lives of simple folks are as soon as the Whites and others stop interfering with the will of the people."

The troops finally arrived at the place in the woods where they would stay overnight. Soldiers were preparing to eat and sleep. This was not the first day of fighting, losing friends, and sleeping outside, nor would it be the last.

5

When Lyuba opened the door and saw her two boys with wide smiles on their faces, she could not contain her tears. "Senya, Anna, come see who is here!" she shouted. Senya and Anna came out and joined in the excitement. The family was together again—what joy, what happiness!

As soon as the boys settled down, everybody was ready for the stories of the past six months of their lives. Yasha and Sergey did not know anything about the events back home and their family did not know anything about the boys. They exchanged their tales of hardship and joy, their thoughts about the revolution, their expectations and dreams, and the actual events that had shaped their lives during the period of separation. Sergey and Yasha were stunned at the news that Countess Rudinsky occupied their room. Lyuba cringed every time they described a battle. But hearing that the boys were not staying for long really upset her. They were on a ten-day vacation for their distinguished contribution to the fight against the counterrevolution. Ten days together, that was all they had, and then... then return to the Red Army with all its associated dangers of war and constant worrying back home.

The family was waiting for Zhenya to come home for dinner. She was still studying in medical school—strangely, some aspects of life had not changed. When Zhenya arrived the stories and dreams were repeated, while Lyuba and Anna set the table for a celebration. The Countess was also called for dinner—she did not leave her room except to go for a walk or eat. And when she saw Yasha and Sergey she was startled but composed herself quickly and, as was expected from her, did not say a word of greeting or ask a single question. The boys had decided not to share the fact that they saw Victor even before they arrived home.

After dinner, the question of finding living quarters for Yasha and Sergey came up. Since the Countess occupied their room, the easy solution was to temporarily move her in with Anna and let the boys have the room back. But it was easier said than done, as she would not even hear of sharing space with another person. The Countess said with her usual arrogance, "I will move back to my own house."

"But how will you survive?" Lyuba asked.

"I can manage. Besides, it's warm now and I don't need to heat the place up."

That sounded reasonable. The first night, the boys slept on the living room floor—they did not mind, they had slept in much worse conditions—and the next day, the Countess moved to her mansion. As soon as Sergey and Yasha brought in the Countess's belongings from their home, they and Anna started cleaning up the house while the Countess walked around, replaying memories of happier times. Once they finished, Anna promised the Countess to visit her every couple of days and bring food. The youngsters departed, leaving the old woman alone in her beautiful but empty mansion.

On the way home, Sergey could not stop talking about the Countess, her arrogance, and her inability to do anything useful.

"She still behaves like these are the old times, and we, also like in the old times, are serving her needs. Why can't she do it herself? And why does she need such a big house?" Sergey asked.

"We are helping her because she is helpless," Anna replied. "We cannot just forget her. Yasha promised Victor to give her a hand if she needed it."

Sergey just waved his hand as if saying, "You don't understand," and kept walking silently. As soon as they returned home, Lyuba took Sergey by the hand and walked him into her bedroom. She picked up something wrapped in cloth and offered it to Sergey, saying, "I collected what you were giving me while working in the print shop. Use it for anything you want."

It was a pack of bills—money. Sergey, bewildered, did not know what to say. He had never thought about the money he was giving to Lyuba, just as Yasha did when they were working together. Seeing it all here, saved and neatly wrapped as a present, made him speechless. After recovering, he said, "Thank you, Mama Lyuba! But I cannot take the money. You always took care of me and the money is yours, for the family. Please keep it for your needs. What you did for me cannot be bought at any price. I am in the army and have my food rations, while you need every ruble to survive. Please, keep the money."

Lyuba could not argue anymore with a young man who felt strongly about his contribution to the family finances. Besides, feeding the family was becoming more difficult. She kissed him and they joined the others in the living room. Time was short—only eight days were left until the boys would have to return to their military duties—and everyone wanted to enjoy each other.

6

The Civil War was raging on. As the troops were returning from the fronts of the First World War, the majority were joining either Red or White forces, swelling the numbers of participants in the brotherly slaughter. Many wanted to be associated with neither side and either tried to sit out the whole thing in their villages and towns or became members of the bands ravaging the countryside, especially in Ukraine, adding to the uncertainty and confusion. Peasants were saying, "Reds are coming and robbing us, Whites are coming and robbing us."

By the middle of 1918, the Bolsheviks were solidifying their influence on people, but people living in towns and cities were hungry. To address the food question, the so-called provision detachments were organized. After their vacation, Yasha and Sergey were assigned to one such unit responsible for the collection of foodstuffs in Central Ukraine. Sergey was actually made a commander of the unit. He always made it to a leadership position in the Red Army. Physically strong and tall, confident in his understanding of the situation, Sergey was a natural leader. Both he and Yasha had joined the Communist Party earlier in the year, when all the Red Guards were asked to join, and many of them did. They wanted to contribute to the process, which they expected would lead to a freer and fairer society. Sergey felt confident that the Communists intended to make people's lives better, while Yasha, although agreeing with many of their ideas and actions, kept finding himself questioning some of the methods of political struggle used by them.

Collecting provisions was not a safe job. Peasants did not like to surrender food for free and sometimes attempted to protect their property aggressively. Then there was always a chance that a White regiment was either nearby for a military purpose or to collect provisions for themselves. That is why the provision detachments looked more like regular army units than collection groups. They were all on horseback, well supplied with guns and ammunition, and included medical personnel.

As soon as Sergey's unit was assigned a specific region to canvass for foodstuffs, it departed. The day was nice and sunny, warm enough to enjoy life, especially since the soldiers in Sergey's detachment were riding slowly through peaceful surroundings, not hearing any shots or screams, only the sound of horses' hooves and the squeaking of wagons' wheels. Sergey, as a commander, was going around the entire detachment making sure everything was all right, and Yasha was shadowing him—they liked being together. Over the last few days they had little opportunity for private conversations and used this time to compensate. One of the topics was—surprise, surprise, they were only twenty!—girls. There were always women-nurses in the army, and with the Bolsheviks there were even women-commissars. Sergey and Yasha noticed the two nurses. On this trip they were sitting in the same wagon and, as Sergey and Yasha observed while riding near them, talking enthusiastically about God knows what. Their conversation was not of interest to the boys. They liked these girls and wanted to get closer to them.

One of them, Tanya, looked at Yasha with a certain deliberateness that led him to believe that she had some interest in him. And the interest was mutual. Yasha began building plans for further acquaintance with the young woman. She had a beautiful face, with brooding brown eyes under the cover of long eyelashes. Her wavy chestnut hair was shoulder length and her smile generated a feeling of tranquility.

Sergey noticed the glances between his friend and Tanya. He decided to pay closer attention to Katya, the other nurse. She was a well-built blonde with large blue eyes and a dynamo spirit—always talking, defending her point of view, arguing, explaining. Sergey was attracted to her more than he wanted to be as a commander. Saying a few words to Katya, he continued his inspection and Yasha followed him.

The girls were left alone, and after giggling about the attention from the boys, resumed their conversation. Tanya and Katya had met when they arrived in the assignment center. They were both from the same region—Katya from Elizavetgrad, Tanya from a small town nearby—and both had just graduated from the expedited course for medical nurses. The army needed medical specialists and, lacking experienced personnel, trained their own. The girls met, liked each other, and stuck together, but this trip was the first opportunity to share their past and their dreams with each other. When the boys' interruption was over, Katya said, "What were you telling me about your family?"

"Well, I was saying that I have four brothers and three sisters and we were always very close, but now we are all over this big country and don't know much about each other."

"Your parents must have been rich to have that many children," Katya said, sounding surprised.

"Rich? No, we were not rich."

Tanya thought about what details of her former life she could share with her new friend. There were a lot of things she could not tell Katya: that her father was a descendant of Polish aristocrats, had a factory where many people worked, that she was well educated and knew several foreign languages, played piano, and designed clothes. She also could not tell her that the Bolsheviks had confiscated their house and the factory, and that her father died of a heart attack right after, leaving her mother and the children without support. She had to keep all of it secret and play the role of an enthusiastic revolutionary to be safe.

Katya said, "In cities like mine, only rich families could have many kids. Poor families could not afford to buy food and clothes for so many. What did your father do?"

"My father had a small business; he made pots, pans, shovels, and things like that. He even had a few young guys working for him when times were good."

"And you are telling me you were not rich? Your father was a bourgeois and a capitalist."

"Of course not!" strongly objected Tanya. "He was just trying to make a living."

"He was exploiting workers for his benefit. That is what's wrong with it!"

"But if my father or somebody else did not offer them jobs, how would they earn money to live?"

Instead of answering Tanya's question, Katya asked another, "Did he pay them good wages?"

"They would not work otherwise." Tanya stopped for a second, as if looking into a distant mirror, and smiled at the memory. Then she continued, "My mother always made sure that her children studied well. Knowledge was the most important thing to her, and she always said that good education opens many doors. We also had responsibilities at home: cleaning, helping her with many things, and she taught us many practical skills, such as clothing design. Actually, my younger brother, Sasha, was the best at it. We were saving a lot of money by buying fabrics and sewing dresses based on our own designs. People always thought that we were buying the most expensive clothes. We made good-looking clothes out of nothing and looked like rich people, but we were not rich."

"So, your brother wanted to become a dressmaker?" Katya asked with a smirk.

"He dreamt of becoming a famous painter and architect."

Wanting to tone down this conversation and shift its focus away from her, Tanya said, "Tell me about your family."

"My father is a worker, a proletarian. He worked at the plant together with my two brothers. They started working young, well before they had learned enough in school. We needed the money because our father's earnings were not enough, but I could continue studying after my older brothers went to work." Katya stopped for a second, hesitating, as if trying to decide what to say next.

"You see, my father liked to drink. He had these comrades-drinkers he spent a lot of time and money with. And then, drunk, he would beat my mother and us. That is, until my brothers had grown big enough, and they would not let him. When they were paid at work, they would just grab my father and take him home before he had a chance to waste himself and the money on drinks. Things became a lot better at home." She stopped again. Something seemed to be on her mind that bothered her.

"What is the matter, Katya?"

Katya shook her head and answered, "No, nothing is the matter. I just thought of my parents. My brothers are in the army somewhere, and I don't know what is taking place at home. Does my father work? Does he drink? I am pretty sure he does without his sons around. And when he drinks, he beats my mom, and I cannot help it at all." Katya's face trembled as she fought back tears, and Tanya moved closer and hugged her warmly.

"It's okay, Katya. You don't know if that's the case. Maybe the situation is completely different."

"You don't know my father. I just want to protect my mother. She is defenseless. When I leave the army, my mother will live with me."

"And what do you want to do after the war is over?"

"I am not sure yet. I want to have a good profession, make a lot of money, and live like a proud human being. I was always poor, but these are new times and the poor will become rich. You know how it is in the 'International': 'Who was nothing will become everything!' That's about me. But I need patience, as we all do."

"So, you become rich and others will think you are that bourgeois who we are fighting against."

"Why?" Katya's face contorted with surprise at Tanya's unexpected comparison.

"Because you would have more than those who do not have a good profession like yours. You will be *everything* to them, while they are *nothing*."

Katya was thinking. She had never seen it that way. Then she smiled, as if remembering something, and said, "But we are building a new society in which everyone will make a lot of money to live on. Everyone will be equal! No reason to think of others in our country as having more than others. This is what we are building. When these temporary difficulties end, life for all good people will be much better than before."

7

Three months, four serious fights, and several injured and dead comrades later, Sergey's detachment was on the way to Miratin,—the next village on their trip, and Katya suddenly fell ill. Chilly rain had been coming down from the heavens for three days, sometimes pouring, transforming the roads into a mess and making people wet and cold. Tanya was with Katya the entire time, feeding her all the medical and folk remedies she had at her disposal, but lying in a wagon and feeling all the bumps on the road was difficult for a sick woman.

One of the soldiers, Ivan, was from Miratin, and he tried to keep Katya's spirits up by telling her how nice and cozy she would feel as soon as they reached the village. Yasha also frequented Katya's wagon to find out the latest status, give her and Tanya support, and inform Sergey, who could not see Katya often. Ivan shared his excitement about approaching Miratin.

"I cannot wait to see my village and my family. I have two brothers— one older, another younger—and a mother, whom I have not seen in almost a year. Our house is the last in the village, and poor, but the lake nearby is full of fish and it is so good to swim there in the summer when it's hot. Or you could hide from the sun in the nearby forest and pick berries and mushrooms."

Ivan's recollections made him smile. And then his facial expression suddenly changed to a frown. "But the first thing I will do in Miratin is shake up a rich neighbor. You cannot imagine the greed of this jerk. My brothers and I worked hard on his land. The harvests were good, but he paid us just with grain and food. We worked long hours, he sold the crops well, and we had little. I am going to remind this son of a bitch of that."

It was early in the afternoon when the detachment arrived in Miratin. The troops knew the process: pairs of soldiers would go through all the houses in the village, taking what they found and then bringing their findings to the central location where the commander, commissar, and a few guards were collecting foodstuffs on the wagons. Then a few soldiers would be dispatched to the regional base with these wagons, while the rest of the detachment moved on, the departing troops usually replaced by those coming back from the previous trip to the base. As the collection process started, Ivan, who knew the village well, took Katya's wagon directly to the house he wanted her to stay in.

"This is a prosperous house and you will be comfortable here. I will make sure you are."

Ivan opened a wicket, walked directly to the porch, opened the front door, and shouted, "Galya, you have guests, where are you?"

Soon a tall woman in her early thirties walked out onto the porch. She had the confident look of a person who knows her own worth, and a long blonde plait set in circles on her head made her look even taller. A traditional Ukrainian shawl—with beautiful, colorful flowers on a dark background—that women used on chilly days, moved on her shoulders in rhythm with her voice as she spoke with anger and almost disgust. "What is the matter with you, Ivan, why are you shouting? Who do you think you are?"

"I am Ivan, remember me? I am the one who had done all this work for you and your brother with no respect and little pay. I am also a Red Guard now! You know what that means."

The expression on Galya's face started to change from disgust to surprise at his forceful answer, while Ivan continued. "First, take this woman," he pointed to Katya, "and put her in bed. She is ill and needs a lot of care. Make sure she is safe or you die. Second, where is your grain surplus? I need to confiscate it for the benefit of the revolution."

"We don't have any surplus."

"Oh, yeah?" With a smirk, Ivan walked off in the direction of the barn.

"Listen, Ivan," Galya changed her tone. "Whatever we have spared we need for sowing next year. Without it we'd starve!"

Ivan kept walking; he knew this property. In the barn he found two sacks of grain and took them, one by one, to the wagon.

"Galya," he turned to the woman again, "make sure you take care of Katya well. I will be checking."

With that he put the sacks in the wagon and started walking toward the next house. Approaching it, he shouted, "Peter, I am back. I am going to get even with you!"

An unexpected sound cut through the turmoil of the small village. Galya, who was watching Ivan walking to her brother's house, saw him fall as Peter appeared in the doorway with a rifle in his hand, shouting obscenities.

"You want to rob me? You think I am a woman who would let you do it? This is my stuff and you cannot steal it from me!" Peter noticed that Ivan was still alive and aimed his gun at him again. "I am going to teach you a lesson; I am going to teach all guys like you a lesson. Do not steal what is not yours, it is dangerous for your life!"

Peter kept cursing Ivan, choking with the excitement of his power over an injured man. He failed to notice when a number of Red Guards, who had heard the shot, assembled around his yard and pointed guns at him. His rage ended only when something hot hit him in the shoulder. He looked around and fell down next to Ivan. The Red Guards rushed toward them, and soon Tanya was working first on Ivan and then Peter.

Ivan was taken to his house, where his mother, sobbing and shouting, was arranging a bed for her wounded son. Although she was in tears, Ivan still enjoyed seeing his mother, as well as his younger brother, who looked thin—so thin! But his older brother was not around. Instead of joining the Reds as Ivan had, he joined the band organized by Peter's son, Grishka.

8

It was time to leave Miratin. Sergey ordered a private to stay with Katya for her protection, left Tanya to take care of the fallen, dispatched a small group of soldiers to the base with the collected provisions, and led his main detachment on the way to the next village. Peter, an injured kulak, was taken prisoner and put on one of the wagons with provisions, to be delivered to the proper authorities. Sergey thought all the day's troubles were over.

Fate had other plans.

Within an hour of departing Miratin, the small group of soldiers with provisions was ambushed by Grishka's band. The surprise worked and the band easily overwhelmed the Red Guards accompanying the wagons. They were all killed and their bellies were sliced open with knives and stuffed with grain—to teach a lesson, as Peter had said.

Grishka's band was one of many roaming the outskirts of towns and cities—pillaging, fighting the Reds or other bands, and always looking for new victims. Some bands were small, like Grishka's--about twenty people, some were huge, like the Makhno army, and they all added to the complexity of the situation in Ukraine.

As soon as the band learned from the freed Peter of the events in Miratin and the fact that some Reds were still there, Grishka ordered them to enter his village and free it from the presence of the disgusting Reds. He also swore to personally kill Ivan—the cause of his father's injury and detainment. The band arrived in Miratin riding at full gallop. They wanted their revenge fast and entered the village without first checking if the main detachment was still there. It was not, and the place was quiet, but as soon as the sound of horses was heard, the villagers, who had been through this before, began hanging the icons on their gates to indicate that no unbelievers—Bolsheviks—were on their property.

Riding through the streets of the village, Grishka was watching for the absent icon—that is where the Reds would be. The band almost reached the other end of the village when he noticed that no icon hung on his aunt Galya's gate. He smiled, as his revenge was near. He drew his gun, nodded to his followers to back him up, and quietly moved toward the house. Just as quietly, Galya opened the door and pointed at the outdoor lavatory. Grishka understood at once. He opened the lavatory's door, and the Red Guard who was sitting there with his trunks down almost choked to death at the sight of a gun pointed at him. A shot rang out and the guard slumped on the lavatory doorstep.

Grishka turned around and asked Galya, "Anybody else?"

"Just this one girl who is in bed sick."

"A girl! Let's see how red her blood is."

Grishka ran inside the house, directly to the room where Katya was. She had heard the earlier shot and had a gun in bed, but she was no trained soldier. Grishka easily overpowered and laid her on the bed, positioning himself on top of the young woman. Katya's golden curls were covering her face and when Grishka moved them away, he saw his prize: a beautiful face with lovely blue eyes that were staring at him, but with an aversion as if they saw a toad. He was pleased with his catch and was about to enjoy it. He pressed his body against Katya hard and with his finger, very slowly, started to touch her hair, her cheeks, her lips, and.... Grishka screamed as if hit with an axe. He looked at his finger. It was bleeding and a part of it was separated and hanging loose. Katya, in desperation, had bitten his finger off. Grinding his teeth and swearing, Grishka took his handgun and smashed Katya's face with it hard. She lost consciousness and the struggle was over.

9

When Ivan's mother heard the band entering the village, she hung the icon outside and told her youngest son to take Ivan's horse and find Sergey's detachment quickly before they were all dead. And then she hid Tanya in the cellar, where they had dug an extra space, small enough that only a child or a diminutive woman would fit in. She moved a wooden barrel over the hideout and positioned whatever small items were lying in the cellar around it so as not to bring attention to that area, in case someone came down to look for the girl. With Tanya secure, the woman thought about what to do with her son.

"Ivan, do you think you can run and hide in the woods? Can you, son?"

"I am so weak, Mother, I don't think I can walk more than a few steps. I'll take my chances here."

Unexpectedly, Fedya, her oldest son, walked into the house. He was not in a good mood after hearing what Peter had told him about Ivan, but he first greeted his mother before turning to Ivan.

"Ivan, you fool, why did you go after Peter?"

"Because he is a bloodsucker."

"Do you think the Reds are any better? You want them to take over, make everything common, and we will still have nothing? If you are so dumb that you cannot see what the Reds are, I'd rather shoot you than let you help them." Fedya began reaching for his gun as their mother screamed, "Stop it! Stop it! I will kill you and myself if you touch Ivan!"

At that moment, the door opened and Grishka walked in with a bandaged hand. "Where is this traitor?" he shouted, and finding Ivan, grabbed him by his shirt.

"Where is the Red bitch you are hiding? I know she is here, my aunt told me. Don't lie to me!"

Ivan's mother, with tears in her eyes, squeezed between Grishka and Ivan and said, "She is not here; she ran to the woods. Go look for her over there!"

"We'll find her, the Red bitch. She could not have gone far. But first I need to waste Ivan-the-traitor."

Hearing that, the woman covered Ivan with her body and, sobbing violently, repeated, "No, no, no...."

Fedya, seeing his mother's suffering, intervened. "Go for the girl, Grishka. The Reds may come back and time is short. I will take care of my former brother myself."

Grishka left, and in a few seconds, he heard a shot and a woman's scream. He crossed himself in the orthodox manner at the sound of a brotherly murder, but he did not know that Fedya had not killed his brother, but had instead shot at the floor while his mother screamed to make the scene believable.

Meanwhile, Ivan's younger brother had reached Sergey quickly, and the whole detachment was coming back to Miratin. Without stopping for even a second to plan an attack, they just rode into the village galloping at full speed. The band was caught off-guard and did not have a chance to organize for the fight, which ended quickly. Several bandits were killed and injured, while the rest regrouped and left the village. Two Red Guards were wounded, including Yasha. Sergey ordered his soldiers to take the prisoners, both nurses, and the injured soldiers. The detachment departed again, this time leaving nobody behind.

10

Anna diligently visited Countess Rudinsky, bringing her food and taking her dirty clothes for washing. Her visits did not last long as she did not want to be around an arrogant woman who thought she was still a member of the elite. One day, as she was approaching the Rudinsky mansion, Anna noticed a commotion around it. Coming closer, she observed unfamiliar people moving into and out of the house, carrying some boards and other items. She stopped, looked around, and saw a young man in a military uniform without any insignia—obviously a former soldier—giving orders and looking official. Anna approached him and asked, "What is going on here?"

The young man replied, "Who are you?"

"I am an acquaintance of the owner of this house."

"Such a pretty girl. Why would you be an acquaintance of bourgeois? Can't you find better friends?"

"And who are you to dictate to me who my friends should be?" It was easy to spark Anna's anger by asking a wrong question.

The man just laughed and introduced himself, "My name is Vasili. I am responsible for the densification."

"What is this densification?"

"Well, as you know, your acquaintance lives alone in a huge mansion. The result is that the density of this building is low, if you think how many people per square meter live in it. We will settle more people here—people who have no place to live—and the density will improve."

Anna just shook her head and walked into the house. The Countess was upstairs in her room. She answered Anna's knock on the door with "Who is it?" and told her to come in. The Countess was sitting by the makeup table and examining herself in a mirror, looking strange, as if out of this world. Anna stood still for a second, deciding what to do, and then, just as usual, put out the food sent by Lyuba to the Countess, who did not, also as usual, say "thank you." Instead, the Countess asked, "What is going on downstairs? They came earlier today, showed me some papers. I could not understand what they were talking about, but they did not listen to me anyway and started building something. I should call the police."

"Countess, those are the new authorities. They decided you have extra space that you don't need, so some people will move in."

"I don't have any extra space! This is my house, it's all mine! My husband's grandfather built it and we always lived here. I don't understand these new authorities and how they can just come in and do what they want. I should call the police."

"Calling the police will not change anything. They represent the same authority. I recommend you just stay upstairs and not argue with them, for your own sake. I will be back in a couple of days."

96

Back at home, Anna described what she had seen to her parents and expressed some apprehension about the same densification applying to them, but Senya calmed her down.

"We have a small house and our boys are in the Red Army. Where would they live when they return?"

Anna visited the Countess every couple of days and noticed more and more people living in the mansion. Every once in a while she saw Vasili but she would not engage with him and any conversations were brief, until one day Vasili offered to escort her and she agreed, thinking she could learn more details about the housing situation on a friendlier ground. Walking home, Vasili asked, "Anna, how do you know Countess Rudinsky?"

"I used to work for her."

"What are you doing here now? I assume you don't work for her any longer, do you?"

"No, no. I just visit her because she is all alone and has no idea how to take care of herself. I come out of pity for her."

"She exploited you and you have pity for her?"

"Well, I would not call her a nice person, but she did not exploit me—she paid for my work. My dad used to have a shoemaking business and he had two guys working for him. They did their job and he paid them for it. Was he exploiting them?"

"Yes, he was. This is why we are building a new society where everyone would work not for some capitalist, but for the state."

"So, working for the state is okay, but not for someone else? This means that the state is exploiting the workers!"

"No, working for the state is the same as working for yourself, because the country now belongs to us," Vasili explained, pleased with what he thought to be a politically right answer.

Anna wanted to steer away from political conversations with a fellow she hardly knew and changed the subject.

"Vasili, why don't you tell me about yourself?"

"About myself? I am just a regular guy. I became an orphan early in life when both my parents died. My uncle took care of me, and at thirteen I went to work at the plant. Before the revolution, I was drafted and became a soldier. Right after the revolution I joined the Communists in building the new state. I fought against the Whites and became a civilian when my right hand was injured. Even now, I have trouble fully using it. So, now I work on densification."

Time passed quickly and they appeared in front of Anna's house. Vasili was surprised and asked, "How many people live here?"

"Are you thinking of densifying us?" Anna jokingly answered with a question.

She opened the door and offered Vasili to come in. Zhenya saw them and reacted with a big smile because she thought Anna was with an admirer, but her sister quickly introduced Vasili, "Zhenya, this is Vasili, the densificator."

"Oh! Are you planning to densify us also?" Zhenya asked with a smirk.

"That depends." Vasili answered with a smile.

Lyuba met the visitor and immediately offered him something to eat. In a few minutes, the sisters and Vasili were sitting at the table, eating and talking about other subjects. Lyuba was observing silently until Vasili finished eating and thanked her for the great food. Then she asked him, "Why are you doing this densification?"

"I was a soldier in the Red Army, and after an injury, I was sent to a different front: fighting with the vestiges of the bourgeoisie. This is my front now and it is not easy. You know, many people don't have a place to live, especially peasants who leave their villages because it is more difficult to survive there."

"Do you like doing this?" Zhenya asked.

"One has to do what is necessary to advance the interests of the new proletarian society. We are breaking new ground on the way to a bright future, where exploitation is no more and everyone is equal in a world of peace and kindness."

Vasili's answer sounded like an article in a political paper and the girls were biting their lips to avoid laughing, while Lyuba, who could control herself better than the youngsters, said with a serious face, "You are explaining these things wonderfully!"

Vasili missed the sarcasm and proudly responded, "These are not my words. Comrade Lenin said it and I remembered! Now the poor will govern workers and peasants."

Senya's voice intervened, "But if only poor people govern the country, it will be poor. They don't know how to make the country rich!"

"We will learn!" Vasili replied.

"And while you're learning, the country will keep deteriorating."

Vasili had no answer. Instead, he switched his attention to Zhenya. Everybody noticed that she attracted him. And when the time came for Vasili to leave, he asked Zhenya, "Can we meet again?"

"You are welcome to come anytime," Zhenya answered.

They liked each other for sure. After the guest left, Anna remarked, "How interesting things are in life! I argued with him and he ended up in my home by chance, only to fall in love with my sister. What a strange turn of events."

11

The Countess was crying. The confident, self-assured, and seemingly eternally strong Countess was crying. Anna had never felt close to the woman, but this change of façade, this despair, moved her.

"What happened?" Anna asked.

"They rob me right in my own home. First, they move in without asking my permission, and now they are taking whatever they want."

"Who are they?"

"The tenants! Those who now live here. When I go for a walk, they take whatever they want."

Anna was in a bad mood when she left the Countess. More than that, she was mad. She abhorred unfairness, even directed at people she did not like. All the way home she was searching for a solution. Coming home, she saw Vasili at the table talking to Zhenya and Senya, while her mother was serving food. Vasili was the guy who had brought all those tenants in, but more importantly, he was the face of the state under whose protection they were stealing the Countess's property. Anna ran to the kitchen and asked Lyuba angrily, "Does he think we are supposed to feed him?"

"We don't feed him. He brought all this food," answered Lyuba.

Then Anna, who had to find an outlet for her anger, joined her family at the table and spoke, without even saying hello, "I am sorry to interrupt your friendly conversation, but I have a question to ask. Is it true that the Soviet state allows robbery?"

"Of course not, Anna. What are you talking about?" answered Vasili.

"I am talking about the tenants in the Rudinskys' house, who steal whatever they see when she is not there, and nobody is protecting her or punishing the thieves."

"You see, Anna, the Countess accumulated all this stuff without working; someone else made it all for her. Now, people are taking back what they consider belongs to them, made with their sweat and blood."

Nobody liked that answer. Zhenya expressed her opinion first, "I think this is just a robbery."

"It is shameful. Taking the house was not enough, now they want to take the rest. Shame, shame," added Senya.

This was the topic of conversation all evening and Vasili, under pressure from the entire family, and himself feeling something was wrong, promised to stop the lawlessness.

The next morning, he went directly to the Rudinsky house, called all the tenants, and said, "We received a complaint from Rudinsky about stealing. In our state, stealing is illegal. This is not what we fought for, and the thieves will be severely punished. You better return all the items that were stolen from Rudinsky before the state comes down on you. And in the future, avoid breaking the law."

Vasili finished and the tenants unhappily went to their rooms to collect what they were supposed to return. Whether everything was returned or not Anna did not know, but she was satisfied that fairness had triumphed.

A few months passed by, and one day, as Anna was going to see the Countess again and was approaching the mansion, the shape of a familiar-looking man attracted her attention. Her heart began beating a little faster as her mind raced through her memory to match the shape with someone she knew. As hard as it was to believe, it was Victor! Their separation had not been amicable, but Anna always thought of him, and taking care of his mother was making her feel only closer to Victor. Anna's steps quickened until she was almost running and, finally, she was next to him. How different he looked though—pale, thin, despondent—but it was Victor. In her mind, she wanted to hug him, squeeze him, kiss him. But what was it with him? He kept talking to some man and did not even want to acknowledge her. She was sure he had noticed her.

Anna did not stop, instead walked by Victor into the house and up the stairs to see the Countess. She delivered food and was about to leave, but decided to ask a question.

"Is Victor back?"

"Yes, he is!" the Countess answered proudly.

"When did he come back?"

"Just yesterday. Now everything will be great for us. He will find a way to get our house and belongings back," proclaimed the Countess.

Then Victor walked in. This time he could not avoid acknowledging Anna's presence.

"Hello, Anna." His demeanor was as though he felt dead inside.

"Hello, Victor," Anna replied, unable to completely suppress all the warmth she wanted him to feel. "I've heard you just came back yesterday. Where have you been, what are you planning to do now?"

Victor's frost began to melt under the rays of female attention. He dropped into a chair, looked down at the floor, and said, "Where I have been is a long story, we will talk about it some other time. What I am planning to do, you are asking? I don't know. For now, I just want to stop people who live in my house from stealing my things, and I don't know how."

"Your mother told me about this a while ago, but not lately. Are they still taking your stuff?"

"Oh, yes. And I am in no position to demand anything from them." These last words just slipped through Victor's defenses; he had not meant to disclose anything pertaining to his relationship with the new system. But Anna jumped from the chair she was sitting in as though boiling water had been poured on her.

Without a single word, she ran downstairs into the tenants' common area, where several women were cooking, and screamed at them, "Did Vasili not tell you that stealing is a capital offence? You better bring everything that belongs to the Rudinskys back to them or you will go to jail. I will make sure Vasili knows what is going on here." Her confidence in what she was saying was so strong that the women were dumbfounded. In a second, they turned around and went to their rooms, only to reappear a few minutes later with some items in their hands, which they carried upstairs and laid on the floor.

Seeing such events unfolding before his eyes, Victor asked, "Is this how you deal with people now? And who is this Vasili?"

"We will talk about it some other time. Right now, we should pack some items we could sell to buy food. We'll take them to our house for safety as this house is like an open barn."

They spread a large tablecloth and piled some clothes, jewelry, and other items they could sell. Wrapping the cloth up, they tied the ends of it into a knot to make a sack, and took it to Anna's house. At the door to her home, Victor passed the sack to Anna and said, "Let's meet tomorrow."

12

A new world, an unexpected new world, was what Victor found in Elizavetgrad. This was not the Russia he had known when he left home before the revolution. Everything was different now: his station in life, his relationship with the government, his ability to acquire living necessities. Even his house—which really was not his any longer as it belonged to the state, which could evict him from his birthplace at any time.

Finding a job was difficult. Opportunities for earning a living were scarce for all, but for a member of the former nobility it was not only tough but dangerous. Disclosing his real pedigree, as was required on a job application, would have been suicidal, while lying that he comes from the proletariat would be even worse. Temporary hard labor jobs were what provided him with some money.

The bright spot for Victor was Anna. He felt good visiting the Nepomnyashchy residence. Being with Anna's family allowed him to experience the warmth he was missing in his own house. His mother behaved strangely, as if she believed that life would return to the prerevolutionary time, and they never had any visitors. Anna was his lifeline, and became even more of a savior when Victor told her one day that he and his mother were being squeezed into one bedroom, while the rest of the second floor was to be divided among additional new tenants. Victor was losing it, and if not for Anna, he would probably have done something foolish. Anna's will took over. She organized a steady movement of Victor's possessions to her house, bringing over whatever could be sold. That provided the source of income to sustain the Rudinskys, and Victor could not do it without Anna.

When Victor was absent, the tenants were not shy around the Countess and would come to her room and take whatever they wanted, ignoring her screams of outrage. Life in the mansion that was full of strangers became unbearable for the Countess and Victor. They chose to move. For the second time, the Rudinskys became the occupants of the boys' room in the Nepomnyashchy house.

The family's economic circumstances were not good. Since Senya's business was not producing much and Victor could not find a job, the only source of income for the entire household was Zhenya's salary as a nurse. But most of the food was coming from Lyuba's shelves—

whatever she had stocked up when they were still making money and could purchase foodstuffs, while some of it was purchased with the money Victor made by selling his ancestral possessions, especially the silver and china. Senya's favorite sayings during that time were, "It is good that we saved some food during capitalism, so now we can survive under socialism," and "What are we going to do if socialism exists longer than we have food for?"

For the Countess this was torture. She would not accept the change and attempted to behave as in the old times. She did not participate in any household activities and did not have any chores on her shoulders. Anna, who was washing the Countess's clothes and cleaning her room, once asked, "Why can't you do it yourself? We are not your servants."

"But I don't know how!"

"Leave her alone, Anna," edified Lyuba. "She is an unfortunate woman who lives in a completely new country without leaving the old one, and her old habits are hard to change. Have pity."

Life was crowded for the inhabitants of the Nepomnyashchy house, when one day Yasha and Sergey appeared on the doorstep of their home.

Initially, after their arrival, Yasha and Sergey did not really have a chance to feel the impact of the Rudinskys becoming part of their household, but when they finally settled in for the night—and they settled in the living room, the only space still available—the boys learned the details of the situation from Anna.

"Why do we have to live under the same roof with the people who want our death? He was shooting at us to kill!" Sergey said to Yasha once they were alone.

"Are we not building a new society? Shouldn't we influence people to accept the new way of life instead of throwing them overboard? This is how I understand our task," Yasha argued.

"Here we go, empathy for everyone, just like Mama Lyuba. Do you think our enemies would have pity for you if the situation was reversed?"

104

"I really don't know what they would do. You may be right and they would destroy me, but we are different. This is what's important to me: we must be different!"

Yasha's speech made an impression on Sergey; he always paid attention to his friend-brother. It was just difficult for him to adjust to this strange situation.

"Promise me you will not tell anyone, anyone, about where we saw Victor, okay?" Yasha requested.

Sergey agreed. He was beginning a new life and wanted to start it clean, without any feelings of hatred and with the confidence of a high moral ground.

Part Two

1

In 1919, after spending two weeks at their home with the family, Yasha and Sergey received a new assignment.

The Civil War was still lingering. The Red Army would beat one attacker only to face another in a different area. Denikin, Kolchak, Yudenich—the waves of counterrevolutionary attempts flooded Russia one after another, but the Bolshevik government was building strength. And although the threat still existed and required most of the country's human and material resources to counter it, the effort to build a new society with all its necessary institutions was underway. Lenin and his compatriots understood well that military victory was only the beginning and if they wanted to govern for a long time they would need cadres of engineers, scientists, bureaucrats, military commanders, diplomats, doctors, skilled workers.... The list was long. The old infrastructure was just about destroyed—not only physical, but also human—and the country would not survive without developing its own. Only a small fraction of the existing skilled personnel was employed in support of the new system, which quickly led to the realization that the sooner the new cadres were developed the better. And who would these new cadres be? Preferably proletarian, literate, and even more importantly—the ones who had risked their lives defending the new state.

Both Yasha and Sergey fit the bill well. Yasha's origin was just a bit suspect because his father had been a small entrepreneur before the revolution, but "small" was an important modifier, and in addition, Yasha had proven himself to be dedicated to the cause and very smart. They were both removed from the military duties and sent back to their hometown for more education and training. This was their new assignment.

They were glad to come home. Yasha wanted to study, to learn more about history, philosophy, and people—everything he had dreamed about as a teenager. Sergey's interests were more in active participation in the creation of the new state. While studying at the university, the actual jobs the state was willing to offer them at this time were based not on their desires but experience. Hence, Yasha went back to his old profession printing papers and books, but at a higher level—he became an assistant manager in the shop. Sergey received an assignment in the local NKVD office.

Going back to work instead of constantly moving and fighting, living in the normal—if there was such a thing at the time—environment of the family was a pleasant change for Yasha and Sergey. An added attraction was the ability to see the women they liked. Katya and Tanya had left the Red Army earlier. Katya had physically recovered from her illness and the beating, but emotionally she was not capable of being in the army anymore. She went home to Elizavetgrad to live with her mother and study economics in the evening college while working in the local NKVD as a secretary during the day. Tanya left the Red Guards and studied to become a teacher, a profession of importance and high prestige in the Soviet state. She studied at night and worked as a librarian during the day. She loved the books so much that in the library she felt in paradise.

Meanwhile, Zhenya—quiet and thoughtful, serious and dedicated to her goals—had already made her choice. She dated Vasili briefly before the couple decided to marry. It came as a surprise to everyone because they had spent only a short amount of time together, but the parents did not mind, as Vasili was an affable, hard-working, and loving person. The tricky issue of where to live was quickly resolved by Senya: "Of course, here, in our house!"

A forthcoming wedding always energizes everyone involved. Under the circumstances, this would not be a typical Jewish wedding. Vasili was not Jewish and had few relations, and the religious aspects of the ceremony disappeared as the Soviet state declared religion an anti-people device harmful to proletarians. The official procedure was a civil transaction in a special government office, which registered birth, death, and other civil acts, including marriage.

The formal portion of Vasili and Zhenya's wedding ended quickly, and then there was a celebration at home with a special meal—Lyuba's resourcefulness came in handy—followed by singing and frolicking around. A new family was born.

At the wedding, Senya and Lyuba met their sons' girlfriends for the first time. How excited Lyuba was to see Katya and Tanya! She knew about the infatuation and had heard good things about both girls, but seeing them alleviated any apprehension a mother could have about other women in her sons' lives. She saw beautiful faces, inquiring eyes, kind smiles, and her heart beat with excitement that one day she would be able to call these nice girls her daughters.

After a wonderful wedding, the expanded family returned to everyday work, concerns, and challenges. Although Senya rearranged his nonfunctional shop into a bedroom to provide more space, their home was still very crowded. However, soon both Yasha and Sergey moved away into a state dormitory thanks to their important occupations. Tenants there lived in small rooms, had a communal kitchen and bathroom, and had to follow many rules. But the cost was minimal and the lucky ones were happy to find themselves in a dormitory. Katya and Tanya were also among those lucky ones—their service in the army had paid off—and together shared a room. They became close friends, and dating Yasha and Sergey created a comfortable situation with all four people liking and enjoying each other. These were good days by the standards of the time.

Vasili also wanted to attain an apartment of his own and filed a request with the appropriate authority, the one in charge of the extremely limited living space. To qualify for an apartment was one thing, to actually get one was another, but Vasili, as an employee of the housing department, had an advantage and was granted an apartment relatively quickly on account of having a family.

One evening, Vasili came home in a strange mood and anxiously shared his thoughts with Lyuba—the wise peacemaker—while Zhenya was still away.

"Mama Lyuba," Vasili had adopted Sergey's way of referring to her, "I have good news. I finally got an apartment for us."

"An apartment? Don't you have a place to live?"

"We do, but our room is small, while the new apartment is larger. We can even put a crib in it."

"A crib! I was hoping my grandchildren would be running around in this house and I would see them every day."

"But the place is not far away and it will be more convenient for us. It is a room in a communal house with a common kitchen and bathroom." Vasili wanted to say something else, but visibly hesitated.

"What's eating you?" Lyuba asked.

"Well... it is Countess Rudinsky's bedroom in her house."

What a turn of events! Vasili always performed his duties as a densificator with the conviction that it was the right thing to do, but now he had to face the people he had lived with for some time and tell them that while they had to stay in somebody else's house in a small room, he would move into their place. Vasili's sense of fairness was confused and he did not know how to deal with the situation.

Lyuba was speechless. The issue was difficult and she was also at a loss. It took her a few seconds to recover and then she said, "My God! This is a problem. And I don't know how to deal with it except finding an appropriate time and telling Victor directly. It is not their house anymore; somebody will live there, so why not you?"

That was the decision.

On Sunday, when the entire family was at home for a traditional weekly gathering, Vasili made an announcement about the apartment. Everybody congratulated him, and then there were questions.

"When are you planning to move?"

"Is the room furnished?"

"How far is this place from here?" Senya asked. He already knew the answer, but wanted to introduce the dangerous topic while everyone was there, possibly to soften the blow to Victor.

Vasili said, "The room is in the Rudinsky mansion. We were assigned it, including the furniture in the room, while it all belongs to the state."

Victor, initially shocked at the coincidence, collected himself quickly and allowed humor to disperse the heavy silence that had set in.

"Well, I will get even with you by moving into your room here!"

Everybody laughed and Vasili could breathe easier.

"Victor, I am sorry it happened this way. You know, I did not pick this particular room. It was assigned to me, and if I reject it, who knows when I would have another chance."

"It's okay, Vasili, I understand. For me this is not such a big deal. I lost much more than this room, which would be given to somebody anyway. I lost my country, I lost myself."

The discussion ended not on the brightest note, but the air was cleared, and when everybody helped the young couple move, the issue was not mentioned anymore. Victor moved into his own small bedroom, which was a huge improvement over staying together with his mother, and life continued in the Nepomnyashchy household with a smaller number of tenants.

2

Senya contributed to the common finances less than others living under the same roof and he hated it. His business had disappeared, since the Soviet system did not allow for private enterprise. Occasionally Anna would sell a pair of shoes he had made in a market, which was all the financial contribution he made. The feeling of helplessness was strong. Many questions without answers were swarming in his head and every time he had a chance to verbalize them, he did. There were two fervent defenders of the new system under his roof: Vasili and Sergey, with Yasha coming at a distant third. All of them thought that the new state was attempting to create a new and better society for the benefit of everyone. Sergey and Vasili believed in every move the new government made and both tried to address Senya's questions with passion, but Sergey was finding himself under the rain of Senya's inquiries more often than Vasili.

"Sergey, how is it that both you and Yasha work for the state but receive different rations?"

"Because I have a position of more responsibility than Yasha."

"But Vasili was telling us these stories about the new system where all are equal and get whatever they need. Do you think Yasha needs less than you?"

"Vasili was probably describing communism to you, where everyone would work according to their abilities and receive according to their needs. But we are now building socialism—the first step on the road to communism—and we don't have enough resources for everybody yet, so right now it is different. You work according to your ability and receive according to your contribution. The state believes that my contribution is greater than Yasha's."

"All right, tell me then, why are so many people hungry? We used to feed half of Europe and now our people don't have enough to eat."

"We are trying the best we can. It takes time to learn, to develop new cadres. These are temporary difficulties."

"Well, I hope you learn quickly, before everybody starves. And what do you mean by *equality*?"

"Everyone is equal. It's as simple as that."

"Everyone?" Senya asked again with a smirk.

"We are building a state of proletarians and peasants who are equal. And we will grow intelligentsia out of them."

"What class do I belong to?"

"You are closer to the proletariat than you think."

"And what are the people who do not work called?"

"Tuneyadtsi. They are our enemies and we will make them work," Sergey enthusiastically replied.

112

"But what if a person wants to work, but cannot find a job?"

"The state would help such people either by finding an opportunity or sending them to learn a new profession."

"Then help Victor find a job."

"He is a bourgeois. We need to open opportunities for our people, not help the dying class."

"What do you mean by that? Nobody chooses their parents and everyone needs to earn money to survive. How would I survive? I am also the son of a count. Does that mean I am undesirable?"

Sergey was stunned. He had never heard that before. In all his years of living with the Nepomnyashchys, it had not come up in conversation. Perplexed and embarrassed, Sergey could not say a word. But this conversation stuck in his mind. Young and idealistic as he was, the sense that life could not be seen in black and white but consisted of many shades of gray was setting in.

Soon after that conversation with Senya, when he saw Victor returning from his regular market trip in a bad mood, Sergey addressed him first, which was unusual. "Hello, Victor, how are you doing?"

"I am fine," Victor answered in a tone that made it obvious he was just keeping his façade up and, as he was unaccustomed to attention from Sergey, wanted to leave the room. Sergey stopped him with another question, "Would you like to have a job in my organization?"

Surprise! Victor did not expect such an offer, especially because Sergey's organization, as he referred to it, was involved in persecuting people like Victor. Sergey understood his hesitation.

"If you are willing, I will help create the right paperwork for you to be considered for a job. We need to think through a new personal history for you."

"Let's make his father a proletarian," chimed in Yasha, who was reading at the table and had heard the conversation, still keeping his eyes on the book.

"Are you serious? Just look at his hands—no calluses. Who would believe he is a worker?"

"Then let's make his father an engineer. That is probably the best we can do," offered Yasha again.

By the end of the evening, a new biography of Victor Rudinsky that was acceptable to the state institutions was created. Then Victor asked, "What will I do?"

"I don't really know yet," Sergey answered and added, "I will probably be moving to Kharkov soon because of my expected promotion. I will know more about open positions there later on, but I wanted to get your agreement and your papers in order first."

Promotion is a good thing for an aspiring employee: more money, more prestige, and more responsibilities. Moving to the capital is also a plus. Leaving the family behind is a big minus. Nobody liked this element of the change, including Sergey, but that was the price for advancement.

"Don't worry, I will get you all to Kharkov!" stated Sergey cheerfully, believing it would be possible with all his loving heart. Then he made another announcement, "I want to go to a new place as a family. Before leaving, I want to marry Katya."

"Congratulations!"

"Mazel Tov!"

All present cheered.

Sergey said, "I want to make a proposal to Katya in such a special way that we will remember it forever. Mama Lyuba, can you make a family dinner next Saturday?"

"Of course," answered Lyuba.

"Let's tell everyone that this is to celebrate my promotion. I will propose to Katya at the right moment. But you have to play along, please."

The next Saturday, everything and everybody at the Nepomnyashchy house was ready at the appropriate time. Dressed in their best clothes, they all looked sharp and full of anticipation. When Yasha and Sergey arrived with their girlfriends, the young women were surprised by the energy emanating from these people, but they eventually assumed that this was just the way this family celebrated.

114

During the meal, at the right moment, Sergey stood up and asked for everyone's attention. Katya expected a toast. Instead, she heard, "Katya, you are my love. Would you marry me?"

It took Katya a few long seconds to catch her breath, while the silence was as sharp as a razor blade. Then, looking into Sergey's eyes and blushing profusely, she replied softly, "Yes."

Everybody clapped, everybody smiled, and Senya proposed a toast to the new family. The excitement moved everyone at the table to talk loudly and share their own moments of surprise in life. And then Yasha tapped on a glass with a fork to attract attention, stood up, and announced, "I want to say something."

With that he turned to Tanya, who was sitting next to him, and quietly said, "Tanya, you will make me the happiest man in the universe if you marry me."

"I will be the happiest woman alive when I marry you!"

A happy commotion ensued. Congratulations were showered and smiles shined on the family, which would soon enlarge. They all missed the knock on the door and were startled when an unfamiliar man entered. Everyone looked with puzzlement at the young, well-dressed man who did not fit the mold of a new Soviet citizen.

"Who are you?" asked Lyuba, breaking the silence.

"Aunt Lyuba, I am Boris, your nephew. Did you not receive my letters that I am coming to help build the first socialist country in the world?"

"Boris, my God! You are so... mature, and this is so unexpected. We haven't had any letters from your family in a long time," Lyuba said and squeezed her nephew. When Senya and the children took Lyuba's place in welcoming their relative, she explained to the others who he was.

The celebration was winding down when Lyuba decided that Boris needed some rest after a long trip. When the visitors left, she made a temporary bed for Boris in the living room and said, "Sleep well, nephew. We have a lot to talk about tomorrow."

"Thank you, Aunt." Boris kissed Lyuba, undressed, and fell asleep faster than he expected.

3

After breakfast the next morning, Senya asked Boris, "How do you live in America?"

"We are doing well. My parents bought a grocery store with the money they saved and a loan from other relatives. It's a small store, but it supports the family. We sell groceries and Mama's baked goods, which she prepares at home."

"Are you married?" Lyuba asked.

"No," laughed Boris, "but I have a fiancée. She even promised to come here and contribute to the prosperity of the first workers' state. She is a devout socialist and talks about creating a socialist state in America too."

Lyuba and Senya looked at each other, puzzled, but let Boris continue.

"We are so proud that you are building a new society here where everyone is to be equal. Nobody is rich, nobody is poor, and everyone has what they need to live on. It's wonderful! And after these temporary difficulties with food shortages and whatever else is not working yet, you make a new society and create a new kind of citizen."

Boris used other phrases familiar to Lyuba and Senya, such as, "A man to a man is a friend in a socialist state," and "Who used to be nothing will be everything." He spoke with the conviction and enthusiasm of a Bolshevik agitator, and Lyuba imagined dropping a bucket of cold water on him to cool his passion. Instead, she said, "It's all well and good, but many people are starving. If not for Sergey's help with food—he is an important man and gets extra—we would be close to starving too."

"Why doesn't Uncle Senya make more shoes then? He is one of the best shoemakers. People loved his products."

"But private business is not allowed under socialism. Everything belongs to the state," sneered Senya. "And if you want socialism in America, your parents' store will be taken over by the state too. Your parents will wait for their kids to help them, unless they've saved foodstuffs for a rainy day, as Aunt Lyuba had."

Boris was startled for a second but then decided these old people didn't really know what they were talking about. He said, "The best solution to provide enough food for the population is to improve agriculture. I studied economics in college and spent time with a good farmer to learn agricultural business. I can help. I am so happy that your revolution happened in my lifetime and I have an opportunity to participate in the creation of the first socialist state! I did not mention the most important news yet. Our Jewish community bought a tractor as a present to Russia and I am taking it to the designated kolkhoz. I will teach the people there how to use it."

Later that day, Boris left to deliver the tractor.

4

Preparations for the double wedding were swift, as Sergey's new assignment had worked out and he had to move to Kharkov in less than a month. When the two couples arrived at the registration office, they saw a tall, lean woman with hair slicked back into a bun. She looked more like a man, and her stiff demeanor was not in line with the occasion. After asking some formal questions, she stated, with no emotion and the seriousness of a judge presiding at a trial, "I pronounce you husband and wife. Congratulations on creating new Soviet families of a new socialist state."

The young couples could hardly contain their laughter, and as soon as they left the room, the youthful enthusiasm of the happy newlyweds erupted into a loud release. They mimicked the woman's expressions and repeated some of the more pompous statements. In this joyful mood, they went home, where guests were waiting for the real wedding.

It was a blissful celebration with music, dancing, and even some delicacies supplied by Sergey via his connections.

Happy days interlaced with routine and sometimes with bad days. The excitement surrounding the wedding provided for happy days; the routine followed. In a couple of weeks, Sergey and Katya moved to Kharkov into a small flat provided by the NKVD. Sergey arranged for Victor to be hired as an administrative clerk, and the Rudinskys— mother and son—also moved to Kharkov into a small flat of their own.

Prior to leaving, Victor's heart was aching. He loved Anna and wanted to propose to her, but lacking a decent job until now prevented him from taking this step, since supporting a family without sufficient income was out of the question. When Sergey had offered him a position in a different city, he thought at first that his time had come. But then where would he take his new wife? He had no reasonable assurance that the job, the apartment, and the living conditions would be satisfactory. He had to wait and experience the new environment by himself. Then he would find a way to bring Anna into his life.

Within days after the Rudinskys departure Yasha and Tanya occupied their empty room, making the house full again.

5

While Sergey's career was going well in Kharkov, Yasha was promoted to director of the print shop. His ration and salary increased, but the food he brought in was still not sufficient for everyone, for besides supporting his family, including a pregnant wife, Yasha always helped his parents and Tanya's relatives, who had lost their provider. He also felt responsibility for his workers. His personal experience in the provision detachment gave him an idea. Always uneasy as a Red Guard coming to a village and taking whatever foodstuffs they found "for the benefit of the proletariat," he now thought about going to the countryside with the fruits of the proletarian labor to be exchanged for food.

Yasha announced his plan at the shop meeting and asked everyone to bring in whatever they could for the exchange. Everybody liked the idea, although some people remained skeptical about such a venture having a positive result. On the scheduled day, most employees gathered at the shop, where several wagons and horses were waiting for them—courtesy of Yasha's efforts. They piled into the wagons whatever had been brought in for the exchange. Yasha even included some of the books and notebooks printed in the shop, in case there was an interest for them in the village. He brought a few pairs of boots that Senya had made and some pots and shovels that Tanya collected from her family. Yasha picked the village for this event based on the advice of his deputy, who happened to know someone in it. It was not too far from Elizavetgrad, but far enough for the villagers not to come to town often.

It was early fall and the day was decent—not too cold, but not one of those beautiful autumn days when the soul, impressed by nature's display of color, is singing. The wagons moved along the dirt road, the people anticipating a good trading day and hoping to see the wagons full of food on the way back. In three hours they reached the village of Kresti. Since it was Sunday, nobody was present at the local soviet and it took a while to find an official capable of gathering people. He was puzzled by the proposition of the exchange and was initially suspicious, but Yasha's confident demeanor and the Red Guard uniform he had put on for the occasion convinced the official that no harm would be done by offering the villagers a bartering opportunity.

The people gathering in the central square of the village were apprehensive when they saw the wagons and the outsiders, who despite looking different from the provision detachment seemed suspicious enough for the people to feel uneasy. Yasha understood their mood well and wanted to explain the offer quickly. He found a barrel, stood on it as a podium, and asked everyone for attention.

"Comrades! We came to you, Soviet peasants, for help. But we also brought something that you would find useful in your life. You know that the food situation in towns is terrible. Many people don't have

119

enough even for their children. We work at the print shop and make books, journals, and other printed materials. We work hard for the state, but foodstuffs are hard to find. We need your help! Look at my wife," Yasha pointed to where Tanya was sitting in the wagon. "As you see, she is pregnant, but we are afraid of what will happen with the baby since she does not have enough nourishment for the two of them. Now, we brought many useful things with us: shovels and pots and furniture and clothes. We want a fair exchange with you. Please help us!"

Yasha finished his speech and noticed with horror that the peasants did not move, did not ask questions, and did not react in any way indicating their understanding and agreement. It was quiet for a few seconds, which felt like eternity to Yasha and his cohorts, until someone among the peasants shouted, "Where are the shovels? I need a couple because my old one just broke." This was like a sign to the crowd, which began transforming from a motionless mass into a vibrant market. Within minutes, negotiations started at every wagon about the exchange of goods. Soon the wagons were full of potatoes, apples, chickens, vegetables, lard, and wheat, while the peasants were dragging home the former possessions of the proletariat. Tanya drew special attention from the women. They brought her milk and even some baby clothes. Everyone seemed to be happy, smiles and handshakes replacing the former suspicious looks. Yasha thanked the local official for gathering the people, and they agreed that such exchanges should take place regularly.

The road back to town felt longer as everyone wanted to share the good fortune with their families. But the first thing they had to do upon arrival was to divide the foodstuffs, which was accomplished in a strictly communist, idealistic way: everything was distributed based on the family sizes. The venture clearly was a success.

When Yasha and Tanya came home with food, Senya was surprised that Yasha's idea had worked. He was surprised but pleased that now—at least for a while—his family was not in danger of hunger. When Yasha described how everything happened, including the food distribution, Senya commented, "So now I see how communism works: you have an idea, you organize everything, you make it happen, and then share the fruits of your labor with everyone."

6

Lyuba's dream of having grandchildren in the house was realized when Tanya brought into the world a baby girl. They named her Lara. She was a beautiful child. Smiling was her favorite activity other than sleeping. She also brought a sense of normalcy into the Nepomnyashchy household. Meanwhile, Yasha's job was satisfying and rewarding as he made a print shop into a well-functioning organization. Food shortages disappeared, thanks to his trips to Kresti, and with a baby in the house the family was satisfied with life, although Lyuba did feel sorry that Sergey was far away and Anna missed Victor.

Victor had learned a new job and was content with the situation. Nobody was suspicious of him, and with time, his education and good work ethic earned the respect of his co-workers. The distant days of his past as a noble were just that—distant. He lived a new life in a new country. His mother, though, still thought of herself as a countess. Victor constantly reminded her not to share her pedigree with anyone so they would stay alive.

After the birth of Yasha and Tanya's child, Sergey offered to help them move to Kharkov. He had his arguments: "We would be together and it would be more exciting to live in the capital than a provincial town." It took Sergey more than a year, but he finally convinced Yasha to move when a job he could not refuse was found: a lecturer at the prestigious High Party School. The Communist Party organized such schools and offered a political education to those in the Party leadership ranks.

Yasha, Tanya, and little Lara moved to Kharkov when Tanya was pregnant again. Sergey helped find an apartment for them, and Tanya was pleasantly surprised to see that it was completely furnished. She was also surprised when the man who showed them in pulled out a furniture list, asked Yasha to check everything and then sign the list. Tanya waited until they were alone and asked, "What are you signing?"

"All this belongs to the state. If something is broken or missing when we leave this place, we will have to pay for it."

"You mean all this furniture used to belong to someone else until the state confiscated it and now calls it its property? Why don't you then ask them to provide us with a piano, the one that they took from my parents? We could teach our kids to play."

"Tanya, I just got this new job. I am not sure I can demand anything, but I'll ask for a piano."

"I know, my dear, I know. It's just when I remember everything my family lost in the revolution, the death of my father.... Someone is playing my piano, while I am asking for another piano, confiscated from another family. Someone is using our furniture while I have to sign for furniture the state confiscated from someone else. It upsets me. I am sorry."

"You should not worry this much. We'll be fine."

That's what Yasha thought at the time as he kissed his wife's cool lips.

Sergey was pleased by Yasha's agreement to move to Kharkov. He wanted to have the entire family together again, but his pleas with Lyuba and Senya went nowhere—they would not give up their house, their home, which they bought a long time ago and where so many memorable events had happened. At the same time, Victor was writing to Anna, asking her to move to Kharkov too. Anna wanted to move but would not leave her parents. The impasse was broken by the Soviet state. Since the house was occupied by a small number of people— Senya, Lyuba, and Anna—the authorities discovered the atrocity and quickly corrected the situation.

While Anna moved to live with her parents in their single room, three families occupied the other rooms. Two adults and two kids in one bedroom, two adults and three kids in another, and two adults and one child in the living room. It was not the Nepomnyashchy house anymore; it was a dormitory with a common kitchen where squabbles broke out regularly. And when the new men came home drunk, fights erupted.

Anna and her parents were afraid. There was nothing to hold onto, so move to Kharkov they did.

Senya found humor even in this situation. "The great state always finds a way to keep a family together!"

In Kharkov, Sergey managed to find a flat for them in the same building where the Rudinskys lived, but on the first floor. Although the first floor was less desirable, as higher levels afforded better security, this was the best he could do, and Lyuba actually liked that she would not have to climb stairs every day.

Kharkov was a big city, the biggest one the newcomers had ever seen in their lives. They were awed by its size, the imposing buildings, wide avenues, and most of all, by the number of people on the streets. It was like an ant house, commented Senya, people moving quickly here and there, here and there, appearing and disappearing with the speed of lightning, or at least that is how it looked to them. Although much impressed with what they saw, Lyuba and Senya were disappointed to find themselves in a place where they had no backyard, no vegetable garden, and no flowers to take care of. Country people since childhood, it was not easy for them to adapt to new ways and live in a multi-story apartment house, which Senya dubbed barracks. But they were happy to be close to all their dear ones, all except Zhenya, who could not move because Vasili did not want to interrupt his studies at the engineering college. The only problem was their complete financial dependence on their children, since they could earn no money of their own. There were not enough jobs even for younger people.

Sergey's career was really taking off at the time. Right when Yasha joined him in Kharkov, he got a new job in the Central Committee of the Ukrainian Communist Party. His title was not catchy, but people with such titles were influential. Sergey's ability to acquire what he needed through his connections increased significantly. It was due to his position that Victor and Yasha found jobs, and it was due to his efforts that they all had apartments.

7

What a year it was for the Nepomnyashchys! A new city, new apartments, new jobs, and... a new family. It did not take Victor long to propose to Anna. It happened at her birthday celebration. He had tested the waters with Anna before her birthday, but she always answered, "I'll think about it." Victor decided to propose publicly, as he had observed back in Elizavetgrad with Sergey and Yasha.

When they were all seated around the table, Victor stood up with his glass full, but instead of making a toast said, "Anna, I was waiting for this a long time. I could not do it before, but now I can. I love you! I want you to be my wife. Would you marry me?"

Everyone waited for the answer. Anna thought for a second, looked straight at Victor, and said, "I need to think it over."

Bang! Victor's mother, the Countess, who usually said nothing at the table, pronounced with indignation, "What is there to think about? He loves you, and you should marry him!"

"Well, I know who your son is, and I am not sure he is from the right family. I am not convinced he would be the right choice for me."

"He is from a great family!"

The Countess was visibly shaken by Anna's attitude. "His family's roots are from ancient times! What better family do you want?"

Anna remained calm. "Yes, I know. And that's what concerns me. We live in a different time, the time of proletarians and peasants, not nobility. I come from a simple family and he does not. In today's terms, I come from a better family!"

Silence. Nobody knew what to say. Victor left the room, his face pale and tragic. Lyuba followed him. Lyuba, the peacemaker, touched Victor's arm and said, "Victor, don't be offended by Anna's behavior. She used this occasion to get even with your mother for what she did to her all these years, even when we were supporting her. She wanted to let you and your mother feel a little of what she had felt. I know she loves you, and in a while she will regret hurting you so. Instead of judging her words, judge her deeds. Remember, Anna was the one who took care of your mother when she was alone. Let her calm down and I am sure she will marry you."

What is the value of the wisdom a person brings to a situation? Whatever it is, it should be multiplied by the number of people protected and saved by its power.

Anna and Victor were married in a week. At the wedding dinner, which took place in Sergey's apartment because it was the largest, the mood was different: laughter and kisses, jokes and sparkling toasts, including one from Lyuba asking for many grandchildren. Even the Countess joined in the celebration and gave Anna a ring that she had kept, a beautiful platinum and sapphire ring that had been in the Rudinsky family for many generations. And when she offered a toast, it was a simple but significant one for her, "Mazel Tov!"

8

"I got a letter from Boris!"

Yasha came running into his parents' flat, waving a paper in his hand.

"Call Anna and Victor."

When everyone assembled, Yasha said, "Boris's letter arrived today. Let's hear it," and began reading aloud.

> *Dear Yasha,*
>
> *It's good you found me and sent your new address. I want to share with all of you what I am doing. I am leaving Russia in a few days.*
>
> *I thought the people in the kolkhoz would be happy to use the tractor and learn new agricultural methods, but they ignored me. I was so surprised that they had no interest in*

learning anything new. The tractor was neglected. They were just laughing at me, and when I complained to their boss they called me a kike.

It seems to me that no one really wants to improve anything. The kolkhoz chairman used to be a poor peasant and is very proud to become such an important man, but he knows nothing about how to manage his kolkhoz and does not want to hear advice either. He drinks vodka with some of his workers while most of the actual work is done by women. Everything seems to be covered by a blanket of corruption. Stealing and avoiding improvements is what people do. And the higher these people are the more they steal. They don't care about the state; it is an abstraction to them. They care about how to prosper in their situation. If this is socialism, I do not want it.

If nothing changes in their attitude, your temporary difficulties will become permanent. I lost hope in helping these people and depart for home. No wonder there is hunger in Russia.

My eyes opened about socialism. It sounds much better when you read about it than when you see it in reality. I will explain all this to those in America whose eyes are still closed. God forbid America will go this way.

I wish you all the best success in life and happiness for the entire family. I am glad I visited you.

Your Boris.

9

Soviet Russia was winning the Civil War. Although the vestiges of the Whites were still fighting for the restoration of the former system, by 1921 the country was under the definite control of the Communist Party. The biggest problems facing the country became economic malaise and hunger. To address economic issues, Lenin proposed a so-called New Economic Policy—NEP. It was new only from the point of view of the Communist ideology; everything else in it was old. It allowed people to create and own small commercial enterprises. From farming to restaurants, from factories making household items to sewing shops—entrepreneurs were allowed to open their own businesses and the country started to come back to life. In big cities the turnaround was remarkable, with new shops, stores, and restaurants opening on every corner. It was a stroke of genius for a leader of the first Communist state to use the financial motivation and benefits of capitalistic free enterprise in difficult times.

Yasha and Sergey had financially supported their parents since they had moved to Kharkov, but Senya did not like their dependency. And when Tanya had her second daughter—Meri—Lyuba and Senya felt an even stronger need to find a moneymaking opportunity. It came along with NEP.

When Anna married Victor, she moved up to the third floor into the apartment where her husband and mother-in-law lived, while her parents stayed in the apartment on the first floor. Senya and Lyuba lived in a two-room apartment, where only one room belonged to them, while a friendly middle-aged family occupied the second one. Quickly, Anna sought to exchange apartments with those other tenants. Since an apartment on the third floor with a balcony was more desirable than one on the first floor, Anna's attempt to exchange succeeded promptly—the Rudinskys moved downstairs and the other family upstairs. The two-room apartment on the first floor now belonged to the members of the same extended family. This was significant, as it provided an opportunity for the next step.

One day, while eating at her mother's and listening to her complaints about the lack of money, Anna said, "Mom, why don't we open a canteen? Your cooking is so tasty, I am sure people will like it."

"A canteen? Who will come here to eat?"

"There are offices all over, plus Yasha and Sergey can tell their colleagues about us. You know people love your food, and I will help you organize and cook. Let's do it!"

"Let me think about it." Lyuba was hesitant to start something so suddenly.

The next day, early in the morning, Anna was already in her parents' bedroom.

"Mother, what do you think?"

"You know, I had a dream that we started some business and the police came and arrested you, and I was crying profusely. I could not stand you being arrested."

"Mother, don't you know about NEP? It is legal now to own a business like this. Don't worry. I promise, everything will be all right."

The deal was made, and Anna devoted her considerable organizational talent to the venture. With Sergey's help, the necessary furniture was found and brought in within days, produce bought, the menu created, and the canteen was ready to open its doors. At first, they put tables for customers in only one room, but soon both rooms were needed. The canteen was a success!

Now, Lyuba and Senya enjoyed earning their own money and even helping their kids by providing meals for them. Everyone was changing, adapting to new circumstances, except Countess Rudinsky, who still could not adjust to the new world.

When the canteen opened, Anna was the one serving customers: taking orders, bringing food to the tables, removing dirty dishes. One day, the Countess came in and sat at the table, expecting Anna to wait on her. Running between the kitchen and the customers, Anna did notice her mother-in-law sitting at the table, but ignored her at first. It was only when the Countess, bored by waiting and offended by the inattention, started shifting in her chair and making strange noises to attract attention that Anna quietly asked her to come to the kitchen. There, Anna sternly said, "Why are you doing this? I don't have time to wait on you. You should be helping me. You know, 'No work, no food!'"

"But what can I do?" the Countess asked.

"You can collect dirty dishes and clean tables!"

"Me? Cleaning tables?"

128

Bewilderment gave way to indignation in the Countess's voice. She could not believe what Anna had asked her to do and was just about to turn around and leave, when Anna simply said, "You can leave, but you will have nothing to eat today if you don't want to help."

Anna left the kitchen. The Countess stood there for a second, made her decision, and followed Anna to the room where the customers were eating. She approached a table and squeamishly began collecting dirty dishes.

When Victor came home, she cried and complained to him about the treatment from Anna. He listened and replied, "You do need to help, Mother." But he also later asked Anna, "Please, go easier on my Mother. She needs time to get used to the new situation. Don't push her too hard, and don't forget that she is my mother and I love her. What can I do for you two to live in peace?"

"You can love her but she still needs to contribute to the family's efforts to survive. Or I can leave and you can stay with your beloved mother."

"What are you talking about, Anna? All I want is for you to treat my mother with understanding."

"Well, let's understand that my mother works all day long to make some money and to feed us all. And your mother does nothing except taking care of herself, and then she tells our neighbors that I am not your wife, but her servant. How do you like that?" Anna's face became red. The conversation was reaching deeper and deeper into her soul, where new incidents were feeding old wounds, and it led nowhere.

Victor understood why Anna was upset, but he also wanted to find a way for the two women in his life to live in peace. He just did not know how to achieve it.

10

After Lenin's death, Stalin became the leader of a newly named country—the USSR. The Civil War abated and more people were back to work, building a bright socialist future. Life seemed to be improving.

129

One way or another, regardless of the encountered pain, if given a small chance people were drawn to what they saw as a normal life. Nobody thought that a heavily accented Georgian would become their father, their leader, their God. People adapt, and they adapted to the new state and found ways to enjoy their lives.

The Nepomnyashchy children were growing with the times. They did not worry about hunger and poverty anymore, but focused on their jobs and families. They were among millions in a new country that promised those who were loyal a tremendous future, not just for the USSR and its people, but for all of humanity. This expectation of better things to come and the fact that they were participants in the new experiment gave their lives meaning, and they dedicated themselves to their jobs, their country, and their family.

Coming home late one day from work, Yasha kissed his wife as usual and noticed that she was fixing her shawl, a warm wool shawl she used on cold days, and that it was considerably smaller than before.

"What happened to your shawl?"

"Today's trend is for smaller sized shawls, so I am making it smaller."

Yasha took the shawl into his own hands and saw it was full of holes.

"Tanya, my love, I am making enough money to buy a new shawl. And by the way, you should make your dresses at the professional dressmaker. Don't waste your time on things like that."

Tanya did not say anything. Yasha gave her his salary to cover the family's needs. He knew some money went to help Tanya's mother and her brother Sasha—an architecture student—but he did not realize that his money actually spread too thin, definitely not enough to custom-make dresses. She just sighed and said, "Okay."

When after a while Yasha did not see a new shawl, he decided to take care of it himself. On her birthday, he went to the market looking for a down shawl. He found one at the counter of an old woman who looked honest. This was a large shawl that would keep his wife warm.

130

He was sure she would appreciate his efforts. The shawl was not cheap, but Yasha did not care. He paid the money; the woman counted it, took the shawl under the counter to pack it in newspapers, and gave the package to Yasha, who was beside himself and full of pride that he did not buy a thrifty present, but an expensive one.

On the way home, he stopped in a few pricey stores that they did not usually patronize and bought some delicacies: German salami, French cheese, Danish pastries. On a street corner, he also purchased flowers. Equipped with presents and in a great mood, he went home. Tanya met him with concern written on her face because she had expected him earlier on such a day.

"Happy birthday, my darling!" Yasha said, giving her all the packages with pride. "This is for you," he pointed to the package with the shawl in it, "but please don't open it until all the guests are in."

"Okay, okay, but where were you? I was worried!"

"You know, walking by the German store I saw a beautiful blonde with blue eyes. She wanted me to try salami, so I did and bought some. Then, walking by the French store I saw a couple of beautiful brunettes, and they wanted me to try some cheese...." Yasha was laughing; he felt full of love and life.

"And when I tried what they offered me, I could not avoid buying it; besides, I could not refuse buying from attractive women. You know how it is in the new stores. They hire beautiful women, and weak men buy whatever these women offer. But I brought everything to you, my beauty, because I love only you!" He kissed his wife.

The guests were arriving and the table was filling with dishes. Everyone sat at the table and talked simultaneously. Yasha stood up and, when everyone quieted down, said, "A toast to my wife, my beauty, my angel. I am so lucky to have found you. I wish you joy and happiness forever. Happy birthday!"

The guests repeated "Happy birthday," clinked glasses, drank their liquids, and turned to eating. A rare quiet ensued and Yasha used the opportunity to ask Tanya to open his present. She took the package and began unwrapping, Yasha restless with anticipation for the big surprise and everybody else watching the birthday girl with interest. The birthday girl kept taking off layer after layer of newspaper until she unwrapped it completely and... such astonishment colored her face that everyone around the table looked at the item that had appeared in her hands and froze, including Yasha. She was holding an empty potato sack!

Tanya stared at the sack with bewilderment until she noticed Yasha's stunned face and she understood. She started laughing. Then she said, "I just wanted to play a practical joke, this is not what Yasha gave me, but I switched it. Here is his present." She went to the drawers and pulled out a scarf she was knitting for herself from two old woolen sweaters that could not be worn anymore. She showed the scarf and everyone expressed delight at such good taste exhibited by a man. Yasha was saved, but his wife knew what had happened: Yasha was not street smart at all. For many years they remembered and laughed at this incident together. Over time, the initial horror of the forgery revelation became a dear moment to them, as a symbol of their tenderness and understanding.

11

Sunday. Day of rest. No need to rise early and rush to the office, or start preparing food for customers, or do whatever it is one has to do during the work week. On Sunday it is time to relax—sleep a little longer, move a little slower.

An early morning knock on the door is a strange sound when no one is expected and the occupants of the abode are still in bed. Now someone has to put on clothes and find out who is the person bothering them. And everyone waits just another second longer, hoping someone else can be faster to the door. Another knock, louder— the person outside is becoming more insistent. Lyuba makes it to the door first.

"Who is it?"

"I am here to see the Rudinskys. I believe they live here, don't they?"

"Victor, it's for you," announced Lyuba loudly, while opening the door. "Come in, Victor will be here in a minute."

A young woman of medium height, dressed in the indistinct clothes of the day—gray and black—walked in. The woman seemed a little apprehensive about the situation, although she was trying to hide her nervousness. There was something in her appearance that reminded Lyuba of someone else, and she was going through her memory when Victor, still half asleep, walked out of his room in a robe. As he was walking toward the stranger, Lyuba already knew who she was.

When the young woman saw Victor, her nervousness disappeared and she threw herself on him with a cry, "My God, Victor, it is you!"

Victor froze, but just for a second, and then returned the hug. They stood in embrace for a few moments, saying nothing, just enjoying their closeness. Tears were rolling down the woman's face when Victor moved a few inches away to see her better.

"Thank God you are alive! We were worried about you. But how did you find us?" Victor asked. He was ecstatic.

"This is my sister, Natasha," he explained to Lyuba, who did not really need any explanation.

"Let's go see Mother," said Victor, opening the door to his room.

The Countess was still in bed, but when she saw Natasha, she jumped from the bed and kissed her daughter, who had been missing since the time of the revolution.

"My dear Natasha, I am so glad you found us. Do you know, we don't have our house in Elizavetgrad any longer? This new power—the new state—these bandits, they took away the place where you were born!"

"I know, Mother, I was there."

Anna, already on her feet, was observing the scene from the corner of the room. Victor finally made the introduction, "Natasha, this is Anna—my wife." The Countess made a face showing her unhappiness about the statement, while Natasha hugged Anna.

Later, when everyone was eating the breakfast Lyuba and Anna had prepared, Natasha narrated her story.

"My husband was called for the army service before the revolution, just like Victor. He left and after the revolution disappeared like many others. No letters, no information. I could not find out anything about him because of the turmoil in the country. Then the new government was set up, which was not interested and did not have the capability to find missing people. Do you know what one official told me? 'Missing husband? The whole country is missing!'

"During the Civil War, our estate was trashed by the bands, and since banks were not functioning, I was left with no resources and became a nurse in the hospital. Luckily there were plenty of wounded requiring care and few professional doctors and nurses to offer it. It was grueling work, sometimes forty-eight hours without sleep or rest, but I could feed myself and had a place to stay. Plus, blending among regular people also helped hide my identity. When the country had begun to settle, I decided to find you. It took me a while to get to Elizavetgrad, and I did not know any better than to go directly to our house. Although I suspected it was taken over by the new regime, that was the only way to search for you, hoping you were still alive. I had actually prepared myself to discover that none of you survived or that you had gone somewhere in this whirlwind of time, leaving me alone in the world. So, finding people living there who had direct knowledge of my family was actually pleasing. Zhenya and Vasili described the situation, and after learning that Victor was married, I thought of the happy ending to my search. Getting from Elizavetgrad to Kharkov was much easier with Vasili's help, including some money he offered for the road. And you know, it's strange that we are together again, together, but in a different world and we are different people."

The relatives spent the entire Sunday talking about the years they were not in contact with each other. There was so much to share, so much to learn. Natasha had nowhere else to go, so Lyuba arranged a folding bed for her.

The next day, Natasha went to look for a job. She had valuable experience, and finding a job as a nurse was not difficult. It was more difficult to locate living quarters. She ended up finding a job in a hospital, which offered her a place to stay until better times. Her room there was actually a closet—a large one, but just a closet nevertheless—with no windows. Despite that, Natasha was glad she had a place where she could sleep and feel secure. On her days off, she went to see the relatives. Anna observed this young woman spending time with them and knew that Natasha needed something different—a family of her own. She asked Victor, "Why don't you find a young man among your colleagues for Natasha?"

Victor had always liked one fellow he worked with. There was a certain chemistry between the two of them, something that was hard to explain but made being together comfortable. He was of the right age, single, well mannered. His name was Aleksandr, and he cheerfully accepted when Victor invited him to join them for a meal on a Sunday.

The Sunday family dinner was the first time Aleksandr visited his friend at home. Previously, Victor had been extremely careful not to introduce his mother, who could at any time say something they would regret later, to his co-workers—it was the NKVD, after all. But his desire to find a suitable husband for his sister was stronger than fear. His mother was trained, again, in what not to say, and the reception went smoothly. The young people liked each other at once, and it was the beginning of a courtship which in a few months materialized into a proposal from Aleksandr. Natasha liked him and was ready to marry. When she announced the upcoming marriage to her family, everybody wanted to mark the occasion.

Preparations for the celebration were joyful. Even the Countess happily contributed to the event. Victor had a special conversation with his mother to remind her of the times they lived in and persuaded her to refrain from mentioning her noble past. On Sunday, at the agreed time, Aleksandr appeared in Victor's flat. Although the decision to tie the knot had been made, Aleksandr knew to ask for Natasha's hand officially, as the old custom dictated. He behaved as a true gentleman, bringing flowers for Natasha, her mother, and Anna, kissing every woman's hand, and exhibiting gallant manners throughout. At the table, he turned to his future mother-in-law and said, using her full name, "Tamara Ivanovna, I love your daughter and want to marry her."

This was the traditional request for the bride's hand, and since the father of the bride was not alive, the mother would have to consent, which she did.

After the toast for the young couple, Tamara Ivanovna, as the drink was loosening her up, asked Aleksandr, "Would you tell us more about yourself and your family?"

Aleksandr stopped for a second and then answered, "I am from a good, simple family. My father was a proletarian and my mother was from a village, a peasant, but they both died in the struggle for the Soviet state, leaving me alone in the world, as I was the only child."

While Aleksandr was talking, it was easy to observe how Tamara Ivanovna wanted to interrupt and add something extremely important, even critical, from her point of view, but she waited until he had finished and then said, "Do you know, young man, that my daughter is from noble stock? Her father is from the family of distinguished counts!"

Victor's hand stopped in midair with a fork full of dangling food. He could not believe what he had just heard. Aleksandr seemed shocked too, but just for a moment, as he took control of himself and simply said, "No, I did not know that."

Anna meanwhile walked behind the Countess and made signs to Aleksandr that Tamara Ivanovna was not playing with a full deck, at which point the Countess said, "Anna, what are you doing behind my back? Go to the kitchen and take care of the dishes." Then, to Aleksandr, "She is our servant."

An uneasy silence covered the room until it was finally broken by Aleksandr offering Victor a cigarette and asking him to go outside for a smoke.

The day was warm and the friends stood outside enjoying a smoke. They were quiet, saying not a word, and there seemed to be a new feeling between them, a feeling they had never experienced before in their relationship. At last, Aleksandr broke the silence.

136

"Victor, you don't have to worry, I will not tell anyone what your mother said." After a quick pause and some hesitation, he continued, "And to prove to you that you have no need to worry, here is my story: I am also from a noble family. I always felt a certain closeness to you and now it is clear why. But I cannot marry Natasha. I love her with all my heart, but your mother is unpredictable and it's too risky for my future family to depend on the whim of her desires. It's too dangerous. I sincerely apologize, but this is my decision. Please convey my regards and love to Natasha."

With that, Aleksandr left and the courtship was over. Victor walked back into the apartment with an expression that required no explanation for anyone to understand what had just happened. Natasha covered her face with both hands and ran out. Victor approached his mother, who was the only one still maintaining a jovial attitude, and said, "Mom, had I not asked you to avoid any talk of our family? Why did you have to mention titles?"

"But I only said that her father was a count, not me?" the Countess replied with sincere surprise.

12

On May 1, a big holiday in the USSR, Yasha stood by the open window and watched people in festive mood moving toward the central square. He was thinking about how this intended glorification of the proletariat had become more of a celebration of the new warm season. People love this time, seeing it as the beginning of pleasant days. It is not yet summer, but the days are longer, rain showers warmer, and the sun brighter. Nature has awoken from its winter slumber, and in Ukraine the trees are green and flowers appear everywhere. In Kharkov, like in all Soviet cities, a demonstration was taking place. Music, smiles, loud conversations abounded. Really, a people's holiday!

Yasha and Tanya were ready to leave their apartment and join the thousands already greeting splendid May. Lara and Meri, who were eight and six respectively, wore the same white and blue dresses, mimicking the sailors' uniform. They were supposed to wait for their parents, but when Tanya and Yasha came to the door, only Lara was there.

"Where is Meri?" Tanya asked.

"She is outside," Lara answered.

"Outside? She is wearing her best dress!" Tanya had recently made new dresses for the children. "I bet she is climbing trees."

The last words were directed to Yasha, who, with a smile, replied, "She would not do that."

He was smiling because Meri was known as an insatiable climber, and sure enough, she was not to be seen until they looked up and there she was, in a tree.

"Meri, come down here. Don't you know today is a holiday?" demanded Tanya. Meri started down the tree, but as soon as she was on the ground, Tanya noticed the torn dress.

"What a child! You are not a boy, why do you have to climb trees or fences all the time?" Tanya was upset because they had been invited to celebrate the holiday with Yasha's boss and now she had an unexpected problem to address. For a few moments Tanya was panicking, but then her creativity took over. She sat down at the table with her sewing implements and in less than half an hour gave Meri a patched-up dress. There were no visible tears in the dress anymore. Tanya had used a cloth anchor she took from another piece of clothing and patched it over the tear in such a way that it looked like it had always been there. Meri loved it! So did Lara, which meant Tanya had to find another anchor to make Lara's dress the same as her sister's.

Finally, the preparations were over, and, an hour later than planned, the family was on its way. The streets were full of people, some going to the demonstration, some just frolicking, enjoying a nice day and an opportunity to dress up around friends and family. The mood on the streets was festive and anyone's worries were displaced by the overwhelming sense of camaraderie and joy: the joy of existence, of belonging, of being human. Yasha's family went directly to his boss's apartment, talking and sharing impressions the entire way.

While Meri was skipping and jumping, Lara was subdued, describing what she had heard in school from the teacher about Russia before the revolution and the bourgeoisie. When Meri heard that word—bourgeoisie—she interrupted her sister and said, "I know about them also. They are fat, with huge bellies, because they are torturing workers and peasants and drink their blood. And they carry large bags full of stolen money. They are terrible, terrible!"

Everybody laughed at the expression on Meri's face at the end of her speech. Knowing the unpredictable nature of his younger daughter, Yasha lifted Meri in his arms before entering the building where his boss lived and said, "Meri, we are going to be at the party with many people, adults. Could you please remember what we discussed before and not say anything without thinking it first? Promise?"

"I promise. I will always think about what to say, but I won't always say what I think," Meri answered confidently, and Yasha rang the bell.

The door opened and his boss graciously asked them to come inside. Meri would not move. Her face reddened and she looked down while pulling Yasha's hand, trying to move him away from the door.

"What's the matter, Meri?" Tanya asked.

Meri pointed a finger directly at the host and angrily shouted, "He is a bourgeois, bourgeois! He will torture you and drink your blood! Don't you see his belly?"

The man was rotund and resembled the figures in the pictures children had seen in books. It was an awkward moment. While Tanya was explaining Meri's reaction with some embarrassment, Yasha was trying to convince his daughter, "I know this man; he is a good, working man. Don't worry, Meri. You'll see he is very nice."

The host laughed and called his wife, "Dear, please come meet our guests."

A young woman, considerably younger than her husband, greeted them, and her husband turned to Meri with a big smile on his face and said, "What a beautiful and smart girl you are."

Meri pointed at the hostess and said, "You also have a nice daughter."

139

Yasha and Tanya were embarrassed and could not lift their eyes to look at the hosts, who both laughed heartily and invited the family in. Fortunately, the rest of the evening did not produce any more pearls of embarrassment. Coming home after the party, Tanya and Yasha were recollecting the events of that evening and laughing.

"We teach our kids to be truthful, to speak their minds. How do you explain to a naïve child that sometimes the truth should not be announced? Your boss's wife really looks like his daughter," Tanya said.

"Don't you know it's fashionable now to divorce old wives and marry young ones? I am the only one still living with the same woman!"

13

Two destructive waves were sweeping the country in 1928: the NEP ending and the annihilation of the kulaks. Yasha had a lot of trouble with the concepts used to justify the attacks on the kulaks. His analytical disposition and a sense of fairness scratched the veneer of the propaganda fed to the public. The only person he could talk to about this was Sergey, who was unable to avoid the difficult questions from his friend.

"Sergey, doesn't the distribution of property confiscated from those we call rich to those who are poor actually make rich out of poor? Should we not then confiscate this property from the newly rich again, to be consistent?"

"We need to build collective farms. Where would we take the equipment and seeds from?"

"Why do we need these collective farms? Russia was producing lots of food before, even feeding half of Europe, and now we cannot feed ourselves. Why is that?"

"Stalin wants to make the country independent of the kulaks. He wants people to work for the common good of their country, not for their private selves."

It kept going like this, Yasha still unsatisfied with the answers, Sergey unable to convince his friend. Real life entered into these discussions.

When Lyuba and Anna's canteen closed its doors due to the end of the NEP, Senya and his wife were left with no independent income, as before. Their children had to support them again. At this point in their lives they were left with nothing: no house, no property except some clothes, no money, and no way to survive without help. Senya was asking his boys, "Where are those promised better times? I thought it was bad before, but now it is even worse."

But the worst was yet to come.

It was about three o'clock in the morning when loud knocking awakened everyone in the apartment. Victor opened the door and saw two men in black leather jackets—not a good sign. They introduced themselves as NKVD agents.

"We need to see Anna."

"But what is the problem?" Victor asked.

"We have an order for her arrest. Where is she?"

Anna heard everything. She did not have to be told twice; she knew that arguments were futile. Anna put on some clothes and came to the door, her face pale, her eyes full of fear.

"I will go with you," Victor said. He was sure they knew he was working for the NKVD.

"It's not allowed, Comrade Rudinsky," was the dry answer.

Before departing with the two scary-looking fellows, Anna kissed her parents, who came out hearing the commotion, and Victor. Senya was trying to calm Lyuba down, saying it was just a mistake and everything would be all right, but Lyuba would not listen. She kept crying and repeating the same phrase over and over, "I knew it; this is what the dream was about."

Victor realized the need to remove Anna from the clutches of the NKVD before it was too late. The question was, how? His inclination was to go to the interrogation center and try to convince whoever was in charge to free his wife, but it was clearly foolish—although he worked for the powerful NKVD, he was a small fish in that huge apparatus and his credentials would not be sufficient for an audience with anybody important. All of a sudden, a clear thought crossed his mind: Sergey! In his position he had to know people high enough in the NKVD who could intervene. It was only a matter of letting Sergey know and he would find a way to help.

A few minutes of dressing up with trembling hands seemed like hours to Victor, and finally he was outside. Walking, almost running, to Sergey's apartment took less than an hour; convincing the building guard to call Sergey to let him in—a few precious minutes; explaining the situation—more time. And the intolerable wait continued as Sergey was frantically making call after call. Finally, he put the phone down and said, "Done! I just talked to the fellow who assured me that Anna would be freed shortly."

Victor sighed with relief. "Are we going to the interrogation center?"

"Yes," Sergey replied. "Let me call a car."

Sergey dialed a number and requested a car. Then he phoned Yasha, who in the middle of the night could not, or would not, believe what had happened, and told him to be outside as soon as possible. By the time Sergey dressed up, the guard had called announcing the car's arrival. Sergey and Victor did not even take the elevator—running down the stairs was faster. In the car, Sergey ordered the driver to first go by Yasha's place to pick him up and then to the other, scarier, location. At last, they reached the interrogation center and parked outside the gate.

Waiting is torture when your loved one is in danger. At that time of night, the street was empty and the silence added to the gravity of the situation. Every sound promised to be Anna's steps, but disappointment reigned. When the door finally opened, Anna appeared supported by a man. She could not walk by herself and her face was bruised and bloody. The man was young, of medium build, and would look like thousands of other men if not for his grin, which showed contempt and malice for other people. It was smug and annoying. When Victor saw Anna, his hands became fists, ready to pound this poor excuse for a human being, and he started moving toward the man, but Sergey pulled him back and held him in his embrace until Yasha safely seated Anna in the car.

She was in bad shape. Victor and Sergey looked at the interrogator with such explicit anger that he felt the need to find an excuse for his actions.

"Nothing personal. I am just doing my job," stated the man and disappeared into the bowels of the building where other prisoners were waiting for his attention.

Now the decision had to be made where to take Anna.

"I will take Anna to our place. Katya will take care of her," Sergey said.

"Right," Victor responded, "right."

The ride to Sergey's home was spent trying to get answers from Anna. They wanted to know what she was accused of and what happened to her, but she was silent. She would not say a word, would not even react to the questions asked by the people who loved her, just stared into the distance, just stared. The men in the car were concerned with her mental state.

By the time Katya had put Anna to bed, the sun was up and Victor went home. The anxious parents heard him say, "Anna is free. She is with Katya."

"Thank God!" Lyuba said, wiping the tears from her eyes.

"Let's go, Lyuba, to see how she is," Senya said.

Victor changed and went to work. He did not have a choice. But in the office he tried to stay away from everyone as much as possible. Aleksandr approached him.

"Victor, how are you?"

"I am fine," Victor answered in a cold, formal manner. "Just busy, have a lot of work to do."

He did not want to discuss anything, but Aleksandr came close to him and whispered, "How is Anna?"

"She is well too."

"I know about the arrest. Someone presumed she was hiding money earned in her business and wanted to recover it. I sincerely wish her to get well. We'll talk more in a different place," Aleksandr finished and left.

After work, Victor went to Sergey's apartment and found Anna peacefully sleeping. Katya told him that most of the time since he left Anna had been inconsolable. She was either crying or staring straight ahead like a wooden doll. She would not eat anything, just drink a little water. She would fall asleep only to toss and turn and scream in her sleep as if she were observing terrible scenes. When she would open her eyes, there was no connection to reality evident in them. Only recently had she quieted down. Anna's parents and Katya started to breathe easier, until Anna became delirious and nobody knew what to do except wait and hope for the best. Lyuba watched her daughter struggle and kept repeating, "Everything will be all right."

It took Anna several weeks to recover, but even then she still often had nightmares. And she still did not want to share exactly what had happened in that interrogation room, except that they had pressured her to disclose where she was hiding the money.

Zhenya came for a few days to see her sister and possibly help, but the best medicine seemed to be time. Returning to normalcy was a difficult process. And all this while Victor had to go to work in surroundings that reminded him of those who tortured Anna. The only person he trusted was Aleksandr, who would often catch Victor on the way home and talk. Once, Aleksandr said, "I know the guy who interrogated Anna. He is a real jerk. He should be punished for what he did, and I can help you with that."

Victor did not respond to the idea and Aleksandr added, "Let me know when you decide and are ready."

One day, Victor came home and Anna was not there. Lyuba said she went to see Katya, but Anna did not usually leave for an extended time without first telling Victor, and after waiting a couple of hours he decided to visit Katya. No Anna there either, and Katya hesitated to tell Victor where she was. At last, she sat him down on a sofa and said,

"I am not supposed to tell you this. Anna asked us because she is ashamed and thinks you might not love her anymore if you knew the truth, but I cannot hide it from you."

Victor was sweating. Katya continued, "When Anna was interrogated she was not only beaten, she was also raped by the same guy. Discovering that she was pregnant, an abortion was the only choice she considered and it went bad. The abortion was done in a doctor's office, but when her condition deteriorated Sergey took Anna to the hospital."

"Which hospital is she in?"

"She is with your sister Natasha. She will take better care...." Katya had not finished the phrase yet and Victor was already out the door. He knew the hospital and did not want to waste any more time.

The head feels empty and cold. There is nothing in it, except the desire to see his wife, to touch her hand, to tell her that he loves her no matter what. But why are the streets filled with people? They are everywhere. It is hard to maneuver around them and they slow him down. How terrible! His wife is suffering and needs him, but he cannot be with her quickly enough. Run, run, run. Finally, the hospital building.

Finding Natasha took a few minutes, and she brought Victor to the ward where Anna was in bed. It was a large room with about forty beds, women lying on almost all of them. And the smell! A mixture of medicine, sweat, and God knows what else made breathing in that room a chore.

Anna was sleeping and Natasha forbade Victor to do anything that could wake her up. She said, "Anna is fine and needs rest, the more sleep the better."

Victor wanted to take her home, away from this terrible room, but Natasha was totally against it. She said that if everything went well, Anna would be home in a couple of days. Victor sat at the bedside for a while, an idea developing in his head. Then he asked Natasha for Aleksandr's address—she would have remembered it from the days they dated—and abruptly left.

Victor walked out of the hospital a different man. All this time, while Anna was improving, he had been living as if in a parallel universe, subjugating his needs to the needs of his wife, living every second in a way that allowed the most energy to flow toward her. And she was not herself either. Victor wanted Anna to become her old self again, but he did not know how to help except by making sure that whatever she asked of him was done. His life did not matter for now, it was all for her, and he was not certain about anything. A better understanding of what his wife had to live through was like an opening. He found out exactly what happened. He knew, he felt with all the fibers of his body, how it affected Anna, and he became calm. What happened—happened, and there was nothing anybody could do about the past. But now he could do something about the future—at least the future of that creep, that sadist.

Finding Aleksandr's apartment house was not difficult. He lived in the center of the city, on the fifth floor of a building similar to Victor's. Victor knocked on the door, but nobody answered. He knocked again and again. Finally, the sound of shuffling feet broke the silence and a sleepy female voice asked, "Who is that?"

"I need to see Aleksandr."

"Are you out of your mind?" the voice inquired. "It's one o'clock in the morning! Can't you wait?"

Victor had not realized what time it was. His thoughts were preoccupied with Anna and then his idea, his plan. He did not have time to know what time it was.

"I am sorry, but it's an urgent matter. I am his colleague from the NKVD and need to talk to him right now. Please open the door."

The woman would not dare to get between two NKVD guys. She opened the door and let Victor in, showing which room was Aleksandr's. As the woman went to her room, Victor knocked on the door, and in a short while, it opened. Aleksandr was surprised to see Victor, but let him in without a word. The room was small. In the dim light Victor saw a narrow bed, a couple of chairs by a table, and a small wardrobe. A single window at the end of this narrow, like a rail car,

146

room was covered with drapes, and a couple of pictures on the walls were the only decoration. Aleksandr noticed Victor's reaction to his living space and bitterly said, "Yes, this is where I live. Before the revolution my servants lived in better quarters."

Then he offered Victor a chair and asked, "What is the urgency, Victor?"

"I am sorry for coming so late. I lost track of time. Let's talk about the guy you wanted to hurt. I want to do it and this is why I am here right now."

"Okay, I am glad you decided. This creep deserves it. He needs to experience his own medicine and we will help him with that. I know when he goes home after work. He usually leaves his so-called office," Aleksandr pronounced the word *office* with such disgust as if it was a part of hell, "early in the morning when it is still dark. I know the route he takes, through the cemetery, and that is where we can wait for him."

"But he would recognize us," Victor said.

"Just cover your face with something like a scarf and he will never recognize you, son of a bitch!"

They discussed the plan just a few minutes longer and agreed to finalize everything in a few days, meeting on the way home after work. Victor left, his mind clear, his heart confident that he was doing the right thing: Anna would be avenged.

Victor was waiting for the sign from Aleksandr to execute their plan. When the day was set, they decided to stay together overnight at Victor's apartment, as it was closer to their nighttime destination. The unexpected visit was explained to the family by claiming that they had to be at work early the next morning and it was the only way for Aleksandr to make it on time.

They woke up at four in the morning, dressed, and left the serenity of the apartment behind. The night was chilly and there were no people outside at that time. They walked briskly toward the church and cemetery that the NKVD guy walked through after work. Aleksandr had researched the path the interrogator took home and knew where to wait for him in a secluded place. Their faces were covered with scarves that not only disguised them, but also kept them warm. They hid behind a monument. It was cold and quiet. Victor's heart was beating so loudly he thought the whole city could hear it. A soldier in the past, Victor had been through many tough situations. He had been scared before, but this night was probably the scariest in his life. Danger was ahead, but he realized that now it was he, a small man, against a cruel state, which could come down with its myriad of means of torture and destruction not only on him, but all his family. His actions this night could spell disaster for his mother, Anna, and her parents. Even Sergey with all his powerful connections could be destroyed if the thread Victor might give the NKVD began to unwind and take the pursuing hyenas on a hunt for more innocent victims. It was scary putting the people close to him in danger, mortal danger, but Victor had made a decision and it was too late to change his mind.

Minutes were flowing by into eternity, and the two conspirators were silent. Both were looking into their souls, dealing with the situation they had created the best they could. The silence was broken only by a cracking sound made by bare tree branches resisting the wind and an occasional crunch of snow, which made Victor and Aleksandr more alert and ready for action. But after the crunching sound nobody appeared in the darkness—it had either been a small animal or a fallen tree branch—and they could relax until the next time.

The steady sound of someone actually walking caught their attention. It was definitely a human, but was it the guy they were waiting for? They had planned what to do and tried to imagine every possibility, but they were not professional thugs and were still thinking if the plan were right. They could now distinguish the outline of the figure approaching them and the sound of feet became clear. They judged it was a man. According to the plan, they had to jump him and make sure it was the right man before beating him, and that is what they did. As the man was passing close to their hiding place, they attacked him on both sides and quickly wrestled him to the ground, then turned his head up for the lunar light to shine on it. It was him! It was the guy they were waiting for, and both Victor and Aleksandr started hitting him with their fists and feet. The man, tired after a long night of hard work, surprised by the attack, and under the flood of blows coming from all directions, could not manage a defense except trying to cover his head and crotch. Seeing the futility of his efforts, he pleaded with them, "Why are you doing this? Let me go! I'll give you what I have with me, money, the watch...."

Aleksandr stopped punching him, made a sign to Victor to stop, and, pulling him by the coat collar, brought the face of the creep closer and said, "This is for all those innocents you tortured."

"But this is my job!"

His scream came to a halt and he slumped, sliding away from Aleksandr's clutch. Victor saw Aleksandr pulling something out of the man's side. It was a knife! And as the body fell down, Aleksandr bent over and stabbed him again.

"And this is for my sister, you scum!" Aleksandr whispered, trying to make sure the dying man grasped the message.

With horror, Victor said, "You killed him! We were not supposed to do that!"

"What he did to hundreds of innocent people should have been avenged through living with torment all his life. Death is a salvation for him," Aleksandr replied and started walking away from the scene of revenge and murder. Victor followed. They did not say a word until the cemetery was far behind and then Aleksandr began speaking.

"I did not want to talk about this before, but now I can tell you. My older sister and her husband opened a bakery when the NEP had started. They were doing okay—enough income to survive and not much more than that. When the NEP began to die, they were among the first to be arrested. This guy I just killed interrogated them. He was a real sadist. He enjoyed humiliating people and seeing them suffer. My sister was six months pregnant, and this creep, this...." Tears were interfering with his story. He had to take a full breath of air to release the lump in his throat and then continued, "He raped my sister. Can you imagine? She was six months pregnant! And he tied down her husband and made him watch. He wanted to find the cruelest, most brutal way to torture people's bodies and minds. I learned about it through colleagues he had bragged to about his heroics. Heroics with tied-down people!"

Victor was listening with horror. He never guessed Aleksandr had hidden his suffering at such a depth that nobody could see it. Aleksandr stopped speaking and was contemplating something, something he probably thought of a million times before. Wanting to bring his friend back to reality, Victor asked, "What happened to your sister and her family?"

"My sister started to give birth while in the interrogation room and they did not know what to do with her. She lost a lot of blood. When they finally called a doctor, it was too late. Where her husband is I don't know. All my attempts to find out brought me nothing. Their four-year-old son, my nephew, was sent to a children's asylum. I see him sometimes on Sundays. He never says a word. He used to be such a happy child, always laughing, always playing, and now he is like a living corpse. He might think his parents left him, and I don't know how to explain to him what actually happened. I told him his parents love him but cannot take him away from the asylum right now. When I have better accommodations, I will take him out. But for now, I have things to do."

"What things?"

"Things!"

"You know, Aleksandr, the war is over and we lost."

"My war is not over yet. I am fighting with them from within. I need to build my career to gain as much power as possible, and then use this power to do damage—this is my plan. The Communists are corrupt, immoral, and power hungry. I will use these qualities of theirs both for my career advancement and for their destruction. I hate them so! And do you see what is happening more and more? The ones that become important and powerful are without any scruples. They just want power at any cost. And then they surround themselves with the same kind, and all together they are at the wheel of this huge train called the USSR. But where is this train going?"

14

In 1934, Kiev became an official seat of the Ukrainian Soviet Socialist Republic. Everything and everyone associated with the government moved to Kiev, and that included Sergey, Victor, and Yasha with their families. Lyuba and Senya moved soon after their children did into an apartment Sergey found for them not far from the center. Not long before the move, Yasha had become an employee of the Central Committee of the Ukrainian Communist Party, just like Sergey, while Victor was still with the NKVD. It promised to be an exciting place to live and work. Kiev—the mother of Russian cities—had been the center of Russia since the time the rest of the world had known it as a place where Rus lived. Slavs joined Scandinavians and created a country that had its golden age about a thousand years ago. But through the centuries, this city had always been the center of Russian religion and spiritualism.

The government offices were located on a hill overlooking river Dnieper. Linden trees lining the streets, old beautiful mansions glowing in the summer sun, and a vast park, adjacent to some of the most interesting historic parts of this ancient city, offering picturesque vistas over the river and opportunities to lose oneself in its walkways— truly a nice place.

Yasha was happy with his new job. He had been getting frustrated in his old one as a lecturer in the Party School. With the Soviet state getting stronger and the new leadership solidifying its power, revisions of the not-so-distant past were beginning to surface. The new leadership meant Comrade Stalin. Yasha, as a lecturer of history, was among the first to be told to remove some of the old names from the Bolshevik past and make Stalin's role more prominent. It was he—Stalin—who was Lenin's right hand in designing the socialist future, it was he who personally combated various insurgencies, and it was he who built a new great country—the USSR. Teaching the Party students a history that was fiction—and he knew many episodes through personal experience—was too much for an honest soul and he needed to find another occupation. Sergey helped again.

Yasha's family was also looking forward to life in Kiev. Tanya found a good position as director of the Party Library. She loved being surrounded by books. It was like a special world to her. The Party Library in Kiev would in time be the most extensive in Ukraine and she was much involved with its operation.

Tanya liked their new apartment: four large furnished rooms, a kitchen, and a fully equipped bathroom. It was in a building for Central Committee employees only—centrally located and with armed guards watching the traffic and making sure no unauthorized people were allowed in.

The apartment came with a maid.

"I don't need a maid," Tanya said when Yasha informed her.

"It's not your choice, I am afraid. We live in an exclusive building with special rules."

He came closer to Tanya and whispered, "Sergey said be careful with the maid. Every apartment here has one, and all maids work for the NKVD. They listen to what we say, pay attention to who visits, and report everything. We need to explain to our children how to behave around her too."

Stunned, Tanya was speechless for a moment and then said, "But we have no extra money to pay her."

"The state pays them. And you need to decide which bedroom she will stay in."

The maid appeared the next day. Answering the doorbell, Tanya observed a tall woman about thirty years of age, with coarse facial features and a stern demeanor.

"Good morning. I am Dina, your new maid," the woman said.

"Come in, please."

Dina walked in, placed her suitcase on the floor by the door, and went through the rooms, familiarizing herself with the surroundings. Her expression was serious and official. Tanya decided to warm up the situation.

"Let's have some tea, Dina."

Sitting at the table, the woman's features eased as she answered questions about herself. It turned out she was a descendant of German repatriates who came to Russia with Peter the Great.

"So do you speak German?" Tanya asked.

"I do."

"Wonderful! Could you speak German with my daughters? I try when I have a chance, but if you do that, their school grades in German would definitely win."

"I can speak German to them, if you wish."

The first meeting of the two women ended warmly.

15

Tanya felt completely content with life in Kiev, and her natural tendencies of kindness and hospitality blossomed. Rare was the day when an interesting visitor did not share dinner or at least tea and jam with the family. Often someone stayed overnight, especially when Yasha was in town, and exciting evening conversations about current or historical events invisibly evolved into philosophical arguments, most of the time made not to prove who was right, but to have a debate and enjoy verbal punch-counterpunch. Time vanished fast, and visitors who were too late to catch a tram home stayed with friends until the morning.

Some visitors were new friends and acquaintances Tanya made at the library, where many writers and poets came in search of literary materials. They came from all over Ukraine to the place containing most, if not all, written thoughts and expressions. Many of them asked for help finding something and ended up talking to a knowledgeable person—Tanya. It was her pleasure. It was their pleasure to make such a friend.

One evening after work, Yasha brought home a man Tanya had not seen before. He looked different—still young, but with the stamp of hard experience on his face.

Yasha introduced the man, "This is Comrade Rafael. He is from Spain. He brought in the children whose parents died in their civil war so we would take care of them."

"Hello, Rafael. My name is Tanya. Welcome to our house," Tanya said and extended her right arm to shake his hand.

Rafael took Tanya's hand and said in broken Russian, "It is great to be here and meet you." With that, he kissed Tanya's hand—an unexpected gesture for the hosts.

"Forgive my bad Russian. I do understand much more than I can express myself in your beautiful language," continued Rafael.

"We can converse in Spanish," Tanya replied.

"You speak Spanish?!"

"I do. Also Italian. I love these melodic languages. I studied them in college."

"Wow, I am impressed. Any other languages?"

"My mother had been instilling the love for languages in her children since we were little. As kids, we all spoke English and German. And, you know, it's easier to learn a new language when you're fluent in more than one."

"I only speak Spanish and a little Russian," Rafael said.

"Your Russian is pretty good," Tanya replied. "Make yourself comfortable. We'll eat soon."

While Tanya was with the guest, Yasha called Sergey and invited him and his wife to come for dinner. "We have an unusual guest. You'll love listening to his stories," he said.

"Be there shortly." Sergey accepted the invitation.

The conversation around the table during dinner was lively. Rafael was answering questions about the war in Spain, his views on its result, and how different people felt about the future. Rafael alternated between trying his Russian and speaking Spanish, with Tanya translating for the rest. It was a wonderful evening. When the time came for the guests to leave, Yasha called for his car service to take Rafael to his hotel.

"Thank you for the great time and for listening to my butchered Russian," Rafael said before leaving.

"I want to talk to you, Yasha," Sergey said when the two of them were away from the others.

"Talk, what's on your mind?"

"I was watching your new friend at the table. Do you know that he is in love with your wife?"

Yasha laughed. "Why are you surprised?"

"I am not surprised, but aren't you jealous?"

"He has good taste. What can I say?"

Sergey shook his head. "I'd be careful if I were you."

Yasha did not share with Tanya his conversation with Sergey. He knew that Rafael would come see them again and did not want to alarm his wife.

For the next three weeks, Rafael visited Yasha and Tanya every few days. Sometimes he stayed for dinner and described what he observed in Kiev. The day before his departure to Spain, he arrived a little earlier than usual, coming before Yasha had returned from work. Tanya opened the door. Rafael walked in, shut the door, and grasped both her hands, looking into her eyes with love and admiration.

"Dear Tanya. I fell in love with you the moment I saw you. I cannot keep you out of my mind. You're beautiful, smart, witty. Tanya, come with me to Spain. Take your children and come with me to my country. Being here over the past month, I learned enough about Russian Socialism. I don't know how you can live like that. In Spain, even during the war you'll be better off. Come with me. I'll make you happy!"

"But I'm already happy," Tanya replied, pulling her hands away from his. "I love my husband, and he loves me. I don't want—"

The sound of the door lock opening stopped the conversation. Yasha walked in, warmly greeted Rafael, and kissed his wife.

"Sorry, I am a little late today. Is the dinner ready?" he asked.

155

"I cannot stay for dinner tonight. Need to pack. I just came to say good-bye," Rafael said. "I want to leave you something to remember me by."

Rafael took out a small box from the pocket of his jacket. "This is a two-color pencil. I have not seen anything like it here. There are not even regular pencils in your stores. Please take it."

"Thank you. I'd like to give you something too," Tanya said.

Rafael pointed to a small applique hanging on a wall. "Someone very talented made this. The flowers are beautiful."

"I made it from the pieces of cloth that remained from some projects we had done. It's yours." Tanya took the applique off the wall, wrapped it in paper, and offered it to Rafael.

"Thank you for everything," Rafael said. "Good-bye, friends."

16

Dvornik Fedor served the building where Tanya and Yasha lived. Every building in Russia's big cities was served by a dvornik who took care of the street cleaning in front of the building and, at the same time, watched what was going on around it, reporting to the authorities if something unusual occurred. Talking to the dvornik every morning before going to work gave Yasha a better appreciation for the mood of the people and every once in a while presented new facts and ideas he could build on. Once, during winter, Yasha saw the dvornik's son, Oleg, aged sixteen, shoveling snow.

"Good morning, Oleg. Where is your father? Why are you not in school?"

"My father fell ill last night and he is in the hospital now. It's something with his heart. I cannot go to school because I need to keep the street clean, otherwise we may lose our apartment."

"Oleg, promise me you will go to school tomorrow. Don't worry about the apartment. I will see what is going on with your dad."

In the evening, Yasha and Tanya visited the dvornik in the hospital. He was very ill and the doctor said he might not survive the heart attack. Fedor was upset.

"I worry what would happen to Oleg if I die. He has nobody else in the world, nobody! He will have no place to live."

Yasha tried to calm Fedor down. "You will be fine, you'll see. And don't worry about Oleg. He will stay with us until you return."

Fedor did not survive the night, and the next day Tanya took Oleg under her wing. A boy could not live alone in the apartment. He moved in with Yasha and Tanya, his apartment destined for the next dvornik.

Everyone in the family enveloped Oleg with warmth and attention. He never stayed alone in the house; someone was always nearby in case the shy young boy needed something. They brought him in for family discussions and encouraged his opinions. Slowly, Oleg transitioned into the new environment and felt a part of it. Their love made an impact.

When the school year ended, Yasha and Tanya decided to discuss with Oleg plans for his future.

"Oleg," Tanya began when they finished dinner one evening, "your future depends on your education. You should apply to a professional school, study well, and then go to college. We would always help and support you. What do you think?"

"I agree. I was thinking about it too."

Attending a professional school qualified Oleg for a dormitory, and when the time came for him to leave his adopted home, Tanya offered him a small package and said, "My dear Oleg, here is some money for you. We want you to have something of your own. Don't forget, we are here when you need us."

"Thank you, Aunt Tanya. I will never forget you and will return the money when I can."

"No, you don't have to do that. Better help someone else who needs it."

Who would think at the time that this selfless act of kindness would blossom into a valued gift many years in the future?

17

Yasha's work consisted of overseeing industrial output in some regions of Ukraine. He was away from home a lot, visiting the plants and factories, analyzing the situation there, paying the most attention to enterprises that did not produce according to plan. It was interesting and important work that allowed Yasha to feel involved with the creation of the people's state. His efforts mattered, his attitude was appreciated by those whose lives he touched, and his only regret was his frequent absence from the family he adored.

When Yasha returned home after another long trip, Sergey called him to his office. He was an important man, but Yasha wondered why he didn't just come in the evening to his apartment to talk.

The first thing Sergey said to him when they met was, "I have something important to discuss with you and it is better done here, away from your maid."

"What's going on?" Yasha asked with alarm.

"You know about the directive from Moscow to treat those industry leaders who are not complying with the plan for their enterprises as enemies of the state. And what do you do with such managers? You change their position to a lower status and elevate other people to replace them. But you do not report those bad managers to the proper authorities."

"What do you expect me to do, put them in jail because they are not smart enough or do not have the right skills?"

"Yasha, don't be naïve. You know the situation and you are part of the system."

"I can't send innocent people to jail or worse. I just can't."

"You know, I worry about you. If you are going to be lenient to others, you may be imprisoned before they are. We need to find you another position. I am going to do some investigation."

Soon after the conversation with Sergey, Yasha's boss, Valov, called him in.

"Comrade Nepomnyashchy, the country needs you in a different place now. We decided to send you to London as part of our diplomatic mission there. Go see Stenko in personnel, and good luck, Yakov Semenovich."

Valov stood up and offered a hand to Yasha across the desk, indicating the meeting was over. Moving into diplomatic service was exciting for Yasha. With his interest in history and world affairs, he could not have a better assignment. He needed to learn English, which, he hoped, would be easier for him because he spoke fluent German. Obviously, it was Sergey who had found this opportunity.

"I love this new assignment," Yasha said when he met Sergey. "Thank you so much. But how did you manage it, and so quickly?"

"I started asking the right people about what positions are becoming open and this one was just being discussed. I sold you and Tanya as educated people, who not only fought for the revolution but were also smart and erudite. So, you would need to learn English, which should not be difficult for you. And Tanya already knows English, which is a bonus. They liked it, and you got the job."

Yasha retained his office in the Party building and spent his time with English lessons and homework that included reading English books and magazines provided by his teacher. Learning a second foreign language might have been easier for Yasha than a complete novice, but it was still a different language that required solid efforts to master.

Winter in Kiev is snowy cold, and the days are short. This time of the year is better spent inside with family and work. When the sun is shining, it is pleasant to be outside and feel the air—so crisp that one can almost cut it into small pieces, wrap it in packages, and store somewhere for later use, when the summer dampness comes in the middle of July and affects everything with its smoldering breath. And the beautiful white snow that talks under one's feet—it speaks of beauty, peace, eternity. Marvelous!

But Yasha and Tanya did not have many chances to enjoy their beautiful surroundings. Yasha's learning schedule was tight and he

159

spent much of his time studying. His kids were proud of him whenever he read them a story from an English book—he was beginning to sound foreign. The kids even spent time following their father's example and learning the foreign language they would use in England.

The winter was also tough that year because somehow both Lara and Meri kept catching colds together. Tanya had a good handle on colds. She had learned how to treat them from Lyuba, who remembered her mother's remedies: feeding the sick raw garlic and onions—natural antibiotics—and putting little saucers with cut onions in every room. The fumes helped fight the illness too. It worked! It worked so well that, in most cases, no medicine was even required. Such was this winter: normal worldly worries, hopes for interesting encounters abroad, and hard work in preparation for a new job.

Life looked promising to them.

18

Lyuba woke up early one morning with eyes full of tears. "Senya," she cried out, "Yasha is going to be arrested!"

Senya sat up in bed, turned to his wife, and hugged her softly. "It was just a dream, Lyuba. Don't worry, Yasha is all right."

Lyuba kept crying.

"Yasha will be arrested, and Tanya, poor Tanya, with her weak heart, how will she survive?" Lyuba insisted. "Don't you know? My dreams always come true!"

The year was 1937. The repressions against old Bolsheviks, industry leaders, military commanders, and others were in full swing. They started after the Kirov affair in 1934, slowly intensifying through the next two years, but focusing primarily on the very top echelon of the Party leaders. When Stalin had finished off the most prominent, those who could challenge him, it was time to purge the country of the next levels down in the social hierarchy. Stalin's paranoia, combined with his limitless ambition, cruelty, and desire to instill fear in the population, required multitudes of victims. He was purging the country of its best hope for the future, justifying his actions with claims of counterrevolutionary activities. The country became a terrifying place to live, where a neighbor spied on a neighbor and one relative denounced the other. Nobody knew whom to fear, whom to trust and share hopes with, and whom to stay away from, so everyone—except the closest people—was a suspect.

Yasha found out about his mother's dream and came to visit his parents in the evening, bringing Tanya and the kids with him. How happy Lyuba was to see them all! She was cheerful and said nothing about the arrest as long as they stayed, but after their departure, Lyuba's laments started again. She remained in that state of mind for a few days, but nothing happened.

A tragedy struck unexpectedly from a different direction. Not long after Lyuba's dream, at about three o'clock in the morning, Yasha woke up to the sound of the telephone. It was a guard downstairs calling about a woman, Laura, who insisted on seeing Yasha immediately. Yasha thought her to be the wife of one of his closest friends, whom he knew from the days of the Civil War. He asked the guard to let the woman in and opened the door, waiting for the night visitor to arrive. He was on edge. She appeared in tears. He remembered how this woman was before—proud and reserved, witty and classy—but now she looked lost.

"What happened, Laura?"

"Aleksey was arrested just about an hour ago."

"My God!" Yasha was shocked. Aleksey—Yasha's old friend—was a general in the Red Army. He was a long-time Party member and a hero of the Civil War. Yasha was looking for the right words to calm down the woman, who was nearly hysterical, but no such words existed. Tanya came in from the bedroom and offered Laura a glass of water and a chair. Yasha was still standing in the middle of the room, trying to figure out what to do and what to say. Laura broke the silence.

"I came to see you because you are the only one I can trust, and I hope you can help us through your connections."

"I will try everything, but have you talked to Aleksey's commander?"

161

"Who would want to get involved? It's too dangerous. You are my only hope. Could you go with me to the NKVD, or wherever they have taken him? Could we try to find out more about his case? I know he was not doing anything illegal."

Yasha did not answer immediately. He knew it was useless to do what she wanted.

"Laura, stay with us and I will call everybody I know in the morning. Going to the prison would not be productive. There is no one there right now who we can talk to."

In the morning, they went to check on Aleksey. As Yasha had suspected, all they found was a crowded room and no answers. Laura did manage to speak for a second to an official who told her what to do next, but Yasha discounted the instructions, which were "Bring some warm clothes and food for your husband." Laura was glad to hear those words—this glimmer of hope that a connection with her husband could be made helped her persevere.

With a new day rising, Yasha made all his Party connections come alive, but in most cases people either could not help or would not risk their positions to find answers. By this time, they clearly understood the danger and did not want to jeopardize their lives. Eventually, through many twists of corrupt connections, Yasha learned that Aleksey had been arrested as part of the huge military counterrevolutionary group operating in Ukraine and headed by a famous commander, Yakir—all made up, of course. He also learned that Aleksey could not withstand the interrogation and died the same night he was taken from his house. Yasha discovered what he needed to know, but now he had to be the one to tell Laura what had happened. Otherwise, she would keep taking food and personal items to the jail, and the dead soul did not have any need for them any longer. He had an intricate task on his hands.

When his office routine allowed it, Yasha, accompanied by Tanya, went with a heavy heart to see Laura. She was at home, more peaceful than Yasha had expected and even smiling at seeing her friends. Her son, Slava, was doing his homework.

"It's nice for you to come. Nobody wants to talk to me any longer, people don't even look at me. They cross to the other side of the street to avoid saying *hello* to me. And Slava was expelled from school as the son of an enemy of the people. But we manage. I brought some food and clothes to the jail earlier today. The guard took it and said Aleksey was okay and asking for more food. I will take some more tomorrow."

Laura smiled, thinking that as long as Aleksey was alive there was hope. Tanya was looking down, hiding her tears. Yasha had to tell the truth.

"Laura, you should not take anything to the jail."

"Why? The guard said Aleksey needed more!" Laura was almost shouting.

"Aleksey is not with us any longer," Yasha said quietly. He was trying to say it with as much softness as he could muster, but thought his words were like huge boulders falling from the sky on the unsuspecting woman.

Laura was in shock for a second, her breathing hard. All of a sudden, she started shouting, "It's not true, I know Aleksey is alive, I know that. It's just a misunderstanding."

As she spoke, her words became louder and louder, her tears fuller, and her entire body shook. She pronounced the words hoping that someone would say, "Yes, you are right, this is just a bad dream," but nobody did, and she was coming to the realization that her life had just changed forever. She was still pronouncing words, but they were less and less recognizable as her sobbing took over.

Tanya hugged Laura, then asked Yasha to bring a glass of water and a wet towel to calm down the grieving woman. She placed the towel on Laura's head and rubbed her hands.

Since hearing about his father's death Slava was frozen. At last, he kneeled before his mother and said, "Mommy, don't cry. I will always be with you. I will take care of you." His words made the tragic situation even more apparent, as if underscoring the finality of their loss.

Hours went by until Yasha and Tanya thought they could leave Laura alone with her son. They left after midnight, promising to visit tomorrow and help them decide what to do. At home, no sleep graced their tired bodies. When they came to see Laura the next day, the door to the apartment was open and there was no Laura or Slava in sight. They found a neighbor who described how in the middle of the night the NKVD had come to arrest both the mother and son.

Tanya's breathing became difficult. She could not say a word and was pushing at her chest with her hands. Yasha recognized these symptoms and immediately took her to the hospital. How right his mother was to be concerned with Tanya's health! Really, what would happen to her if he were arrested? While Yasha was thinking, the hospital personnel helped his wife. It was a Central Committee hospital they were privy to and the care there was good, so after Tanya's condition improved, Yasha decided to visit Sergey in his office and talk about Laura and Slava.

Listening to Yasha's full story of the events made Sergey drop his head. He had nothing encouraging to say. Had he known about such cases? Of course he had. There was nothing he could do though. It was too late for Aleksey, and Laura, and the thousands and thousands of those already arrested and those who would be arrested soon. The meat grinder was operating at full capacity and needed more and more meat.

"Yasha, please, listen to me. You cannot do anything for them; nobody can. Think of yourself and your family. Any one of us could be next, and the more waves you create, the more chances for you to be drowned in them and drag your family down too."

"But the boy was only thirteen! How could they arrest a thirteen-year-old boy?"

"Don't you remember the law of 1935, which permitted the prosecution of children twelve and over? They could even be given a death sentence."

"I would like to know what that boy has been accused of. And I would really like to find a way to free him."

"Please, Yasha, pay attention to what I am saying. These are difficult times and we must live through them. We need to survive. Don't do anything stupid."

164

"I have been hearing these words since the revolution—difficult times, temporary difficulties. When will the difficulties be replaced by something good, or at least subside? So far it's getting worse and worse."

19

What a time to be a citizen of the first socialist state! While the country improved economically, people's lives seemed to be worth nothing, as the state could pick up at will a person of any standing and make him or her disappear. Arrests were everywhere. No segment of society was immune, the ones ordering and making the arrests often becoming victims of the same meat grinder. There was no sense to what was going on. Sometimes, after certain people were arrested, newspaper articles described the atrocities they had committed against the state and revolution. What was true? What to believe? Nobody knew. Only fear existed, permeating all aspects of life in the USSR.

Yasha came home earlier than usual.

"What happened?" Tanya asked.

"My dear," Yasha kissed his wife, "don't worry, I am on vacation now."

"Vacation?"

Peace and tranquility were written all over Yasha's face, but he could not fool his wife. After a few long seconds, Yasha said, "I was asked to write about some of the arrested colleagues, their strange behavior, and denounce them as enemies of the people. I refused. I said I am not a writer and will never write fictional stories, especially when people can die from such writing. So, I was told to take a vacation."

Tanya became pale and felt weak. "Now I understand why Dina was not home when I came from work. Now it makes sense."

Yasha moved a chair over for her to sit on. He lifted her hands and kissed them.

"My love, I am sorry, but I could not do it any other way. I would lose all self-respect and be unable to look into my children's eyes if I had done what they asked me to do."

Tanya looked at her husband, her eyes full of admiration and fear. She knew what would come next.

"You know, Tanya, they may even come for me tonight. You should pack and go to your brother in Moscow. Sasha will find a way to hide you and it will be safer there, far away from this place. I don't want you to be arrested and sent to Siberia. You should move fast."

"I will not leave you alone. Don't even talk about it. Let's better call the children and prepare them."

When Lara and Meri walked into the room, they understood. Children of their time, teenagers, they knew well what was going on; they sensed that the meat grinder was nearing their home. Lara hugged her father and asked, "Daddy, is it our turn?"

"My dear daughter, we raised you to be strong. Now you have to be strong. You know that whatever they say about me would not be true, as it is not true with the thousands of others in our country. I promise to fight for my life as long as I know you are waiting for me. And you have to support each other."

Yasha's words were drowned out by a loud knock on the door. It stirred everyone into an expectation of evil, but it was Sergey. He looked alarmed. When the girls left the room, Sergey said, "Yasha, after you called me I could not compose myself, and I am still in shock. Don't you understand that the fate of those they asked you to write about had already been sealed? You are not helping them at all, only endangering yourself and our families."

"Don't you understand, Sergey, that I cannot do it? I am not a jerk to sign somebody's death warrant. How would I live with myself?"

Tanya was quiet, tears rolling down her cheeks. Sergey looked at her, came close, hugging her without saying a word. Yasha stood still, looking down at the floor, his brain consumed by thoughts of his family's future.

"Sergey, if I am arrested, please help my family. Maybe they can move to Moscow and weather the storm there."

"I will, I definitely will—if I am not arrested right after you." Sergey kissed Tanya on the forehead and left. Outside, walking on the street, he felt lost. His mind was searching for the right answers. He felt numb from everything he had seen in the last couple of months and his inability to make any sense out of it. Where was that light at the end of the tunnel, where was that promised better future? He asked himself those questions while walking through a street park. Noticing a bench, he sat down to organize his thoughts. In a few minutes, a man sat down at the other end of the bench and opened a newspaper. He was reading an article about a group of counterrevolutionaries discovered by the brave and dedicated security organs. He muttered, "Enemies of the people are sabotaging the economic development of the country." Then he turned to face Sergey.

"Can you imagine, you live next to someone and do not realize he is an enemy? My neighbor turned out to be one of them. It's terrible for these people to organize against the country that feeds and protects them. And he pretended to be a nice guy."

Sergey could not bear it any longer. "How do you know it is true?"

"He confessed!"

Sergey got up and started walking toward his place. He was upset with himself; a question like that on the street could cost him his life. It was outrageous behavior on his part, and he needed to control himself better. Deep in thought, he did not notice how he arrived home, where his anxious wife could hardly wait to hear the answer to her question: "What happened, Sergey? I was so worried about you being late that I called your secretary, and she said you had left. I called your driver and he said you decided to walk home. What happened?"

"I just went to see Yasha. He was given vacation time. Actually, he did not want to sign bad characteristics for some people who had already been arrested. He worries me."

"Why would he do that? They must be guilty if they've been arrested," Katya said, hugging Sergey. "I have a surprise for you."

"A surprise? This is not a good time for surprises. What is it?"

"I am pregnant!"

"Pregnant?" Sergey looked at his wife with astonishment. "How can we bring a child into this world?"

"What are you saying, Sergey? You scare me!"

"I am saying I can be arrested any minute and—at best—you will have to raise the child alone. And I don't want to think what could be at worst."

"I don't understand. Why would anybody arrest you? You have not done anything wrong."

"And what do you think those thousands already in jails had done? Do you really believe one has to be guilty to be arrested? Do you know how many of my comrades and their families are already destroyed? Don't you see what is happening?"

Sergey was desperate. He hugged his crying wife and kept her close for a long while, as if trying to absorb as much as possible of someone he loved.

20

In their minds, Tanya and Yasha had accepted the inevitability of Yasha's arrest and wanted to be ready when the guys in black leather jackets came at night. A small suitcase with Yasha's shaving implements, some clothes, a toothbrush, and such things was readied and put in a corner. It was hard to fall asleep; they lay on the bed fully dressed, with every sound outside the building attracting their attention. Every sound of a car engine tightened all their muscles, and when it disappeared, they relaxed only to keep their ears attuned to the sounds of the external world. They knew what was coming, but did not want to know it.

The sound of a car engine was approaching again, and this time it stopped abruptly instead of fading after a few seconds. Tanya looked at the clock. It was a little after two in the morning. She glanced at Yasha, tears wetting her cheeks. Yasha looked through a window. Sure enough, there was a black raven by their building. Yasha put his coat on, took the suitcase, and moved closer to the door, asking Tanya to join him and whispering to her, "I don't want to wake up the kids. I don't want them to see their father being arrested. Please tell Lara and Meri I love them very much. And I love you and hope you can take care of yourself while this terrible situation exists. We will be together soon. Be strong, be strong for our kids and for me."

Tanya nodded, tears stopping her from saying anything. Yasha kissed her wet face.

In the silence of the night, they could hear the heavy steps of the NKVD men, their bodies anticipating the beginning of terror as they had never known it before. The steps sounded louder, and then the steps were quieter again—the men kept going up past their floor. It was not Yasha's time yet; it was someone else's turn. Someone else happened to be a family upstairs. Both a husband and wife were arrested. The woman walked down the stairs screaming, "My baby, what will happen to my baby? Please, have pity!"

The screams stopped as soon as the arrested people were pushed into the car. But soon there was another scream, this time with the high pitch of a child, "Mommy, mommy, help me...." These were the screams of the five-year-old daughter, who was being taken to a children's asylum.

A few days after the start of vacation, a knock on the door in the middle of the night woke up everyone in the apartment. Now, it was Yasha's turn. In the bustle of the moment, nobody actually opened the door and the knocking became more aggressive, until finally Yasha turned the key and let two men in leather jackets in.

"Yakov Nepomnyashchy, you are under arrest."

Tanya was pale and could not breathe. She was slumping down, almost falling to the floor before Yasha caught her. Lara brought some water. Yasha positioned Tanya on a chair, whispering words of encouragement to give her strength.

One of the NKVD men was looking around the apartment, especially focusing on the bookshelves. He collected everything he found in English—books, magazines, notebooks Yasha used for homework. He looked under the furniture, in the drawers, everywhere. A little notebook with the telephone numbers of Yasha's friends generated particular interest. He also found a unique item—a pocket-size Bible that was in a small jewelry-like box. It was a present from Yasha's American aunt, Elena, so it was in English.

"What is it?"

"It's a family heirloom, a Bible, like a toy. My parents had it since a long time ago."

"We are confiscating this junk. Religion is the opium of the masses," concluded the man, putting the box with the Bible in his pocket.

Tanya was feeling worse. Drinking water, hand rubbing, her daughters' hugs—nothing was making Tanya feel any stronger. Yasha asked Lara to call for an ambulance.

"Let's go!" The command was thrown at Yasha.

"I can't now. Let me see my wife improve a little."

"We won't wait for an ambulance. It's time to go. We have things to do."

Yasha came close to the guy who was directing him to leave and quietly, avoiding Tanya hearing it, said, "My wife has a bad heart. If I leave now, she may have a heart attack and my two children will see their mother die on their hands. Would you like your children to have such an experience? Let me wait until the ambulance comes. Please! The prison won't go anywhere."

The man thought for a second and replied, "Okay."

The ambulance showed up in fifteen minutes. The medics took Tanya and left. It was time for Yasha to go too. He looked around, saw a devastated household, and suddenly realized that there was no money at home for his children to buy food.

"Anya, sell the books and use the money for food," Yasha said. He immediately heard a voice of the NKVD: "The books now belong to the state. Don't you dare touch them! The state will take care of them."

"But I bought them with my own money!"

"Not your, the people's money. And now you betrayed the people and they take back what is theirs."

With that, he motioned to Yasha to leave the apartment. The distraught father kissed his children hurriedly, took the suitcase, and walked out the door, two men following him. Yasha had thought he was ready for this. But he was not. Nobody can be ready for such cruelty. Nobody! He felt helpless against the inhumane and omnipresent state, which, for some reason, saw benefit in destroying the lives of its citizens. "Why? Why?" Yasha was asking himself, "Why are we being punished for a crime we had never committed?" Millions of Soviet citizens were asking that question. There was no answer.

21

The NKVD interrogation place was in the center of Kiev. The front of the building faced a historic and beautiful plaza revered in the Soviet Union. This was where the golden domes of the ancient St. Sophia Cathedral were gleaming. This was where a magnificent monument to Bogdan Khmelnitsky—a Ukrainian Cossack leader who defeated the Poles and united Ukraine with Russia—stood surrounded by flowers. This was where chestnut trees bloomed in the spring and boys beat chestnuts down to the ground with sticks in the early fall. Yasha had loved to stroll around the square with his family. It was a beautiful place! But not for the prisoners inside the infamous building.

Yasha was walking through a long, narrow corridor—one guard in front of him and another behind. It was a long walk and they passed many doors. He heard screams and shouts behind some of the doors, and Yasha's guts tightened in anticipation of what was waiting for him. The guard stopped and knocked on a door. "Come in," was the reply, and the three of them crossed the threshold of Yasha's innocence.

The room was in semi-darkness. Yasha could make out only the silhouette of a man sitting behind a desk. The man offered Yasha a seat facing him across the desk and turned the desk lamp to shine directly at his face. The guards left the room and Yasha sat down, immediately asking, "Why am I here?"

"I will ask the questions, you will provide the answers."

"I am not guilty of anything and you cannot blame me for something I have not done."

"We'll find what you have done, and if not, we will make something up." He looked at Yasha carefully—a short and slender man. "We've broken stronger guys than you, give it time." He looked down at the desk and seemed to be reading from a dossier.

"Aha, I can see we found English books and magazines in your apartment. Are you an English spy?"

"Of course not! I was studying English because of my new work assignment in London. I speak German. Does that make me a German spy?"

"I see. I will indicate here that you are not only an English spy, but a German spy too." He stopped for a second and smiled mysteriously. "I told you we would find something."

The interrogator looked down, shuffled some papers on his desk, and picked up Yasha's notebook that had been taken from his home. He opened the book and read, "'Vasili.' What was his role in your organization?"

"I had no organization! I am not a traitor!"

One by one, the interrogator read aloud the names of the people in the notebook.

"You have to describe the role of each of these people in your organization."

"I repeat, there is no organization!"

"We'll see what your collaborators say!"

It dawned on Yasha that all the people listed in his notebook were now in danger. He thought of Sergey and the likelihood of his arrest. He had counted on Sergey to help his family, but there was no way to help from behind bars! Suddenly, Yasha heard a voice breaking his thoughts, "Would you sign your confession if we bring your wife and children here?"

"I... will... not... sign... anything!"

The interrogator stood up, walked around the desk closer to Yasha, and looked at him intently.

"Are you trying to make my job difficult?" he asked slowly, with a smirk, and without warning hit Yasha in the face with a force that sent him to the floor.

The next second, Yasha felt something hard hitting him in the stomach. He caught his breath and realized that the hard thing was the interrogator's boot, and when the boot was nearing his body again, he grabbed it with both hands and pulled with all his strength. Now, both of them were on the floor, struggling to overcome each other. Then Yasha heard a cry of "Help, help!" from his interrogator, and in a moment, the door opened and the two guards rushed in. It was all over for Yasha. He was lifted by the two strong fellows and, with his feet on the floor and his arms twisted by the guards, could not defend himself as the interrogator pounded his body with both fists. In such a heroic manner Yasha was subdued quickly. He was taken to the basement and thrown into one of the cells designated for special troublemakers: it was no more than three feet high. Before fading into some sort of sleep, the last vision of the real world for this exhausted and bleeding former member of the Central Committee was of the dark space with a cement floor and ceiling so close that it felt they were squeezing the life out of him.

22

When Victor and Anna learned of Yasha's arrest, they decided to divorce immediately. Since it was common for relatives to follow those arrested, they wanted to protect at least someone in the family from a terrible fate. They divorced the following day and were waiting for what would happen next. Anna expected to be arrested.

The NKVD appeared in their apartment in the middle of the night, as usual. Anna was ready with her things packed. She kissed Victor, picked up her bag, and....

"Victor Rudinsky, you are under arrest, bring your things with you," the voice boomed as if from a loudspeaker.

Victor took it stoically. Maybe he had prepared for such a possibility. He was definitely relieved that it was him and not his wife being arrested. Anna was shocked. She started shouting, "Why are you arresting him? He is not even my husband!"

"Hey, little beauty," answered one of them with a grin. "We are not taking you... yet."

When Victor walked out onto the street with his guards, the black car door opened to let him in and the familiar faces of Sergey and Katya appeared from the gray depths.

"Oh my God! They even detained Sergey. What are we going to do?" thought Victor, surprised to see Sergey and his wife in the same car for prisoners. They were not even Yasha's blood relatives, and Sergey had such strong connections that he was the hope for all of them in these dangerous times. The three prisoners sat looking at each other. With guards sitting next to them, communicating was out of the question, so they spent these minutes of their lives contemplating the situation.

They arrived at the NKVD interrogation center. After a short while, Victor was asked to follow two guards to his destination. He glanced at Sergey, as if asking for reassurance. Sergey was not looking at him. Any word, any gesture could be used against them, and it was only prudent to be careful.

Time moved slowly. There was nothing to do and nothing to say, even to a spouse sitting a few inches away. It was torture for Sergey to trace the past years of his life and figure out his mistakes. He must have made some mistakes to end up here, and Katya was suffering because of him. He had worked hard to establish good contacts with the right people. As an outgoing and companionship-loving person, Sergey had never had problems making friends, and these qualities had served him well throughout his military and Party career. In the 1930s, when terror was saturating the air Soviet citizens breathed, whom you knew became even more important than just as a benefit to one's career. It could save one's life, and Sergey understood it well. He remembered an episode

174

from a few months ago, when he came home drunk and was not able to talk to Katya, who was mad at him. She was so mad that the next morning, as soon as he woke up, she jumped on him.

"Sergey, I cannot live with you any longer," she said with such passion that he clearly understood how serious it was. "You are spending more time with your buddies than with me and coming home drunk more and more often. I suffered enough from my father. I don't want to have a drunk for a husband! I am leaving you."

At that time, he had convinced Katya to stay by telling the truth.

"Katya, do you think I like to be drunk? You know that connections are important. How do you think your mother has such a nice apartment in Kiev? How do you think you eat and wear what you want? Don't you know that most people cannot buy these things at will? I have connections. I develop connections! And you know our customs: you meet friends—you drink. Every time there is a celebration, you've got to drink with them, especially if they want to thank me for a favor. The more people I know, the more I need to spend time away from you, and the more benefits I can hope for. This is the way it works and I am a part of it. I wish it were different."

"And why doesn't Yasha behave the same way?"

"Yasha can be a nice, honest intellectual when someone—I—behind his back helps him stay afloat. If not for me, possibly all of the Nepomnyashchys would be in prison by now. I can smooth things out through my friends. And I have to drink with my friends."

Sergey's thoughts were interrupted when he heard his name. He looked up and saw a relatively young man in the NKVD uniform standing by him. He knew this man; he remembered drinking with him a number of times.

"What are you doing here?" the man asked.

"I don't really know," Sergey answered with as much calm as he could muster. He shrugged his shoulders and continued, "It must be a mistake. I am sure we'll be out of here soon."

"We?"

"Oh, yes. This is my wife, Katya." Katya did not have the strength to greet the NKVD officer. "Listen, Stepan, could you do me a favor? Could you arrange for both of us to be together with the same detective? She is pregnant and I don't want her to worry unnecessarily."

"I'll try," Stepan replied and left the room.

They were called, together—what a relief! They walked behind a guard through the corridor Yasha had experienced just a few days earlier. The same long walk until they reached the right door. It took them less than a minute, but it felt much longer, especially when through the doors on the left and right they heard moans and cries of pain.

A small, semi-dark room with a desk, a chair, and a man behind the desk. Sergey recognized this man who held their lives in his hands for now. Sergey once did a favor for him, but now his demeanor was formal, as if they had never met before.

"We know of your activities with the Nepomnyashchy group. All you have to do is sign this. It will be easier for all of us," said the man, looking at Sergey as if saying, "You know what I mean, don't you?"

Sergey knew. He glanced over the document, took a pen, and quickly signed it. He was reading a grotesque story of the subversive group activity headed by Yakov Nepomnyashchy. Katya and Sergey, according to the paper, were a part of it. It was totally ridiculous but he signed it anyway; he knew better.

Sergey gave the pen to Katya and said, "Katya, sign anything they give you. You don't have to read it, just sign it."

She signed it without reading, her heart pounding as if trying to escape from its ribcage and leave this person who just signed her life away, and probably her unborn child too.

The interrogator took the signed document, checked the signatures, and grinned.

"Very good. It took only a couple of minutes to obtain your confessions. Do you think someone may view me as too soft of an interrogator?" He was addressing Sergey and approaching him at the same time. Sergey wanted to take it as a joke and smiled, when he felt a sudden pain in his nose. The interrogator, a former friend and recipient of Sergey's favors, had struck his face with a quick blow, almost cutting him down like a sick, unwanted tree. Sergey did not fall down, but his nose was bleeding profusely.

"Now it looks more believable," his former friend concluded with satisfaction, and both of them heard the sound of a body falling. It was Katya. She could not handle the pressure any longer, and her husband's blood was the last drop in this cup of life she had been drinking all day. She dropped to the floor like a bird shot by a mean hunter just for the fun of it.

23

Lyuba had lived through the worst day of her life many years ago, when a mob attacked her family only because they were Jews. The pogrom had killed her parents and the unborn baby she was carrying inside her. The pogrom also affected an important part of her and Senya's life—the extended family, since some of her closest relations left for America, never to be seen or touched again. Once in a lifetime is enough for anyone to experience the shock treatment like that. The second time is even more difficult, especially in older age when the children are threatened. But this was exactly what happened to Senya and Lyuba: first, their daughter was arrested, and now their entire family was attacked for an unknown reason, but to Lyuba it was another pogrom. They came, took what they wanted, and left. The Nepomnyashchy family was decimated: most were arrested; Tanya and the children survived the arrest, but had to leave Kiev to avoid being jailed; Zhenya's husband, Vasili, was arrested in Elizavetgrad, and in a few days she was told he went on a hunger strike and starved. Starved in a few days? Zhenya knew better. She was sure he had been tortured to death. Zhenya decided to leave town and join her parents in Kiev. Anna was heartbroken after her husband's arrest. All the previous horrors she had experienced when she was arrested years ago came back to haunt her again. Such was the state of the family. The ones who had not been arrested could expect persecution at any time and knew nothing about the fate of the arrested ones.

The arrested did not know what was happening with other family members and friends either. None of them saw each other, except once. Yasha still had not signed a confession. He was interrogated again and again, but would not sign anything to betray himself and the people he loved. Once again, Yasha was taken to that dreaded room, but when the door opened he saw another person there besides the interrogator.

"Sit down, Nepomnyashchy," the interrogator commanded. "Your friends have already accepted responsibility for participation in the subversive group you organized. They implicated you as the leader. There is no reason for you to maintain your stupid denials. Sign the protocol and your suffering is over."

Yasha did not move and did not say a word. The interrogator waited a few seconds and then continued, "We brought one of your accomplices, who already signed a confession," and he pointed to the man sitting in a corner. It was dark in the room—the light was shining only directly in Yasha's face. He looked intently but could only make out an outline of a man slumping in a chair. The man was in bad shape. All of a sudden, a light illuminated the corner where the man was sitting and Yasha recognized him—it was Victor, beaten and broken. Victor kept his head down to avoid meeting Yasha's eyes. He had signed the confession and felt terrible that he could not withstand the beatings any longer.

"My God, Victor, what did they do to you?"

Yasha was angry, very angry—with himself for being the reason the people close to him were tortured, and with the interrogator for being an animal—especially with the interrogator. Yasha wanted to kill this guy with his bare hands. He jumped up from the chair and put his hands on it as if trying to lift it. He wanted to throw it at the interrogator—and could not do it. The chair was bolted to the floor.

"You son of a bitch! I cannot imagine a woman gave birth to you. I am not the first one who wanted to kill you with this chair! I can see

178

the day you'll die of torture in this room." Yasha was shouting because he felt impotent to fight this man, and when the son of a bitch came closer and hit him, Yasha had no mental strength to resist. The interrogator was beating Yasha while Victor sat helplessly sobbing in his corner, blaming himself for his weakness and inability to help his friend.

24

The trip to Moscow was difficult for Tanya. She had to move after Yasha's arrest to protect herself and the children, but her heart was back in Kiev with her husband. She knew that the chances of hearing from Yasha were nonexistent, but she was hoping that her brother Sasha, who was an established architect in Moscow, could help.

Sasha was glad to see his sister.

"What happened, my dear?"

Tanya wanted to answer, but tears were choking her.

"Daddy was arrested," Lara intervened.

"When?"

"Two days ago."

"Let's talk later. I am sure you are all tired and hungry. Children, why don't you go to the kitchen and help Aunt Shura? We will eat soon."

When the children left the room, he hugged Tanya and said, "You have to disappear. Moscow is not a good place to hide, and you know that in many cases wives are arrested when their husbands are. I have a good friend. He is a school principal in Krasnaya Polyana—a small town not far from Moscow. I am sure he could find some employment for you. Take Meri and I will keep Lara here. She is old enough not to disclose where her father is, and she can study at the university. Remember, don't tell anybody about Yasha. Just say you are divorced and have no idea where your ex-husband is. The children must remember it too."

This sounded like a good plan. The next day, Sasha hired a car and took Tanya and Meri to Krasnaya Polyana, where his friend met them joyfully and offered Tanya a job as a librarian. He also helped find a small unoccupied house in the tiny village of Chashkino. The old woman—a former teacher—who used to live there had died recently. Small villages like Chashkino were losing young people to big cities and there was no demand for housing. A walk to Krasnaya Polyana was about forty minutes—not too far by village standards. Tanya and Meri settled down, alone in a new place.

Living in the country required certain things, including a basic minimum of farm animals. They started by acquiring a few chickens and a rooster, and then, a goat. The neighbors taught Tanya and Meri how to take care of the farm animals so they could have milk and eggs, and how to start a vegetable garden.

Sasha and Lara visited them when time allowed. Sasha promised Tanya to find the right connections and learn about Yasha's fate, but every time he came, the answer was the same, "So far, no news."

Tanya missed Yasha desperately. She was imagining their future meeting, how they make love, feeling so happy. In her dreams, they were often together. In real life, some men were attracted to her, but she was desperate to stay away from them. One such man was the math teacher of Meri's class, who kept asking the young girl about her mother. Meri, as she had been taught, explained that her mother was divorced, and the teacher found more and more reasons to use the library. He would always bring sweets, and sometimes even chocolate, which was hard to find. Tanya understood his interest but could not accept his courtship.

One evening, Tanya answered a knock on her door and the math teacher appeared in front of her: neatly dressed, smiling, and holding a bouquet of flowers in one hand and a bag in the other.

"Hello, Tanya. I brought you something from my garden." He offered the bag to Tanya. It was full of fruits and vegetables.

Tanya thanked him for the gifts and set the flowers in the vase. Offering the teacher a place to sit, she asked Meri to serve tea with handmade jam. She had a small house—just two rooms and a kitchen, the furniture basic and old. Meri poured tea into glasses, put food on the table, and went to the bedroom to read. Tanya remained alone with the teacher. He was a little nervous and started the conversation by praising Meri's efforts in math. Gradually he relaxed, settling into a reasonable comfort, and said, "I lost my wife three years ago. She was ill. I felt alone all this time, and then I saw you. I liked you from the first time we met. My heart was pounding so hard, I was afraid you would hear it. You are beautiful and also tranquil. When you are around, everything lights up as though in heaven. And you are such a good mother—just look at Meri!"

The teacher stopped for a second, inhaled, and finished his speech, "Marry me, Tanya, and I will give you a beautiful life!"

Tanya found herself in a difficult situation. She did not want to offend her visitor, who was a decent man, but she could not accept his offer either. She was looking for the right words, but what came out sounded not the way she intended it, "I am not ready yet to marry again."

"Is that because I am German or because I am a country boy?" the teacher asked nervously.

Tanya could not handle the situation any longer. She started crying and, through the tears, said, "You are a great guy and any woman would be happy to marry you, but I am not ready at this time."

The teacher approached Tanya and kissed her hand.

"I am so sorry. I did not want to upset you. My proposal is open until you are ready to accept it."

With that, he left. Tanya continued crying all the tears she had been holding back for months. She felt bad. What did she do to deserve such a fate? What did Yasha do to suffer imprisonment or worse?

25

If you close your eyes and just listen to the rhythmic and monotonous sound of train wheels, after a while it is easy to imagine being on a trip to some exciting and beautiful place. Just pick the destination. Let's say, Venice. Or the French Riviera. Or, maybe, Jerusalem. Yasha had always wanted to see this place—Jerusalem! There was so much associated with it: history, religions, philosophy. His ancestors probably saw Jerusalem, maybe even lived in it, who knows. Yasha did not know anything about his Jewish roots beyond his grandparents. It would be nice to know. His family would also be here, with him, in this ancient place. During the day they walk the streets, and in the evening they are in a restaurant, eating exotic dishes. What do they eat in Jerusalem? And then at night—a cozy hotel, children sleeping comfortably or also dreaming about something beautiful....

"Hey! Move a little, I don't have enough space here."

Yasha's introspection came to an end with a push from a big fellow sitting next to him on the floor of the cargo wagon, which was full of prisoners—mostly political, some criminal—on their way to a labor camp. They did not know the destination, but judging from the scenery observed through the cracks in the wagon walls, the snow was deeper— they were moving north. This was not good. Labor camps and prisons were located everywhere in the country. They could have ended up in a warmer climate, or at least close to a big population center, but it was not their luck; they kept going north, farther and farther away. For four days in transit they had little to eat, it was hard to sleep in the crowded space, and there was nothing to do.

Yasha's daydreaming of vacationing with the family was rare. Most of his thoughts were about his loved ones in real life, the life that was completely hidden from him. Did Tanya manage to get to Moscow? Is she healthy? How are the kids adjusting? Where is Sergey, Victor? Poor Victor, he was crushed. Maybe they threatened him with Anna's arrest and he signed. So many people he missed, so many people.... It hurt so much.

After the interrogation in Victor's presence, Yasha thought he had been forgotten by the NKVD machine, as for months nobody had any interest in him. He was just transported from one prison in Kiev to another, seemingly without a purpose. Then he was called in only one more time, and a man who looked like a doctor, but probably was an administrative type, read the court's decision: "Yakov Nepomnyashchy, for your subversive anti-Soviet activity and spying for foreign powers, you are sentenced to twenty-five years of hard labor."

That was it. No court hearings, no defense attorney, no opportunity to even hear an intelligent accusation. His life was over. These camps were not places people usually returned from after twenty-five years of hard labor. No more family, no Tanya's hands, no children's voices, just existence. Shortly after the sentencing, he was taken to the train station and joined dozens of others on a trip to a Russian wasteland.

After another twelve days on the cold, crowded train, the destination was finally reached: Vorkuta—one of the worst places a human being could live in. It was no more than a labor camp then, one of many in the Northern Russian tundra above the Arctic Circle. At the train station they were met by armed guards with dogs and marched to the camp. It was dark in the middle of the day. Coming from Ukraine, they had never seen a place as drab as the one they were walking through. Rays of light coming from projectors located high up on poles pulled out from the darkness piles of snow—just snow, nothing else. Although there was some satisfaction in finally reaching their destination, the surroundings were gloomy, with not an ounce of positive feeling that could help the prisoners.

They reached the camp gate, walked inside, and lined up. After a short introduction about debt to society and obeying the rules, the group was split into smaller contingents and taken to the assigned barracks. Among twenty others, Yasha walked to a barracks.

Inside, the new group lined up again, and the lead guard introduced them to a man standing in the middle of the barracks.

"This is your team leader. He will tell you the rules. Pay attention."

Even with the man's heavy clothes, facial hair, and lifeless look, Yasha still recognized him. It was Sergey! Skinny, pale, and haggard, but Sergey nevertheless. The first emotion Yasha experienced was joy— there was someone here he could talk to and count on. But this also meant Sergey could not help anyone.

Yasha could not wait to talk with Sergey about Tanya, Katya, and the others, but he had to wait. Sergey was talking about the rules in the barracks and did not make eye contact. Yasha patiently waited. After Sergey distributed warm working clothes and talked to everyone, it was Yasha's turn.

Sergey quietly said, "Do not tell anyone we know each other and be alert. Not everybody here is a political prisoner, many are criminals and you have to be careful with them. Three days ago, they killed the guy who was the team leader and I was assigned to this duty. Don't react to whatever they say and do. I will try to talk to you tomorrow at work."

Criminals were easy to spot—they had the air of owners of this godforsaken place. Their behavior was explicitly hostile to politicals, who did not have the experience or the guts of the criminals. The first evening Yasha witnessed a scene that repeated itself many times all over the Gulag: the criminals played cards for something valuable they could take from the politicals. Their leader looked over the newcomers and noticed that one fellow had warm underwear.

"I will play for those," he announced, and the game started.

Yasha's bunk was on the first level and right above him was the guy with warm underwear. He was a large man, built like a wrestler. They shook hands.

"My name is Yasha. I was spying for Germany and England."

"I am Mamut. My charge—spying for Turkey."

Both chuckled.

"Where are you coming from?" Mamut asked.

"Kiev. I worked for the Party. You?"

"I came to Russia from Turkey after the revolution to help build socialism, so everyone would be equal, no poor and no rich people. I am from a rich family, but I did not like seeing so many poor people on the streets. I was young and dumb. Now I am paying for the lesson."

"What did you do before the arrest?"

"I was a math teacher in Mahachkala."

They were tired and wanted to rest, but the card game was noisy and was going on and on. Yasha finally fell asleep after a few unsuccessful attempts interrupted by loud shouts of "Uhbyuh, gad!" (*I'll kill you, viper!*) He woke up from pressure on his foot. Opening his eyes, he saw a man trying to climb to Mamut's bunk.

"What are you doing?" Yasha asked quietly because it was dark and everyone seemed to be asleep.

"Shut your mouth if you want to live." The man kept trying to reach something, and Yasha raised his voice, now wanting to attract the attention of others, "What are you doing?"

And seeing that his words had no impact, Yasha pushed the man away from his bunk. The man fell noisily to the floor and, angered by Yasha's strange and stupid behavior, took a knife out and said, "Pray, political swine. This is your last moment alive."

Yasha did not have a chance to get scared; he just saw a huge body falling down from the upper bunk right onto the attacking criminal, pressing him down like an empty bag. The noise woke up the rest of the prisoners and the lines were quickly drawn: criminals against politicals. The smaller number of criminals lost this time, but the danger was still there and the politicals decided to keep a sentry at night, just in case.

Early in the morning, the prisoners had hot water with stale bread and left for work. As Sergey's team was digging trenches for pipes, everyone received either a shovel or a pick from a grim-looking guard and lined up, ready to march. It was cold and dark. Yasha was anxious to start working so he could warm up. Then he noticed that the man who wanted to kill Mamut last night made a sign with his hand at him, moving it close to his throat to indicate Yasha's fate. In the darkness, when the guards did not really care what happened to the prisoners as long as they were all accounted for, anything was possible. Others also saw the criminal's body language, and both Sergey and Mamut moved closer to Yasha. They marched to a construction site surrounded by guards. In this minus-forty-degree weather, only felt boots saved people from freezing their toes off. The work started. A few men loosened permafrost-glued dirt with picks and the rest shoveled it out of the trenches and moved it away in little wheelbarrows. Sergey, as the team

185

leader, assigned Yasha to work next to him. They could talk, as long as they made sure their conversation did not attract unwanted attention.

"When did you arrive?" Yasha asked.

"I've been here almost a year."

"Do you know anything about Tanya?"

"I helped her get train tickets to Moscow and she left before I was arrested."

Yasha's heavy heart felt lighter knowing that his family had escaped a devastating situation.

"And Katya?"

"She was arrested together with me. I know nothing about what happened to her."

Sergey cursed and spat on the snow. With horror, Yasha noticed color where Sergey had spat. It was dark in the trench—little light from the projectors reached it—and he could not distinguish the color, but he knew it was red. Sergey was spitting blood.

"What is it, Sergey?"

"Scurvy. With the terrible food here, many people develop it. You saw what we eat in the morning, in the evening—lean soup with some meatless dumplings. That's it. Plus an eighteen-hour work day. You know, we are just cheap slave labor for Stalin, who sends us to the camps to build a future for him and at the same time relieve the pressure of food scarcity on the rest of the people. We build new cities and nobody will remember how they were built. We die, and the great Stalin will be cheered as the heroic builder, but these cities will stand on our bones."

Suddenly, Sergey heard a thumping sound and saw Yasha falling on his face. Behind Yasha stood the criminal who had threatened him earlier, holding the shovel he had just used as a weapon. Full of rage, Sergey rushed at the guy with all the strength he had. The criminal fell, and Sergey noticed Mamut running in to help. But help was no longer needed as the criminal had hit his head on a rock that ended his life.

At the end of the day, Mamut brought still weak Yasha to the barracks on his back, and the criminals were carrying a dead associate for a burial. On that day, the rule of the criminals in Sergey's barracks ended, and the political prisoners could breathe a little easier.

26

By March, a polar night became a polar day. No need for projectors anymore, but how difficult it was to sleep! The body was confused. It did not believe the time was right for dreams. Grueling work, though, made the transition from night to day easier for the prisoners. They returned to the barracks after a long day, ate something that looked like slop, and, tired, dropped into their bunks for rest.

Yasha was concerned about Sergey's health, which was not improving at all, and with the kind of diet the prisoners consumed, little hope existed. Sergey was not the only one suffering, and those who did not have scurvy yet could develop it at any time. People needed vegetables and fruits to fight scurvy, but where would they find them? Trying to find a solution, Yasha, over Sergey's objections, finally found a way to talk to someone in the camp management. What he proposed was simple and based on the observations of his mother, who always had plants growing inside her apartment in the city—he proposed to build a greenhouse. The idea was accepted because the primary beneficiaries would be those in charge. The greenhouse was to be built.

Now Yasha had contacts within the camp administration that could be valuable. Later, he used those contacts for acquiring books he needed to study Nenets—the language of the local Nentsy people. The study gave him something to occupy his brain with and provided tools that might come in handy one day. When asked, "Why do you need to study this?" he always answered, "We came to their place and should study their way of life."

Summer came and left within a few short weeks, bringing warm sun and swarms of mosquitoes. Oh, those mosquitoes! They were everywhere and they were fighting hard to leave memories of their short active lives on humans. Then winter again, gray and snowy. The summer sun had not helped Sergey; his health kept worsening. Yasha

187

decided to take extreme steps to save him and ask for the management's permission to exchange flour, which the Nentsy craved, for a reindeer.

"Are you out of your mind, Nepomnyashchy?" said the camp officer that Yasha had approached. "It's winter. It's freezing cold. It's dark. Where are you going to find them?"

"I noticed some distant smoke from where we were working the last few days. It should not be more than two or three kilometers. If you allow me to take a few guys with me, we should be back promptly."

"I don't know. Your ideas.... What is it going to do, this one reindeer?"

"It will help people with scurvy. They will be stronger and work harder. And it's not just for the prisoners."

The officer was thinking. He turned his head away from Yasha, as if looking for someone to help him decide. Yasha stood waiting for the answer, nervously rubbing his hands. The officer's head turned back with a smile.

"All right. Go. Take three guys and go. I will tell the kitchen to give you a bag of flour."

"Thank you, grahzhdanin nachalnik," said Yasha, using the formal title *citizen chief* to address the officer.

To search for the nomadic Nentsy no guards were necessary. If a prisoner thought to escape, where would he go and how would he survive in the middle of the frozen tundra? Besides, even if someone tried such a stupid idea, the Nentsy were always watching for fugitives because they could exchange them for flour, which was clearly more valuable than unwanted enemies of the people. So the four of them went, pulling the bag of flour along the plentiful snow. They went in the direction of the smoke stacks Yasha had noticed before, and in about three hours approached the Nentsy's chums.

They entered the first chum on their path. A chum is all reindeer skin: hanging on the outside of the planks holding the chum, lining the floor inside, and in stacks by the chum's perimeter to be used as blankets. A small fire was burning in the middle of the chum. Several men and a woman holding a baby—that's how they assumed it was a

188

woman—were sitting around. A strange, unfamiliar smell hit the prisoners in the face and startled them. The people in the chum were also startled by the unexpected visitors, whom they immediately recognized as prisoners.

Yasha, using his acquired language skills, explained what they had come for. The host listened, offered them seats around the fire, and produced a pipe. Nothing could be discussed before the pipe had made its way around the circle of men. The host put the pipe in his mouth and inhaled a few times, then took the pipe out and passed it on. When the pipe reached Yasha, the first of the prisoners sitting around the fire, he slowly took it. Forcing himself not to show any disgust, he put it in his mouth, inhaled, and passed it to the next guy, feeling uneasy with the procedure but knowing that it had to be done.

When the smoking ended, the host went out, returning soon with two reindeer caught from among his herd. Both were slaughtered and one was taken inside the chum for a feast. The host cut the reindeer flesh with a knife and offered pieces of meat to all present. Raw meat tasted strange, but the prisoners were hungry and could not offend the host anyway. For Yasha, this was another trial, but he succeeded in displaying no discourtesy. Then he thanked the host for his hospitality and said it was time for them to go.

A surprise waited for them outside: as soon as they exited the chum, several men jumped them, tied their hands up, and put them on sleds. They were about to be driven away, when Yasha started screaming, "You forgot a reindeer, reindeer. We paid for it!"

The host grinned, but brought a killed reindeer and put it on the sled next to Yasha, who was also grinning. Going back to the camp in a sled pulled by reindeer was a lot better than carrying a huge animal on their backs through deep snow in the dark. Coming to the camp was a disappointment to the enterprising Nentsy. They demanded flour for the prisoners they caught but extracted only laughs. Everyone had an opportunity to laugh, and for the prisoners any laughter is good. And the meat—cooked meat this time—tasted so wonderful that even the criminals in Yasha's barracks developed some respect for him.

But it was too late for Sergey. His strength rapidly diminished. One evening he called Yasha to his bunk.

"I think it's time to say good-bye, Yasha. I doubt I can talk and even breathe much longer. I want to ask—"

Yasha interrupted his friend-brother, "Stop it, Sergey! I will find something else to help you."

"No, nothing will help, I know. Please, listen to me. I want to ask you to do everything you can to find Katya and tell her how much I loved her, and how sorry I am that I could not protect her. I am so sorry, so sorry."

"It's not your fault, Sergey, not your fault," Yasha said almost in a whisper, thinking that it could have been his fault. "I am a prisoner, and who knows how long I can survive here. But if I ever get out of this hellhole, I'll do anything to find Katya, I promise."

That was the last conversation between two people who had stood by each other all their lives. Soon after the reindeer affair, Sergey succumbed to scurvy.

Losing a brother was awful and made Yasha's survival more difficult. For a long time, he was in a fog of depression. Only Mamut supported him, bringing him back to the living. But Yasha had to survive. He promised his family to return and he would do everything possible to keep his word.

27

After spending more than six months in jail, Victor began wondering what was going on. Since his imprisonment, he had never been in a single cell, which would had made his existence even more difficult. It made a big difference whether one could talk to people or not; deprivation was a lot easier to handle among company. That memorable encounter with Yasha was Victor's last call for any interrogation. Then, Victor had returned to his cell shaken up. Although nobody had physically touched him, the scene of his brother-in-law being beaten affected him enormously. Exhausted by the torment, he fell asleep. Sleeping was the way to escape. Sometimes he dreamt of his wife, sometimes he was traveling in unknown places, sometimes he saw himself as a little boy running around in a green field, but often the dreams were as hard as reality and did not bring any relief.

Since then, he had just spent his time in a cell, meeting different people every couple of weeks. And what a gallery of characters he observed: quiet scholars, loud military men, strange people with shifting eyes and questionable manners, young and old, poor and well-to-do, weak and strong—all were under the same heel of the tyrannical state out of control. Some of those men were important figures outside the prison walls and knew a lot about the purges. From them, Victor learned that most of those arrested were quickly moved to labor camps with horrendous living conditions, and that being in jail in Kiev was a good thing. After a while he began wondering why he was still in the same place. Month after month, nobody seemed to be interested in him. Then he heard a rumor that the detective who had interrogated him had been arrested and took his share of suffering somewhere in this building too.

A human adapts to new surroundings. Victor adapted to his. He had nothing to do but think, and sometimes he came up with interesting observations while contemplating his life. Was it not amazing, he thought, how a Count and a Czarist officer had lived through all the turmoil of 1920s and '30s with no problems from the state, minus the stolen mansion, and had even worked for the fiercest Soviet creation—the NKVD—only to be finally put in jail not for what he had done or who he was, but because of his relation to a loyal Communist toiler, someone who had spent his life helping to build and improve the country? Just like in the song, "Fate plays with a man." Victor's fate from his birth was to be part of the nobility in an important empire stretching from the Pacific Ocean in the east to the Black and Baltic Seas in the west, and from northern ice to southern deserts. Instead, he had lost his livelihood, his abode, and his money; his wife was imprisoned and raped and thus far could not have children; and finally, he ended up in jail. Something to be angry about! At that moment, he hated this state which promised so much to so many and delivered only terror to its citizens. And why was the state killing off its best and brightest? If a real enemy of the state wished it harm, this is what he would do: destroy its best people.

Different thoughts were coming together. He remembered Aleksandr, who always said he wanted as much power as he could acquire in his career so he could use it against the state. And then it dawned on him: maybe Aleksandr did go high up, maybe he was an important man now, even in Moscow—who knew.

Current events were entering Victor's world with new prisoners, whose steady stream provided information. Learning about the start of the Second World War when Hitler attacked Poland was shocking. Europe was boiling, but the start of a world war was still a huge event. After September, most news had been about the war in Europe and the reaction in the Soviet Union, which was not at war at that time. What would be next?

Very early on the morning of June 22, 1941, Victor woke up to a blasting sound coming from outside. He had never heard such a loud sound in his life; the closest thing he could think of was the sound of artillery during the war many years ago. He and the other prisoners learned quickly that the sound was of German bombs falling from the skies. Hitler had declared war on the Soviet Union. Kiev was in the center of Ukraine and not far from the western border where thousands of German troops entered the country, and the Luftwaffe— the German air force—had a short flight to reach one of the main population centers of the USSR.

Later that day, Victor and the other inmates received a state offer: join the army and fight, with the survivors' prison terms to be annulled. The caveat was that the former inmates would be organized into special "penalty battalions" to be used in the most dangerous activities. Victor decided quickly. He signed up. The next day, he and the others from Kiev prisons were uniformed and sent to the front. They had only a few rifles because even regular army units did not have enough. They were told that guns could be taken from the dead soldiers right there in the middle of a battle.

Soon after appearing in the front area, Victor's battalion, as part of a bigger formation, was surrounded by the overwhelming German forces. The situation was confusing and changing fast. There was no common directive to the troops, and the commanders of the surrounded units were making decisions based only on their local information, primarily trying to save the troops from slaughter. It was hell.

When the commander of Victor's battalion was killed, there was nobody to take his place, as such units were not expected to survive for long and thus were not given a sufficient complement of professional officers. People started to panic and the situation was becoming disastrous. Victor decided it was time to act. Nobody knew he was an educated officer, his military training still in him. It just happened that Victor's detachment was in an area familiar to him since his days as an officer fighting for the Whites. He took over simply by stating, "I know the area. Whoever wants a chance to survive, follow me."

Everyone did. In two days, going through marshes and woods, the battalion escaped the enemy with no losses. When they appeared as apparitions from the woods, their loud shouts of "Svohyee, svohyee" stopped the shooting by the Red Army soldiers at them in time.

And then Victor was reporting to a colonel, "Comrade Colonel, the fifth battalion of the second regiment escaped the encirclement and is ready for service."

"And what is your name?"

"Sergeant Rudinsky."

"Thank you, Sergeant Rudinsky, for taking the troops out of encirclement."

"Serve the Soviet Union!" Victor answered as it was prescribed by the regulations.

Victor actually attained more than a thank you. For his actions in saving the troops, his imprisonment was expunged, he was promoted to lieutenant and given a few days' leave to see his family. That same day, he hitchhiked in army vehicles toward Kiev, and by nightfall he was standing at the door to his apartment.

Anna had not seen Victor for more than four years. She opened the door and could not believe her eyes. "Victor, is it you?" She almost fainted, so unexpected was his arrival, but Victor caught her and carried her into the room.

He had left a broken civilian and returned a confident officer. They kissed for a long time. Victor's mother cried, hugging him with an overwhelming feeling of happiness. The three of them had a lot to talk about, but quickly the topic of conversation turned to war.

"Many people have already evacuated east, far away from the front. Some are evacuating with their enterprises, some are leaving on their own. And these are mostly women, children, and old people; the men are all in the army," Anna said.

Victor immediately jumped in: "You both have to leave too, the sooner the better. It's dangerous to stay."

"Why would I leave? The Germans will give us freedom from the Communists. I am not going anywhere!" replied his mother.

"Who told you this fairytale, Mother?"

"I know, the Germans came here to fight the Communists."

"Where are your parents?" Victor asked Anna, changing the topic.

"They are home. And Zhenya lives with them too after Vasili died in prison."

"Then let's go see them; they should leave Kiev too. As an officer I can help evacuate all of you but we need to move quickly. I have to be back with my troop soon."

Meeting Anna's parents and Zhenya was also emotional, but also brought an unexpected conclusion.

Senya said, "We are old; it is difficult for us to move. Where would we go? Why would the Germans bother us?"

"I cannot leave the sick and the injured," was Zhenya's answer.

Later, when Victor found his sister Natasha, her answer was the same as Zhenya's. Anna was the only one he had convinced to leave. When Victor put her on the train, he could not let go of his wife,

194

hugging her hard, as if scared to lose her again. The train moved and Victor stepped backwards, trying to see his wife for a few more seconds, and said, "I'll find you, Anna, when the war is over. Take care of yourself."

Anna stood by the window, watching Victor fade away. She was going east. Victor went west to find his regiment.

28

Victor had visited Kiev right in time. In a few days, the enemy troops came close to the ancient Russian city. They came close, but could not enter for about two months—such was the fierce defense. Kiev was occupied in the second half of September, and soon after, the Nazi SS entered the city.

Khreshchatik is the main street in Kiev. It is a short and beautiful street located in the city center. From Khreshchatik one can go up the hill to the prestigious parts of the city overlooking the Dnieper, where Yasha and Sergey used to work, or up another hill—in the opposite direction—toward the oldest part of town, where Yasha and Sergey had been in jail. One of the streets going up in this direction was actually the first part of a long arterial road traversing the city. It was a straight road, with sections of it having different names, and it would take someone close to two hours to walk from Khreshchatik to the outskirts of the city. A few days after the SS entered the city, a proclamation was distributed that required all Jews to assemble along this road with their valuables—it was all for their safety, the proclamation announced. Many feeder streets connected to that artery, and on September 29, the streams of Jews on these streets were flowing into the artery, becoming a human river. The Jews were not to stand still, but to move along the road away from the center toward the outskirts, and the German soldiers were there to motivate people to obey the commands. Mostly women, children, and old people, all with some belongings—they were moving slowly, not knowing what to expect, hoping for the best. They were walking toward Babi Yar; they were about to become part of history.

Within two days, more than thirty thousand Jews moved along that road toward Babi Yar—a ravine on the city's outskirts—where they were to undress, leave their belongings, and stand by the ravine's edge to be executed, their bodies falling into the ravine. They were shot by Ukrainian polizai and watched by the SS surrounding the place. Babi Yar became a concentration camp where in two years more than a hundred thousand Soviet citizens, mostly Jews, eventually died.

Hearing about the proclamation, Lyuba cried. She was planning to go. But not Senya. He said, "I will not let you go. I am not a Jew, you are my wife, and Zhenya is my daughter. She is not Jewish either. After all, who would know you did not show up?"

The knock on their door startled them. The door opened and a neighbor, Glusha, came in without waiting for the invitation.

"Are you ready to go where all the Jews supposed to be?" she asked.

"Why are you asking? Do you think something good will happen to us?" Senya responded. "What is it to you? You know I am not even Jewish."

"How do I know that? And your wife is definitely a Jew. You should comply with the directive from the new authority, you know."

Glusha's eyes scanned the room. Here she had hidden from her drunken son. Here she had asked for and received food when her son spent all their money on vodka. She knew this room and its contents well.

"Would you like to switch your room for mine? It is smaller but you can stay there and nobody would tell the Germans you are Jewish."

Senya and Zhenya looked at each other in disbelieve. Lyuba closed her face with her hands and started crying again.

"Glusha, what are you talking about after everything we had done for you? You want our room?" Senya said.

"Yes. Why not? And I really admire that exquisite china set. Deal?"

Senya's look told Glusha everything. She turned around and left the room. Coming to the street she looked left and right, and as soon as a

German detail appeared, she approached them with the words, "Yude, Yude," pointing to her building.

The soldiers came to the apartment, found three souls hoping to escape the enemy, and in a few seconds the souls splattered all over the room, painting its walls red. The soldiers left. The neighbor gained the china. Three human beings disappeared.

29

Sunday was usually when Tanya allowed herself to sleep a little longer. No reason to hurry anywhere, just a day of relaxation. Sunday, June 22, 1941, was planned as a day of garden work. Tanya was up at about nine and went to the kitchen to make breakfast. She turned the radio on—on Sunday mornings they sometimes played fine music. Walking around the house, she noticed that the radio announcers were not coming on as usual and only the music kept playing. Then there was a pause and the deep voice of a famous radio announcer, Levitan, came through:

"Comrades! Last night, the military forces of Nazi Germany treacherously crossed the border of the USSR. We are at war. The brave Red Army troops are currently fighting German forces on the entire length of the western border. The fights are tough, but we will win. Listen for more war announcements during the day."

Each word of Levitan's was like a bullet hitting Tanya's body. Millions of Soviet citizens had the same feeling at exactly the same time. People had expected a war, but hoped it wouldn't happen. The news was unexpected nevertheless.

From that day on, the radio was never turned off. The country was mobilizing its resources to withstand the invaders and everyone was involved. Tiny Chashkino was away from the news and most of the activity, but in Krasnaya Polyana changes were everywhere. Soon, an army detachment was building defense structures in case the enemy appeared close to Moscow. Although the resistance of the Red Army in Ukraine and Belarus significantly delayed German advancement and changed their plans, in September their troops were positioned still far from the capital but close enough to threaten its stability, and every week they came closer. Their still overwhelming superiority in troops and equipment was checked by the bravery of the defenders, but it was not quite enough, and German generals still nursed their plans of a New Year celebration in Moscow.

In November, the front was so near the city that many state institutions had to evacuate, but the will of the government was to defend its capital with everything they had. Women were building ditches and barricades, young college students were grouped into quickly assembled units and sent to the front. Stalin was using every resource available, unfortunately not always carefully thinking through the situation, and many of the students, who had no training and almost no guns, were dying without impacting the enemy, while additional regular troops were being moved from the remote eastern parts of the country to defend the capital.

The front was a moving, breathing line, sometimes pushed in toward Moscow, sometimes pushed out. Some towns changed hands many times. Krasnaya Polyana was close to the front line and it was time for Tanya and Meri to leave their village, where they could hear the steady cannonade. Lara, who was still in Moscow, finally succeeded in renting a wagon with a horse and went to Chashkino to remove her family from the danger zone. The country roads in November were usually a mess, unless early frost helped the situation. It did this time, and Lara found no problem reaching the village. They quickly collected what was reasonable to take and departed. On their way to Moscow they observed military vehicles, infantry units, and cavalry going in the opposite direction—to the front. They saw artillery pieces being set up right in the vegetable gardens in the villages they were moving through and many more wagons with people like them going away from their land, leaving most possessions behind. The scene was heartbreaking and Tanya's weak heart gave out: she fainted. In the first sizable town on the way to Moscow, Lara found a hospital and asked for help. There were few medics in the hospital, most working close to the front line on injured soldiers, but the relative quiet and serenity it offered was comforting to Tanya.

"Anya, take Meri and keep moving to the city. I'll stay here until I feel better and I'll find you afterward," insisted the mother in an effort to place her children as far from the killing fields as possible.

The children left and she stayed. Every day, the cannonade was louder and louder. She learned to imagine where the front was by the intensity of the sound. As the front was coming closer, more people were accumulating in the hospital—first mostly civilians, then soldiers. Tanya helped the hospital personnel with the injured, using her experience during the Civil War. People told stories. It had been about a week since Tanya's unplanned stop at the hospital when an injured woman was admitted. The woman was in a state of shock and initially would not talk much, until she learned that Tanya had been a librarian in Krasnaya Polyana. Then, after crying for a while, she spoke up.

"Three days ago, German troops entered the town. They immediately started searching for Jews and Communists. They were actually after anybody who resembled the intelligentsia: managers, teachers, government workers—anybody they suspected could be an undesirable element. They were going through the streets, house to house, collecting the unlucky ones and taking them to the school. They squeezed as many people in as they could, closed all the doors and windows, and set the school on fire." The woman stopped for a moment to fight the emotions stirred up by this terrible vision.

"There were children inside, teachers, old women; they were shouting loudly to let them out. Children were crying. I saw everything from a nearby house that had been ruined by bombs. Some people broke through the windows, but the SS, who surrounded the church, just sprayed them with bullets. You were a librarian, right? Do you remember a history teacher—a young woman? She was pregnant, but was taken together with her three-year-old. They were Jewish. Do you remember the math teacher? He was German, but when his pupils were taken, he volunteered to go with them. They burned them all!"

Tanya was terrified listening to the tale, and when the math teacher was mentioned—the man who had courted her—tears burst out of her eyes and both women could not stop crying. Who would think cultured people were capable of such savage crimes?

Injured soldiers arriving in the hospital had heard rumors, just rumors, about the entire situation around Moscow. As it happened, Krasnaya Polyana was the closest the German army came to the capital, and the Red Army took the town back quickly. Soon the cannonade was more difficult to hear, until finally the sound of it disappeared completely. By the beginning of December 1941, the Red Army started pushing the enemy further and further away from the Soviet capital. There would not be a New Year celebration in Moscow for the German generals; there would not be a successful completion of Barbarossa. There would be thousands of dead and injured and frostbitten German soldiers; there would be Hitler's wrath at his commanders; there would be defeat. But in 1941, defeat was still a long time and millions of lives away.

Part Three

1

The smiling faces, festive music, and loud chatting everywhere on the streets of Moscow were extraordinary after so much time spent in grief, worries, and tears. People had forgotten happiness, but they had not forgotten how to resurrect it. At last, on May 9, 1945, they received the welcome news of the victory. Happiness burst out like a colorful spring flower with all its glory and beauty. For four long years—four long years!—the war had killed, ruined, destroyed, and humiliated, and now it was over. Germany had capitulated! Life was going to be life again, not a constant state of apprehension: where is the front, is my son alive, will I ever see my husband again, when can we go back to our town? For four years, there had been no life apart from death.

When Tanya first heard of the war's end, her instinct was to go outside. There, on the streets, her countrymen were celebrating the end of cruelty and terror. Tanya wanted to be with them. The human whirlwind took her and moved from street to street. It was amazing to feel part of a nation that just defeated the Nazi hydra so powerful, so fearsome, that—had it not been stopped—could have devoured the entire world. The first hour on the sunlit Moscow streets full of joyful people was intoxicating and Tanya had almost forgotten her personal pain beyond the war—she was still trying to find her husband who had disappeared, victim to another hydra. This domestic hydra created grief and pain comparable to the Nazis' if your loved ones were her victims, and Tanya could not know in the spring of 1945 whether that hydra was still alive and hungry. She had not really forgotten—she just allowed herself to feel the sun, feel the breeze, feel human again, but she had not forgotten.

Ever since Yasha was taken away nine years ago, Tanya had not stopped thinking of him and hoping to have a family again. Now the hope of finding her husband sprang up. She asked Sasha to use his connections for this purpose, and within a couple of months, good news arrived: he was alive in Vorkuta!

A train station. Last hugs with Sasha and his family. The train departing—its wheels churning slowly, then faster, faster, faster, until a certain pitch is reached. As Tanya watched the Moscow buildings melt into the past, her heart was racing toward the future in unison with the wheels, the sweet wheels that carried her to Yasha. Faster, faster, higher pitch, faster! Tanya and her daughters, all reunited as soon as the Germans were pushed away from Moscow, could not wait. But wait they had to, because the trip was long. They would stop at many stations—large and small, cross many rivers—wide and narrow, and see different landscapes as they rode across a big part of Russia going north-east, but mostly north.

And finally, after a two-week journey, Vorkuta—just a small town built by zehkee, the prisoners, to support coal mining in the area, the place populated primarily by former prisoners and some volunteers attracted by the double salaries of the remote North. It looked gray and uninviting, but to Tanya it was better than Moscow because her husband was here. They found a place to stay overnight, and the next day the search began. They needed jobs, a place to live, and, most importantly, find their husband and father. They went out on the streets, which, they did not realize, Yasha had helped create. Vorkuta had grown significantly since his arrival and looked like a real town, with a central square, administrative buildings, and wooden houses.

Finding out the location of the labor camp was easy. While walking in the given direction, Tanya was thinking, "Will I be able to see him?" and "Is he in a condition to recognize me?"

The camp appeared suddenly. Tall poles topped with large stars flanked the entrance gate, the crosspiece connecting them high, the entire structure affecting people underneath it not unlike a cathedral with its powerful impact on small humans. The placard on the crosspiece pronounced that work in the USSR was a matter of honor, glory, and valor—one of the postulates of the Soviet state religion of Communism.

"My Yasha has to be secured inside this concoction?" thought Tanya of the enclosed camp as she was approaching the gate. Coming closer, she saw a booth. Inhaling deeply, as if preparing for a difficult task, she walked to it. A young sentry with a rifle asked her for their credentials.

"I have just arrived and need to find my husband." Her voice cracked from all the tears waiting to come out, but she controlled herself. "I was told in Moscow that he is here. Can I see the camp director?"

"The camp director does not meet with every person who comes here with questions."

"Who can I talk to about my husband? It is such a long way from Moscow, I need to find him."

"I don't know. All I know is that you cannot come through."

"I would really appreciate it if you tell me what I can do to find him. I just want to know if he is here."

"Please leave the premises."

Tanya walked out and stood by the entrance, her daughters calming her down: "Mom, we'll find Father, don't worry."

She looked up at the placard, she read the words carefully again, and thought, "Honor, valor—what kind of honor is there in being a prisoner when no crime has been committed? What right does a state have to force people to become slaves? What glory is there in punishment without crime? And who are these words for in this desolate place? For those who suffer and struggle to survive and who don't have a choice but to perform the tasks that the camp staff want? This is ridiculous!" Tanya recalled what she had read in a newspaper, that at the gate of the most famous concentration camp built by the Germans to exterminate the Jews—Auschwitz—a similar sign proclaimed, "Work makes people free!" Different states, different facades—the same slogans.

At last, the guard, seeing the tears of the women, relented, came out and said, "Prisoners usually come back by eight o'clock."

Later in the day, Tanya returned alone while her daughters were looking for jobs and food. In the middle of the polar summer, none of the usual signs of time change existed, and Tanya's brain, unaccustomed to this phenomenon, registered no significant passing of time when she saw a column of people moving toward the entrance. Tanya focused on those people and quickly figured out that they were prisoners, surrounded by the guards, coming back to the camp. They were prisoners; Yasha could be among them! Tanya started to walk briskly toward the approaching column. And here they were: tired, grim, and haggard. Tanya's eyes analyzed each face in the column, looking for the one she hoped to recognize and worrying, "What if he changed so much that I would not be able to recognize him?"

"Yasha, Yasha Nepomnyashchy, Yashenka, Yasha!"

The guards were looking at her suspiciously, saying nothing.

"Yasha, Yasha Nepomnyashchy!"

"He is not here!" somebody yelled from inside the column. "He is in the print shop in town."

Tanya's face lit up.

"Thank you, comrade!"

Tanya was happy; she started crying. The column passed and Tanya still stood there, exhausted by her efforts and overwhelmed with emotion. Yasha was alive! Now it was only a matter of finding the print shop in town and she would see her husband.

The print shop was housed in a medium-sized wooden building, which looked like many others in Vorkuta. But by this building's front door stood an armed guard.

"I seek my husband, Yasha Nepomnyashchy. I was told he works here," Tanya said to the guard.

"Wait here," the guard replied and disappeared into the building.

Soon, a small figure dressed in drab clothes walked out. The figure was shriveled and haggard, only the eyes signifying life in that body, but it was enough for Tanya because those were Yasha's eyes. When Yasha's gaze focused on his wife, he was shocked.

"How did you find me?" Yasha's lips widened into a smile.

So they stood opposite each other, incredulous at their luck, enjoying what they saw. "Yasha looks awful," Tanya thought, "no teeth, balding, and colorless, but he is alive!" That was all she asked for, and she was granted her wish in full. They embraced, they kissed, they could not separate.

The guard interrupted the couple. "You have thirty minutes. Go inside; I will be outside. When I come back, you leave."

They had half an hour. After the long years of separation—a half-hour together.

Yasha asked first, "How are the children, you, everybody else?"

"Anya and Meri are here, looking for jobs today. They are grown women now. I am all right. Things were not good in Kiev. Your parents and Zhenya were killed by the Nazis." Tanya stopped because Yasha's face twisted, tears poured from his eyes, and he began sobbing uncontrollably. She hugged him and stayed quiet to let him grieve for a while, without telling the entire story of betrayal and murder. He would learn it in due time. Then he wiped the tears and said, "What about Anna?"

"She and Victor are back in Kiev. Victor was an officer in the army and came from the front with many medals. He is free now."

"And Vasili?"

"He was arrested right after you and died within a week. Zhenya thought they tortured him to death."

They were quiet for a few seconds and then Tanya continued, "I know nothing about Sergey and Katya."

"I saw Sergey."

"Really? Where is he?"

"He is dead. He was here before I came and he died."

It was Tanya's turn to cry. The arrests and war had taken half of their family. How the other half would live was not clear yet either, with Yasha still a prisoner and Katya not accounted for at all. Such was the toll of the last nine years. But those were past years; they were gone, and the survivors needed to live in the present and plan for a brighter future. They had to; otherwise, the tortured and tormented would not be avenged.

Tanya felt it was time to change the conversation topic.

"What about this shop, Yasha? Are you still a prisoner here?"

"Oh, this shop! You know, it is my savior. We started it a few years ago. Because of my experience, I was asked to build and manage it. I was able to bring with me whoever I wanted. I took the weakest ones who would probably not survive in the camp. But I am still a prisoner, although the work is not back breaking in the freezing air, and after work it is quiet and safe here."

Yasha stopped, looked around, and lowered his voice. "It is possible that I could get the status of an exile and live almost free, in Vorkuta only, of course, but free from a guard looking over my shoulder all the time. I think it may happen soon!" Yasha was excited about the prospect, especially now that his family had joined him.

They heard the deliberate steps of the guard. It was time for Tanya to leave. She hugged Yasha and said, "I am going to look for a job and will let you know where we are."

"Why don't you try the local library? They don't have anybody who really knows what to do."

At the dormitory, she found two jubilant faces—her daughters'—who proudly announced that they had found jobs: Lara with a construction company—she had graduated from a university, and Meri as a secretary. In addition, Lara was granted a small room in a barracks—really small, but with a kitchen on premises. And when they heard of Tanya's success, the cries and laughter would not stop. It was a good day!

2

The next day, Tanya found a job at the library. It was a small library, quite neglected without appropriate professional attention, but she was in her environment once again, plus the job paid wages. Spending most of her career in libraries, Tanya was one of those lucky people who sincerely enjoyed their vocation and always looked forward to the next working day. It was like that in Kiev in the largest Ukrainian library, and it was the same here in Vorkuta. Cleaning, filing, learning what was needed—the day was a blast, and in the evening she was hoping to meet her husband again. Now was a good opportunity to plan the future; at least this was Tanya's thinking, propelled by their successes in Vorkuta. When an experience is positive, humans think it will never end.

Yasha was finally released from the camp and assigned to run the print shop. From a prisoner he became an exile and could not leave Vorkuta, but life with his wife and children was far superior to his former existence. They all moved into a small room, where all three women in his life were present, but not for long. The older daughter, Lara, married one of Yasha's closest compatriots—Mamut, who had also been released and, as a technical person, had found a job in the same company as Lara. They liked each other so much that in less than a month decided to marry. Lara left her parents' room and moved in with Mamut in another barracks. One loving event after another!

One afternoon, an old woman knocked on the door tagged "Director" in the print shop. The shop was not guarded anymore, since all the people working in it had been transformed into *free* citizens of Vorkuta, and Yasha was the director. When the woman walked in, they both could not say a word for a few seconds.

"Is that you, Katya?"

"Yasha, is that you?"

They had not seen each other in a while, and hard times had changed them considerably. Katya had come looking for a job and found a long-lost friend.

"Katya, my dear! I am glad to see you, but what are you doing here?"

Katya did not answer. Instead she hugged Yasha and kept him close, afraid of losing him again. Yasha walked Katya to the chair and let her sit. She still could not talk, so Yasha just observed her. She had always been beautiful, with her blonde hair and sparkling blue eyes, and now Yasha saw an old, wrinkled woman with a gray face and dim eyes full of sorrow. And then she talked.

"I was sent to Vorkuta after the birth of my daughter."

"Daughter? What daughter?"

"When we were arrested, I was pregnant. She was given—thank God!—to my mother, and I was sent here in 1938. Last week, I was freed—with no right to leave this town, but freed—and now I need a job."

"Don't worry about the job. I'll find something for you in the shop. But how did you do over these years, and where is your daughter?"

"My daughter is here with me. My mother raised her and after the war came to Vorkuta so we could be together. It was tough during all these years, and I still don't know anything about my husband." Katya began sobbing again, as did Yasha; he had to tell her.

"Sergey was here since 1937. I joined him the next year and was with him when he died."

When Yasha pronounced that word, Katya started to shake almost silently. It was as if she had already thought it all through, was ready for such an end, and did not have much energy to grieve louder.

"What did he do to them to deserve such a fate?" Katya was asking a rhetorical question and Yasha did not respond. There was nothing he could say to make her feel better, so he just waited for Katya to come back from the state of despair.

When she did, Katya wanted to know how he had died and, after contemplating Yasha's answer for a few seconds, shook her head and said, "Tell me about yourself; how did you manage?"

"It was not easy. As you know, surviving in this environment could be a matter of luck. Mine was the print shop, but only after a while, a long while. Before the shop, it was the support of my friends that sustained me and the hope of seeing my family again. Now, Tanya is here with both our daughters. We survived, but many others have not." And he explained the fate of those they both knew. "You should come to our place tonight with your daughter and mother. Tanya will be ecstatic to see you, and we have much more to talk about."

When it was time for Katya to leave, Yasha accompanied her to the street and then stood there watching the small figure slowly walking

208

away. It was obvious she carried an awful weight on her shoulders that pressed her body down to the ground, making her movements not slow, but struggling—struggling to live against what seemed to be an overwhelming force that created pain and disasters for no apparent reason. Sad, sad, sad destruction of such a vigorous family, which had to live through so much terror. And Yasha did not even know all of it yet.

3

After many years of deprivation and suffering, Yasha enjoyed *freedom*. Yes, he was not actually free, but it was freedom nevertheless, compared to his prior existence. Having his family together satisfied many, many needs. So what if he could not leave Vorkuta or do what he wanted to do? Yasha felt content and happy.

It did not last long.

Tanya's heart problems reappeared with gusto, impacted by the Vorkuta climate. Worse, there were no special facilities for heart patients and no medicine. Yasha begged her, "Please, dear, go to Moscow. Sasha will find the best care to help you."

"I lived long enough without you; I am not going away alone. Whatever my fate, I want to meet it with my family around."

Tanya's health was deteriorating. And then one morning she said, "I saw myself walking in a vineyard. The sun was shining; I was pulling off grapes and eating them—they were so sweet and juicy! When I woke up, I still tasted them in my mouth. And I still crave them!"

"I promise to bring you grapes!"

Yasha grabbed his coat and ran to the airport. He knew some pilots flying back and forth between Vorkuta and the "big land"—big cities. Luckily, one pilot was just about to walk to his plane, and Yasha asked him to buy grapes for his wife. The price was his monthly salary but it was irrelevant. If his suffering wife wanted grapes, she would have grapes.

Tanya died before the desired grapes and Sasha's medicine that Yasha had requested arrived. Passed away an exceptional human being, full of kindness, love, creativity, and joy. She could have brought a lot more to many people, but it was not to be. Her loving heart was her weakest point. At the cemetery, Yasha watched the casket being lowered into the ground. He threw some dirt on the casket, trying to be strong and not cry, but it was difficult. It hurt a great deal. Something inside him was so distraught and out of balance that no physical pain could compare with this torture. As more dirt piled up on top of the casket, Yasha's suffering became more acute. It would have been totally unbearable if not for his children, who hugged him and cried with him.

Yasha was working and was surrounded by his daughters and friends. But the pain would not subside, especially in the evenings when he was alone. Life, though, is a dynamo. Soon after the tragic event, Meri came home with a man and announced, "Daddy, this is Kusma, my husband. We decided to register today."

Yasha shook hands with his new and unexpected son-in-law and in his present state of mind, which did not have much room for joy, offered him tea. Sitting at the table sipping tea, Yasha said, "This is so sudden. I now have a new son-in-law, but I don't know anything about you."

"I am from Kharkov."

"Oh, we were neighbors at one time! And how did you find your way to this lucky place?"

"I was a lieutenant on the western front. We were surrounded by the Germans in the first days of the war, and I, among thousands of others, became a prisoner. I ripped off the officer's insignia to have a chance at surviving, and I did survive until the Red Army freed us, but was sent here as a traitor. Now I work in the mine and also coach the gymnastics teams."

"So, you were an officer?"

"Yes, I was, but kind of by accident. I did study in a military school, although did not complete it, but I had some training. So, when new recruits lined up for a roll call, I answered in a loud, confident voice, and they called me afterward and said I am a lieutenant now commanding a platoon. They gave us one rifle and some bullets for every ten soldiers. It was pretty bad in the beginning."

"And why are you here as a traitor?"

"Well, we were not supposed to be captured alive," Kusma said with some sarcasm, and then, as if remembering something, added, "I am not complaining. Comrade Stalin is right—we should not have been captured."

The last statement really irritated Yasha, and in a different tone of voice, he asked, "And how were you supposed to do that in your situation?"

"I should have left one bullet and shot myself," proudly answered Kusma, which was followed by the cold reply of his annoyed father-in-law:

"And what about those who did not have any guns, should you not have left bullets for them also, instead of shooting at the enemy?"

Meri decided to interrupt the conversation, which was going downhill fast.

"Dad, Kusma lives in the dormitory for single men, we cannot stay there together."

Yasha thought for a second and replied, "You can stay here. I will temporarily move to the shop and then we'll see."

In the morning, he took some clothes, a pillow, and a blanket, and settled in his office. Two months later, a room in the new barracks became available and Yasha moved in. The room was larger than before and more comfortable. Soon after, Meri announced that she was pregnant. It was great news for Yasha. He would have a grandchild, maybe even a granddaughter resembling Tanya. Something to look forward to!

But fate was not good to them. This time it was Lara. After arriving in Vorkuta, she also developed heart problems and, just like with her mother, not much could be done when the pain began. Sasha did send medicine, but she needed a good doctor to diagnose her disease, and she could not travel to Moscow alone in her condition. Since both Yasha and Mamut were not free to travel and a pregnant Meri could not, Lara was stuck.

Worries about Meri's pregnancy and Lara's heart preoccupied the family until a bundle of joy finally arrived. It was a girl, and they named her Svetlana, a name rooted in the word "svet"—light in Russian. It was Yasha's light, Yasha's hope for a better future. But this light could not help Lara. Within a month of Svetlana's birth, she expired. Two precious lives melted away within a short time and left Yasha devastated. Only his little granddaughter sustained his desire to live. He needed her and, although she did not realize it yet, she needed him—his love, his wisdom, his guidance, his protection.

Yasha knew that.

Four years later, both Svetlana and Vorkuta had grown. Vorkuta acquired many more buildings that made it look more like a real city. Svetlana and her parents moved to live with Yasha as their room was so small that the three of them could hardly walk in it. Yasha's was a corner room—larger than others in the barracks—and the family enjoyed better living conditions.

The building was constructed from logs packed with oakum between them, so the more outside walls there were—a corner room!—the colder it was in the winter. But in a larger room Svetlana could ride a bike around the table in the middle of the room. Besides the table and chairs, there were three beds: Yasha's stood by the stove—the warmest place, Svetlana's—on the outside wall, and her parents'—on the inside. On especially cold days, the oakum was covered with rime and Svetlana played with it right in her bed.

Svetlana was a happy and curious child, hungry for knowledge, hungry for play. She loved dancing and singing, and she enjoyed fairytales, especially read by her grandpa.

Their mornings usually began with Yasha starting the stove and Svetlana taking her clothes to bed and clutching them under her body to warm them up. When it was safe to put them on, she did it under the blanket, then jumped out of bed and heard her grandfather's voice, "Wash off your zoo," which meant to wash the microbes from her hands—he had told her stories about the millions of microbes crawling all over the skin and the need to be clean. Actually, washing was not as simple as it sounded because before using the water kept in a bucket by the door, Yasha had to break the web of thin ice that appeared overnight over the liquid. The water was freezing cold, which made Svetlana always think of it as of little animals biting her when splashed it on her face, and she looked for ways to avoid it.

"Washing with cold water indoors makes it easier to tolerate the cold outside," Yasha reminded his granddaughter.

It was true, she learned, and she followed the directions of her grandfather. She was confident that he knew everything and absorbed his stories, which he was always ready to dispense. It was Yasha's pleasure to spend time with his little granddaughter, and he had plenty of opportunities. She was such a joy in his life, and he was becoming everything to her. Many a time little Svetlana saw her grandfather looking at her with such love and admiration that she would cling to him, her small arms pulling him close, and then she would hear him say, "My sheineh punim," and feel his kiss on her eyes, which, he always said, reminded him of his father.

After washing, dressing, and eating, Yasha put his Svetlana into a sled to take her to the kindergarten. He covered her with a blanket and tied a woolen scarf around her face so only her eyes sparkled out of the bundle. Then Yasha went to work.

When not in a kindergarten, children played games outside, if the weather allowed it. One of their favorites was "Russians and Germans"—the heroes and villains game, with the villains, obviously, being the Germans. Nobody wanted to be "German" because they were bad and had to lose, so the decision was usually made by throwing a coin. There were many Russified ethnic Germans among the exiles—

those who had stayed in Russia since the time of Peter the Great—deported as potential spies when the war began. Their children did not always know they were of German descent. The neighbors, though, knew. Once, Svetlana's friends, Petr and Vova, argued who should be Russian and who German.

"I was German last time! It's my turn to be Russian," Vova said.

"Vova, you are a German anyway; why don't you want to be German in the game?"

Vova stopped arguing, thought for a second, and started crying.

"Why are you crying?" Svetlana asked.

"I am not German!"

"German, German. My father said you are Germans," Petr shouted.

"It's okay to be German," Svetlana said, but Vova would not stop crying. Then she found a solution.

"Vova, don't cry; I will always play German and you can be Russian." That did not work either, so Svetlana added, "I will marry you."

Vova stopped crying and smiled, while Petr shouted, "But you promised to marry me! You can't have two husbands."

The boys started pushing each other until Svetlana intervened. "Boys, don't fight. My grandfather told me that in some countries men have many wives, and he is smart—he knows everything. I am sure we can find a country where a woman can have a few husbands and we will go there."

"But how would we leave this country?" Petr asked. "I heard my parents saying that our country is a big prison."

"My grandpa thinks everyone will be free one day and will go anywhere they want," said Svetlana. Their conversation was interrupted by the voice of her grandpa: "Svetlanka, come home. We have to go to the theater."

"Are the Germans bad?" were the first words Svetlana pronounced at home.

"There are no good or bad nationalities. There are only good or bad people. Some Germans are bad, like those who killed my parents, and some are good."

"What is my nationality?"

"You have a little of everything, like a beautiful bouquet of flowers, each flower a different nationality. And we cannot talk more right now. Remember, we have tickets to the theater."

"Just one small thing," Svetlana said, showing how small it was with her hands. "Why do men have so much hair on their bodies and women don't?"

Yasha was not ready for this. He moved his glasses up toward his forehead and looked intently at his granddaughter.

"Scientists believe that people evolved from apes. Apes had a lot of hair to protect them from the cold, but when some of them descended from the trees and began living on land, after hunting and working for thousands of years they became people and covered themselves with animal skins. They did not need hair any longer."

"I got it! Women came down from the trees thousands of years before men did. So, they lost their hair earlier, while men are still losing it!" finished Svetlana triumphantly, and Yasha, in disbelief, replied, "Sounds logical. Let's go to the theater."

Food for the soul in Vorkuta was supplied by a theater company where many professional actors, musicians, and other so-called workers of culture residing in the town (not of their own volition) performed. The local theater, built of logs like everything else in town, staged plays, ballets, and concerts. Today, it was a ballet. Yasha and Meri always took Svetlana with them when attending a performance, but most of all she enjoyed the ballet. After a performance, Svetlana would not stop dancing, repeating the movements and poses she saw on stage—she loved dancing. One day, Yasha collected Svetlana at the kindergarten and said, "We are going to the ballet school."

Svetlana was thrilled; she wanted to run, not walk. The ballet school director, who knew Yasha well, was not thrilled at all to accept such a little child.

He said, "It would be too difficult for her."

Yasha insisted, "She is dancing all day anyway. At least she would do it right." The director finally gave in and Svetlana became a student.

As it was the beginning of December, the ballet school was practicing for the New Year performance. All the roles had already been given out, and Svetlana was too little to dance anything complicated anyway. Nevertheless, to make her part of the team, she was assigned a small role at the end of the show. All she had to do was walk out on stage, take the hand of the first dancer, and lead her and the rest of the crew away from the stage. Svetlana was practicing every day, but she became concerned with her role and shared her thoughts with her grandpa.

"My role is so small, I have nothing to do."

"But you were given a solo part. Not everybody dances solo."

"But it's so short!"

"Do you recall a movie about the circus? Do you recall a small man who appeared for a few seconds, but everyone remembers his performance? It's not the length of the role but how well you perform that counts."

Svetlana understood well what he meant and kept practicing with extra concentration. She did not bother Grandpa any more with her doubts, and he forgot the conversation. The day of the New Year performance came quickly. Svetlana took her teddy bear—her grandpa's present. Hugging her grandfather, she whispered into his ear, "Today I will dance for you."

The theater was packed. Yasha, Meri, Katya, her daughter Irina, and her mother were in attendance waiting for their ballet star. The music began, then the dance. One after another, the scenes changed, and finally the end was near. It was time for Svetlana's little solo. Her family was breathless. And there she was, a little—the smallest of all dancers—girl coming out from behind the curtain. She was supposed to approach the first dancer, but what was this? The little star made ballet figures, imitating what she had seen before; she danced and danced around the others, without approaching them as planned. Everyone now saw a teddy bear in her hands. She lifted it up and took it down as she danced. The school director was almost dying of laughter, affected by Svetlana's unexpected performance. The other girls reminded her what to do: "Pull the string! Pull." But she had her own plan. Finally, she approached the dancers and took them away. The audience clapped enthusiastically, as if they had just observed a performance by the best dancer in the world.

In her grandfather's arms, Svetlana asked, "Do you think they will remember me?"

"Absolutely!"

4

Meri's married life was not going well. Almost right after the marriage, Kusma's behavior indicated affairs. He was not helping much with the child and was disappearing often. Meri threatened to divorce him, and Kusma begged her not to do it. He promised to change, but he loved himself and the women around him too much.

The disappearing acts continued. Every time, when asked, Kusma said he was with one friend or another who was off work on vacation. Most people could not leave Vorkuta for a vacation. Where would they go? Any reasonable place of attraction was far and getting there was expensive. They stayed put and ended up quickly drinking through all the vacation pay, going back to work within a few days. Kusma did not drink at all, but he always claimed to attend such gatherings. Finally, a disappointed and frustrated Meri succumbed to the letters from Moscow and Yasha's exhortation, and bought a ticket to the capital. She knew her father could handle Svetlana while she traveled to the past. The letters were from an admirer. They had met during the war and had not married only because he did not want to follow Meri to Vorkuta and she did not want to live far from her family. Now she thought of a second chance. One morning, after saying good-bye to her father and daughter, she boarded a train for the long journey to Moscow.

The next day, Svetlana fell ill. It was something different from a simple cold and Yasha took Svetlana to the hospital. It turned out that there was an epidemic of scarlet fever in the kindergarten and a few of Svetlana's friends were already in the hospital. Yasha knew that many children died in Vorkuta because of the combination of bad climate, poor diet, and lack of medicine. He was distressed and went to talk with the doctor.

"Do you have the medicine the kids need? Tell me now and I will send an urgent telegram to Moscow. We will get the medicine."

"No need."

Yasha visited the clinic often to observe his little light and saw her condition worsening. She lay in bed with a high fever, and the doctor explained Svetlana had also contracted measles and that the combination of diseases was dangerous.

"How did she contract measles?"

"She is in the infectious diseases ward; children often contract diseases from other children."

"Then why do you keep them all together?"

"There is not enough room to separate them and we need to protect the rest of the population by keeping the sick ones here—that's our main task. Besides, antibiotics are scarce."

"But you are killing our children! I asked you if you needed any medicine and you said no."

"I don't have to explain anything to you. I am doing my job the best I can."

"I warn you," angrily said the usually calm Yasha, "if our children die, you will be in trouble. I will have nothing to lose. For you, they are just the zehkee's children, but for us, they are the hope we live for."

Yasha left the hospital, collected all the money he had at home, and went to a nurse who was known to dispense scarce medicine for a significant fee. The fee was not important to Yasha; he was about to lose another member of his shrinking family and he would fight to preclude it. The nurse had the necessary antibiotics. Clearly, they were from the hospital supplies. Yasha bought enough antibiotics for all the kids in the hospital and soon they were going home, one by one. It was cold outside, but when Yasha carried Svetlana, he felt warmth and happiness—she was saved, she did not leave him, she would grow up and give light to him and other people.

So far, the year 1953 had not been good. Meri had to leave, Svetlana was very ill, and the weather seemed more brutal than usual. One blizzard came after another, and the prickly wind hit faces with a vengeance as never before. Electricity disappeared consistently and then the candles came out with their dim light that barely allowed reading. It was a depressing winter. And then came March 6. On this day, Stalin's death was officially announced. A tyrant had died, a sadist personally responsible for the destruction of millions. Better news would be hard to imagine in a place where most people were sent because of him. People wanted to cheer, but they were obligated to cry. Nobody—neither prisoners nor guards—knew what to expect next. Would the prisoners be released? Would more arrests follow? Who would run the country and how? Would Beria—that bloodsucker—take over the government?

The safest action to take was to stay calm and invisible, crying and acting sad in public. Svetlana, a small but observant child, came home that day from the kindergarten and asked, "Grandpa, why are all the adults crying?"

"Because they are afraid of him even when he is dead," Yasha answered, forgetting in his happiness that he was talking to a little child. He added, "But don't tell this to anyone because I can be arrested, you understand?"

"Yes, Grandfather. Can I tell my friend Vova?"

"Nobody means nobody, including Vova. Promise me."

The evening was spent with Katya and her family. The mood was festive, but their behavior was subdued to avoid giving anyone an opportunity to denounce them. Coming home after the quiet celebration, Yasha put Svetlana to bed and read her a fairytale. Svetlana loved these minutes before falling asleep: her beloved grandfather putting her in bed, tucking her blanket neatly, feeling secure and warm, and listening to those thrilling tales of remote places and wonderful heroes. Yasha opened the book where they had left off the day before and announced the title of the new tale in his most mysterious voice, "Eternal Dragon."

Svetlana, full of anticipation, curled her legs under the blanket and was all attention.

"There was a beautiful village where everyone was happy, until one day a fire-spewing dragon appeared and demanded the most gorgeous young woman. The dragon burned down a house to show his power and threatened to destroy the entire village. The villagers gave in. With tears in their eyes, they selected the most beautiful maiden and the dragon left with her, commanding them to bring to his palace a maiden every year. And every year the villagers cried and selected a beautiful maiden for the dragon. Life in the village changed, as there was always the threat for any family to lose a child to the dragon. Strong warriors wanted to defeat the dragon and every year a young man would tempt his fate, but nobody ever came back, and the village kept feeding the dragon. Many years passed, and an exceptional warrior was raised in the village who decided to try his luck and liberate the people. The best blacksmith made him a sword and chain armor, and he went to the dragon's palace." Yasha stopped for a second to observe his granddaughter, but she was not asleep yet.

"The warrior was very strong, and the fight with the dragon was even. At last, the warrior managed to strike the dragon right in the heart and he fell down, bleeding and dying. Then the dragon said, 'Once, I was a strong warrior too and wanted to liberate my village. I defeated the dragon and walked into his palace, where I found riches beyond anybody's belief. I was in awe, and the minute I touched the riches, I was transformed into the dragon and became just as terrible as the one I killed. Be careful, don't touch anything, just leave.' And the dragon died.

"The warrior thought for a second and decided to take a look inside. He walked into the palace and saw jewels and gold and other unimaginable riches. His mind was clouded by what he saw and he could not leave. He wanted to touch the jewels, he wanted to take some with him, but the moment he took one, he became the dragon."

5

"They arrested Irina!" were Katya's first words when she walked into Yasha's room.

Katya cried. She was so distressed her body shook uncontrollably. Yasha offered her some water, but she could not even hold the glass without spilling its contents.

"Katya, what happened?"

"Irina was in school when Stalin's death was announced. Some children cried, and she said, 'Why are you crying? There will be another Stalin.'"

Yasha wanted to calm Katya down. He sat next to her and quietly said, "Katya, Stalin is gone. I am sure everything will be different from now on. They arrested her as they arrested millions before, but the situation is changed and she should be out soon, she is just a child."

"You don't understand!" Katya shouted suddenly. Her eyes were sparkling with anger and then she cried again.

"What do you mean?"

"Stalin is dead, but all those sadists who work in jails and interrogate prisoners—they are still there, they are still the same! And do you know what they do to women? I was pregnant and they raped me. They raped me every day, one after another, those bastards. Do you know what it feels like when people strip you of your dignity and do whatever they like because they have the power and you are a nothing, nothing? I saw women losing their minds. What do you think they would do to a beautiful young girl, like my Irina?"

Katya was wailing and Yasha was in shock. He felt Katya's pain and anger with every fiber of his being. After losing so many of his loved ones, he was familiar with this pain, but just imagining his child being raped brought him to tears and curled his fingers into fists. But what could he do?

Taking Katya home was a chore. She wanted to go to the jail, but Yasha persuaded her not to encounter the authorities. Yasha's heart was also heavy with the thought of his possible arrest. At home, he talked to his granddaughter:

"Svetlanka, last night Irina was arrested because she said something inappropriate. This is important, do not share whatever you hear from me or other adults with anybody. Remember."

"Can I share what I have heard from kids?"

"Sure you can," Yasha answered quickly, and then felt uneasy about his permission. "What exactly have you heard from children?"

"I remember someone saying our country is a big prison."

Yasha felt sweat gathering on his forehead. "Please, Svetlana, don't repeat this to anyone."

"Is it true?"

"You cannot say this. Have you shared it with anybody else?"

"No, I forgot it."

"Then forget it again. And remember, if they arrest me, Aunt Klava will take care of you until I return. I promise to return quickly, and you know I always keep my word."

That night, two men came to arrest him. Svetlana heard them, jumped on Yasha, and yelled, "Don't go, Grandpa, they are bad people!" She started crying.

"Don't cry, Svetlanka! Be strong. I will be back soon."

Yasha kissed Svetlana and was ready to go.

"Where are her parents?" asked one of the men.

"They work a night shift," Yasha replied, lying in order to avoid them taking Svetlana to the children's asylum.

Yasha left. Svetlana was still crying when a neighbor—Aunt Klava—walked in and hugged her.

"Don't worry, child. I will stay with you, and your grandfather will be back soon."

Klava took care of Svetlana, who did not go to the kindergarten anymore but sat at the window looking for her beloved grandfather to come home. She did not want to miss him. One day, a group of

222

prisoners arrived right in front of her barracks. They were digging a trench and Svetlana saw them. A child of exiles, she immediately knew they were prisoners. Her grandfather was also a prisoner—he must be there. Svetlana quickly put on her warm clothes and ran outside.

"Grandfather, Grandfather!" Svetlana shouted, running along the line of prisoners working on the trench.

The guard observed a child running around and calling for her grandfather. He laughed; for him, it was funny.

"What's your name?" asked one of the prisoners.

"Svetlana."

"I don't think your grandfather is here, Svetlana."

"But he was arrested, he must be among you!"

Another prisoner working nearby looked at the child. "My daughter's name is also Svetlana. She was as little as you are when I was arrested. Where she is now—I don't know." His voice grew louder and louder, approaching a hysterical level. "I know nothing about my wife, my child, nothing!"

Suddenly, he dropped the shovel and started running away, still shouting. A loud bang punched through the winter air and the prisoner fell down, the snow around him reddening. Svetlana understood that something terrible had just happened. She screamed and ran home, where a blanket over her head and a teddy bear—Grandpa's present—pressed to her heart provided some comfort while she cried herself to sleep.

A few days later, Svetlana was sitting at the window and saw her grandfather on the street, walking toward their barracks. When he walked in, she jumped on him and said, "Grandfather, you came back, you kept your word! But promise me you will never leave me alone and we will always be together."

"I promise!" Yasha squeezed the child tightly, as if afraid to lose her.

6

The Gulag started to come apart, slowly but definitively. Yasha, along with thousands of others, was still exiled. Was his latest arrest just a result of the inertia of a large bureaucracy that took time to change, was it in reaction to the uncertainty after the death of the despot, was it a mistake, or did somebody denounce him? There was no way to know. He returned alive, which all he and Svetlana wanted.

Yasha was hungry for information about his family. A letter from Meri was waiting for him. Meri had good news: she met the fellow she used to date and had decided to divorce Kusma and move with Svetlana to Moscow to marry the old friend. Yasha liked this development because he knew Kusma would always be just a visiting husband with no responsibilities and no intention of helping the family. The other part of the letter was depressing: even in death Stalin killed people. The crowd in Moscow to see Stalin's coffin was so large that many people were crushed to death.

The next thing on Yasha's mind was Katya.

"Has Katya visited you?" He asked Svetlana.

"No, she has not."

"It is strange she has not come!" thought Yasha and asked Svetlana to stay home while he went to Katya's place. He found Katya's neighbor who told him what had happened. A few days after Irina's arrest, Katya learned that her daughter died of pneumonia. This terrible event had devastating consequences. When Katya took possession of her baby's corpse she noticed—it was difficult not to notice!—that the body of her daughter had bruises and bite marks all over it. She did not die of pneumonia; she was tortured to death! Katya's mother had a heart attack and died. A few days later, neighbors found Katya's body hanging in her room. Sergey's family was finished.

Yasha ran away from Katya's apartment. He could not bear losing dear people like this. Tears were streaming down his cheeks as he walked briskly to the cemetery. He now had more people he loved in the Vorkuta cemetery than alive. He could spend hours at the cemetery talking to his wife, daughter, and friends about life. There was no one at home but a child, just a little child, who did not understand all this yet, and Yasha did not really want her to understand it. How could he explain the reason they were all here? Yasha's shoulders stooped as he thought, "And one day I will also end up here." Then he shook himself. "Stop it! Stop it! You have a beautiful child to help raise. She needs you. Without you, who knows what her destiny would be? You have to live for her, and she will be better off with you around." With that, Yasha walked away from the cemetery, leaving the dead behind and looking forward to seeing his light.

In a week, Meri came back and began preparations for the divorce. Kusma did not appreciate that. He liked women, but also wanted a family. He begged Meri for forgiveness and promised to change. He focused on their daughter. "Do you think a stranger is going to be a better father than me?"

Meri wanted to believe him and decided to give him one last chance. They agreed to move to Kharkov, where his parents lived, as soon as he was free.

They left in the spring.

A few months later, Yasha was also freed. He went to Kiev to join his sister Anna. Coming to the place where his sister used to live was a disappointment as she did not live there any longer. He had to find out her new address in an inquiry office. The new address pointed to an older part of town that he needed to take a tram to. The apartment was on the first floor of a solid building, just a few steps up and....

Yasha rang the bell and a short woman opened the door. They looked at each other and did not know whether to smile or cry. Almost twenty years had been lost, and they hardly recognized each other. They hugged and absorbed what they saw: a gray-haired sister and a bald, thin, toothless brother.

"Yasha, my God! How thin you are! I felt your ribs. Come in, come in."

Yasha walked into a small, dimly lit corridor and looked around. Four doors faced the corridor, at whose end he noticed a small kitchen.

The doors were to three tenant rooms and a common restroom. Anna opened one door and they stepped into her living quarters, which consisted of a tiny room furnished with two beds—one for Anna and Victor, another for his mother—a couch, and a small table in the center of the room surrounded by four chairs. Moving in the room required turning sideways.

Victor was sitting on the couch and reading a newspaper. He saw Yasha and froze for a moment, not believing his eyes. Then he stood up and *ran* toward Yasha to hug him, tears in his eyes.

"I thought we would never see each other again. I am so glad to see you! Anna, serve dinner—let's celebrate. And we have a lot to talk about."

They talked. Yasha shared the fates of Tanya, Sergey, Katya, and all their children. He talked and cried about all the murdered and tortured souls. Then Anna and Victor described their travails and how they had survived.

"How is Natasha?" Yasha asked.

"My sister? She is alive. That is the best I can say about her. Fate was not kind to her. She had not evacuated from Kiev, and when the Germans came, they took her, like many other young women, and sent her to Germany as a slave worker. She worked for a rich family who treated her like dirt, worse than dirt. They did whatever they wanted with her. After the war ended she was repatriated, but instead of letting her live and recover, the Soviet government sent her to the labor camp as a traitor. How could she be a traitor? Was she responsible for the Germans taking over Kiev? Now she is allowed to write letters and she asks me all the time to petition for her freedom, as if my petition would mean anything to them. Can you imagine, she waited for the end of the war so she could return to the motherland, only to be imprisoned!"

The atmosphere in the room was gloomy after the sad tales and to raise everyone's spirit it was timely for Anna to serve the table for the celebration. Anna had always been a good cook, and Yasha could not wait to taste some homemade food made by a skilled chef with normal ingredients—something he had not experienced in years. The first toast was for all the victims of terror, Nazi and Soviet.

7

Making life normal was not easy for Yasha. The years of imprisonment and hard work in Vorkuta couldn't disappear without leaving a significant residue. Emotionally, he still struggled with the past. But he was finally free; he was looking forward to normalcy, to being with family and friends, to feeling human again. Feeling human required having a place he could call home. Anna let him sleep in her small room, but the neighbors in her communal apartment complained: "There is little space for us; you can't bring another person to live here." That's when Anna found a woman willing to rent out *a corner* in her room to Yasha.

Every morning, Yasha left for his job in a print shop and returned late in the evening. On Sundays, he visited the farmers market, bought full bags of foodstuffs, and brought it to Anna's apartment, where he would spend time with his family. One Sunday, the quarrelsome woman he rented a corner from complained, "You are never home, you behave like a tenant and spend no time with me. I don't like it."

"But I am a tenant and pay rent."

"I want you to marry me and be my husband."

"But I don't want it."

"You either marry me or I will tell the police that you stole something."

"What could anyone steal from you? There is nothing here to steal!" Yasha gestured toward the items in the small room—two narrow beds, a table, some chairs, a sideboard with dishes, and a clock.

"I will say you stole this clock. This is an old clock...."

"You're right, it's quite old; it should be thrown out to the garbage!"

Yasha gathered his belongings and left. Finding another place to stay loomed as an impossible task ahead, but the next day at work his boss intervened. Having solid connections in the right places helped locating a new home. After moving in, Yasha visited Anna at the first opportunity and declared, "Finally, I have a room of my own!"

"Wonderful!" responded Anna. "How many rooms in that apartment?"

"Twenty-four rooms, two communal kitchens, and two toilets. Most of the rooms are occupied by families of three to five people. I think I am the only single guy there, but I have my own room and I can now move Svetlanka in to live with me."

"That is a large communal apartment," said Victor.

"I don't mind. I am getting tired of working and want to enjoy my home and my granddaughter."

Yasha focused on finding a way for Svetlana to join him in his new apartment. She lived in Kharkov with her parents, and legal residence in a new town required permission from the authorities. Getting that permission to move into cities like Kiev was difficult. Yasha discussed his efforts with Victor and Anna at each visit.

"Tell me, Yasha, any progress in securing Svetlana's permit to live with you?" Victor asked while Anna was busy around the table.

"No, not really. You know how difficult it is with the bureaucrats. They keep up an appearance of importance and wait for a bribe. But I don't know how to offer it. I am afraid it will be too little, or I will do something wrong. So, I just keep going from office to office and hoping to find someone who could help. But all I hear in response to my inquiries is *neht*."

"But how do you expect this to be resolved?"

"In a few days, I have an audience at the city hall with an important man. If this does not work out, I don't know what to do next."

The day of the audience arrived, and Yasha worried about results. He went to the city hall dressed in a suit. When the secretary called his name, he opened a door into the office. It was a large—very large—office. Deep inside, he saw a man sitting behind a monstrous desk. His facial expression communicated the same message he had observed with other officials he visited: "You are a bother."

The official did not lift his eyes, just said, "Take a seat. What is it?"

228

"I want to register my granddaughter to live with me in my apartment."

The man was lazily examining the papers when, all of a sudden, he was jolted out of his torpor and looked at Yasha intently.

"Uncle Yasha? Do you remember me? I am Oleg. You helped me when my father died."

It was difficult to recognize a boy in this flabby, middle-aged man with the drink-affected reddish face who sat in his chair like a king on a throne.

"I was looking for you all these years with no success."

"I was exiled. In Vorkuta. My wife and my older daughter died there. As did Sergey and his family. You remember Sergey? And when I returned to Kiev, I did not want to look for you and affect your life," Yasha said with pain.

"Uncle Yasha, I am gratified you are alive; it's so good to see you again."

"I see you are an important man now. All those people waiting in the reception room for an audience with you, and you will decide their fate."

"Well, you are exaggerating, Uncle Yasha. But what can I do for you? I always wanted to thank you for what you had done for me."

"All I want is permission for my granddaughter to live with me in my apartment."

Oleg took the written request, wrote in the left top corner "Approved," and signed it.

"Uncle Yasha, summon your granddaughter. And let's celebrate her coming to the capital together!"

"See, you do decide people's fate," Yasha said with a smile.

8

Oleg cared for Yasha's needs since their meeting. Although Yasha was happy sharing a room in the communal apartment with his granddaughter, Oleg found a way to move them into an apartment in a new development, where they enjoyed the privacy of a studio with a bathroom and kitchen of their own. Plus, an unexpected luxury: a telephone.

With Svetlana around, Yasha's life retained meaning. Long gone were the days of mental terror. New friends and acquaintances, in addition to some surviving old ones, provided intellectual stimulation for his still probing mind. Life was worth living.

Svetlana's days were busy, her time divided between work, college, and friends, but she always found a way to be with her life tutor—her grandfather. They were happy together during this time that fate gave them as a respite from the hardship of former years, but not for long. Yasha's body began to misfire. The doctors said he had lung cancer. Those cigarettes—so desirable in Vorkuta because they'd provided just about the only comfort—had had an effect on already weakened humans. Yasha's prognosis was not good, but he was ready for a fight to stay alive.

One morning, a phone call interrupted the rhythm of their daily life. It was a phone call from the past. Boris, Yasha's American cousin, unexpectedly appeared. In his respectable age, Boris had decided to visit the place where he grew up, as he had never lost the feeling of connection to this country.

"I am here on a group tour and pretended to be ill to have a day to myself," he explained on the phone. "I would love to see you!"

Yasha gave him the address, and an hour later a taxi brought in a man who was totally dumbfounded by the sameness of what surrounded him. Their hug was sweet, the tears were tears of joy, and finally Yasha, who had spent most of that hour waiting for Boris outside, took him to his third-floor flat.

"How did you find me?"

"Through a telephone operator. I had no idea if you lived in Kiev or not. I am glad I found you."

Boris looked intently at the cousin he had not seen in many years. They were close in age, but Yasha looked a lot older than Boris, his face showing the results of a hard life.

"So, this is where you live now with your family?"

"I live with my granddaughter. Tanya and Lara died in Vorkuta.... I survived a jail, labor camp, the death of my wife and daughter. I try not to talk about that horrendous time. I am content now and happy to live with my granddaughter, Svetlana."

"Two of you living in this small flat?"

"The flat is small, but we are lucky to have it: our own kitchen and bathroom, even a telephone. But my granddaughter is the biggest blessing. You'll see her soon."

"And Meri?"

"She is in Kharkov. Married and works in a library. Svetlana is her daughter."

The sound of a key opening the door interrupted their conversation. A young, attractive woman with brown hair and blue eyes walked in and, surprised by the unexpected guest, looked at her grandfather.

"This is my Svetlanka. Svetlana, this is my cousin from America, Boris."

Boris hugged his young relative, looked at her attentively, and said, "I can see the resemblance. I remember those large blue eyes—just like Uncle Senya's."

"You are from America?! I read a lot about it. What a great surprise! I'd like to learn more. But first let's eat," Svetlana said as she stored her bag in a closet and went to work preparing the treats.

"What a beautiful woman your granddaughter is," Boris said to Yasha while Svetlana busied herself in the kitchen. "What does she do?"

"She is a kindergarten teacher. Luckily for you, she only worked an early shift today because later she attends lectures at the Pedagogical College. And lucky for her to see you too."

Soon the small kitchen smelled of potatoes, bread, canned fish (kept for just such occasions), and vegetables. Plates and utensils were set on the kitchen table, and the three relatives sat down to eat.

Svetlana could not wait to talk. "I have so, so many questions about America. Tell me all about it. From the beginning. I've heard stories about your family, but I'd rather hear it from you."

"From the beginning? Right. A long, long time ago.... It's been a long time, right, Yasha? And it was not easy. We moved to America, driven from Russia by the pogroms. My parents told me how tough it was to separate from the others who stayed behind. Really tough, especially in the beginning. You understand—a new language, new city, new everything. I was a little kid, and I still remember how children were laughing at me because I could not speak English, could not really play with them.

"The parents found all kinds of work to make money. Slowly, they collected enough to buy a small grocery store, which became our foundation. And Aunt Elena helped with the down payment."

"Aunt Elena?" Svetlana asked.

Yasha answered, "Remember my father's sister who moved to America and came back to find him?"

"Yes, yes, and she was always trying to help, such a good woman!" Boris added and continued:

"That store put me through college. We all helped in the store. It's not an easy business, but we did well. I went to college to study economics first, but then decided to become an engineer. After graduation, a large corporation hired me with a good salary. I married a gorgeous woman; smart too—she was an architect. We both worked for the same company. We married, bought a house. After the birth of our first son, she stayed home. Did some work here and there to help financially, but from home. She was good, people liked her work."

"She could make a lot of money working from home?" Svetlana asked.

"No, no, not a lot. But she liked doing it, more to satisfy her need for a challenge than to earn something."

"But how did you manage? A house, kids, and you probably had two cars, right? I read somewhere that most families in America have two cars."

"It was not the easiest. We did need a car for each of us to go where we needed: work, shopping, school, whatever. You must have a car."

"There is no public transport in New York?" Yasha asked.

"Yes, but our house was outside the city and there was little public transportation there."

"Poor you," jumped in Svetlana. "You must have a car per person. Here, a car is a luxury and only rich and well-connected people have them. Or those who call themselves people's servants."

"What? Servants?"

Yasha laughed and explained, "Those in power, those who occupy important political positions call themselves people's servants. By the way, did you marry that woman who wanted to build socialism in America?"

"I did. She changed her mind when I described what I had seen in Russia. She decided to stick with capitalism. We had a good life, two great kids...." Boris stopped talking and looked down.

"What happened?" Yasha asked.

"I lost her last year. Cancer."

"I am so sorry," Svetlana said.

"Yes. I don't like to talk about the painful times. I'd rather tell you about my sons. My older son built a successful advertisement company. He has two daughters, both studying in college. My younger son is a doctor and he has two sons, also students. I have a full set of grandchildren, whom I love. They are good kids and call me often."

Boris's voice was strained with the emotion brought out by talking about his family. He then decided it was his turn to ask questions.

"So, tell me, how do Soviet people live? From the bus windows, it looks like everyone has everything they need."

"People with money live well enough," Svetlana replied.

"In America you also need money to live well."

"But when you have the money, do you need connections to buy necessities?"

"No."

"Here, even if you have the money, you also need connections."

"This is not what our local guides told us."

"What do you expect they would tell you, the truth? They have to say only good things or lose their jobs. I am tired of hearing lies from our so-called leaders. They are all hypocrites and concern themselves only with their own wellbeing. They enjoy Communism right now, you know—you get what you want, while the rest of us have many obligations and few rights. You can't go here, you can't go there. They told us stories about how we live better than people in any other country, but would not let us travel and actually witness it. The only people allowed to go abroad are those who live so well here that they would not jump ship. I dream of the time when I could leave this country. I dream to live in America."

This was an interesting opening for Boris's initiation into the real Soviet life. He wanted to converse more with the passionate and opinionated Svetlana, but she looked at her watch and said, "I will leave you alone to talk. I need to be at a lecture in college."

Svetlana kissed her grandpa and the guest before departing.

"So sorry I could not spend more time with you, Uncle Boris," were her last words as she left.

The two elderly boys continued their discussion in the kitchen. They talked about relatives lost to the war and purges, about Yasha's life, about America and Boris's children—everything they had missed during years of separation.

The sound of a doorbell broke their conversation. Slowly, Yasha opened the door. It was a neighbor.

"Bella, if it is not an emergency, could you try calling from a public phone?"

"Oh, no, I don't need a telephone. I wanted to tell you that I saved you a place in the line for eggs; don't be late," replied Bella and left.

Boris stared at Yasha with a big question in his eyes. Yasha even laughed seeing this expression of bewilderment.

"Poor you, a member of a rotten capitalist society; you don't know what it means not to have a phone. Here, I am the only one in the building who has a phone because I earned it in the fight for the

234

revolution. That is, after they almost killed me as an enemy of that revolution."

"One in a building?"

"And you don't know what it means to stay in line for eggs and be happy about it. When a product is scarce, you better hurry up and get what you can or you may not see it again for a long time."

"Eggs?" Boris asked with mistrust. "There are not enough eggs in the Soviet Union?"

Yasha just waved his hand and said, "Do you want to go with me to the store?"

"Of course I will go with you. How can I miss such an opportunity?"

Standing in line for eggs next to the thoughtful neighbor, Yasha took a net out of his pocket and offered it to Boris.

"What is this?" Boris asked.

"One person can only buy ten eggs. You can purchase ten more and put them in this net."

"Why do I need a net? Don't they package purchases in boxes or bags?"

"What do you mean, Boris, what bags?" It was Yasha's turn to be bewildered. They clearly did not understand each other—people from two different worlds.

Eggs bought, the cousins walked home. Yasha asked, "Aren't you glad you came with me to the store?"

"Sure. Where else would I stay in line for an hour and worry if by the time I reach the counter they will still have it? This is the stuff for comedians!"

"And we have to live with it every day."

"What a day!" Boris said.

"Nothing special," Yasha smiled.

Boris walked absorbed in his thoughts and Yasha did not interrupt. At home, they sat down at the kitchen table.

"I remember," Boris began, "the first time we received news of the revolution in Russia, we were so proud of our countrymen that they plowed clean the road in front of the entire human race and showed the way to a better life. A life based on liberty and equality would be better for all of us. So, here is the revolution, the chance to start from scratch and make a magnificent society for everybody: no poor, no rich, no masters, no slaves, no better or worse nationalities. And what had happened? What happened to those Communist goals?"

"We were young and eager to participate in the Communist experiment, but the longer I live, the better I realize that the experiment had failed. We still have the powerful and the insignificant. What used to be called nobility is now the Party oligarchy, people's servants, and the majority of people are still insignificant.

"You know, Boris, some people in this country invoke Stalin's name every time something is not working. For instance, they would say, 'There was plenty of food under Stalin.' Once I lost my patience and said to this ignoramus, 'You had enough food with Stalin because you had eaten my share, while I worked in the labor camp barely surviving.' People don't know much about what is happening, and with the government-controlled press, they will never know."

"But on our tour we have seen beautiful cities, well-organized factories, stores full of products, cheerful, smiling people. They explained about free education and free medicine. They took us to a ballet performance—it was a very impressive show of a very progressive state. No wonder many professors in America are advocating the socialist system of government."

"Well, there is a cure for those professors," Yasha answered, smiling. "Just let them live in our country as citizens, not tourists, and they will run away in a month. This socialism we had built is like a punishment for the entire people. Yes, the ballet is great, and the cities the foreigners visit, like Kiev, are well maintained and quite beautiful, but everything else is good only for those in power or with connections. Medicine is a joke. We have a saying, 'To be treated for free is to be free of treatment.' Anytime people suspect something serious, they immediately look for a well-known specialist and pay for the visit. The big shots—they don't have to worry about medicine, they have the best. And all these *temporary* difficulties! They never end. Why do you think the Soviet system is afraid of having a real democracy with debates and votes and free opinions? Why do you think the Communists cannot stand other parties with different views? Why are we a closed society? Our borders are protected not so much from intruders as to keep our own citizens from leaving. We did not solve the equality issue; we just changed who is on top."

Yasha took a breather and Boris was also quiet, still absorbing Yasha's opinions. Voices from the street indicated that school was over and pupils were going home, playing around and loudly discussing the events of their day.

"A new Soviet generation," Boris said. "Will these kids see a different life in their country when they grow up?"

Yasha just shrugged his shoulders.

"I can't know when, but I do know it will definitely happen," Boris said and looked at his watch. "I wish I could stay longer, but it's time for me to leave."

Upset about the forthcoming parting, Yasha took Boris outside to catch a taxi When one stopped, the cousins froze in an embrace that lasted a long while. They did not want the moment to end, understanding that this was the last time they would see each other, tears sparkling in their eyes. When the taxi took Boris away, Yasha slowly walked back home to the empty apartment, where the eggs reminded him of the adventure with the envoy from a different world. He felt that his time in this realm was close to its end.

9

Bare tree branches accented the gray sky and a chilly wind blew through a cemetery not far from the residential apartment buildings built over the years in this part of Kiev, no longer new. The final resting place of Yasha Nepomnyashchy—descendant of people rich in history, events, and emotions—was close to his last home. Years had passed since he had succumbed to a vicious disease, but for Svetlana he was still a role model, her guide in life, her protector.

"Thank you for everything. I am the luckiest girl alive to have you for a grandfather. I remember your lessons, and I remember your love. They will always be mine."

A cool breeze touched her cheeks.

"I am with you, Svetlanka," the breeze whispered and she knew it was he, her grandpa. "Be brave, be strong—I promise, everything will be all right."

Svetlana's dream to leave the kingdom of the unjustly punished was near. Soon, soon she would be on her way to another world.

"You're always with me, Grandpa. I am going into the future, but I will never forget the past."

Historical and Ethnic Notes

- *Nepomnyashchy* — in Russian it means *someone who does not remember.*
- February Revolution — The revolution of February 1917, forcing Czar's abdication.
- October (November) Revolution — The Great October Revolution that propelled the Communist Party to power. It took place in October 1917 by the old Russian calendar; it is celebrated in Russia on November 7 by the current calendar.
- *Kulak* — *a fist* in Russian. The more affluent peasants were called *kulaks* to differentiate them from the peasants of lesser means. The word acquired a political meaning after the Revolution as anyone who owned grain and resisted parting with it for the benefit of the proletariat was labelled a kulak. These peasants were later exterminated or resettled in the remote places in large numbers. Many of the relocated peasants died in the unhospitable environment. The effect was devastating on the food supplies, especially in Ukraine.
- NEP — *The New Economic Policy.* Lenin instituted the policy to help economically devastated Russia climb out of famine and hardship by allowing some private entrepreneurship (limited Capitalism). The policy did help as many people opened small business catering to the population. As soon as the Communist Party felt that the experiment was not needed anymore, many of such entrepreneurs were imprisoned and murdered as anti-revolutionaries.
- Soviet — *Soveht* in Russian, meaning *a council.* A group of citizens elected to govern a region, such as a town, a county, or a country.
- Makhno — the leader of an influential guerrilla army in Ukraine.
- *Sheineh punim* — Yiddish for *a beautiful face.*

- *Svohyee* — A Russian word meaning *we are the same as you.*
- *NKVD* — the feared internal affairs arm of the government responsible for the investigation, persecution, and safeguarding of the people deemed undesirable for the country, mostly on political grounds. It was created right after The October Revolution as ChK, then called OGPU, GPU, NKVD. For simplicity, in this book all those names are covered by NKVD.
- Gulag — GULAG: an acronym for the Government Department of Camps.
- USSR/The Soviet Union — Union of Soviet Socialist Republics. A new entity created after the dissolution of the Russian Empire in 1922.

www.ingramcontent.com/pod-product-compliance
Lightning Source LLC
LaVergne TN
LVHW011221080426
835509LV00005B/244